NUTRITION FOR CLIMBERS
Fuel for the Send

Marisa Michael, MSc, RDN, CSSD

WARRANTY DISCLAIMER. The author and publisher have used their best efforts in preparing this book. The author and publisher make no representations or warranties with respect to the accuracy or completeness of the contents of this book and specifically disclaim any implied warranties of merchantability or fitness for any particular purpose.

LIMITATION OF LIABILITY. In no event shall the author or publisher be liable in any respect for any damages relating to the contents of this book including without limitation special, incidental, consequential or other damages, whether or not the author or publisher has been advised of the possibility of such damages.

GENERAL INFORMATION. The contents of this book contain general information about nutrition for rock climbing enthusiasts, including information and opinions about various foods and food groups; recipes and ingredients; supplements; and the consumption of certain foods in relation to training and fitness, climbing, the enthusiast's age, and related items. All of this information and related opinions have been prepared and are intended for the general reader. Such information and opinions are not designed for any specific reader or individual circumstance. Readers are strongly encouraged and recommended to contact their own individual physician or dietician for individual nutrition information and dietary advice suitable for the reader's own, individual circumstance.

PRODUCTS AND SERVICES IN THIS BOOK. This book may include information about third-party products and services and their providers. The author and publisher do not at any time endorse such products or services, nor does the author or publisher operate or control such providers. Such providers are solely responsible for their products and services and all aspects of order processing, fulfillment, billing and customer services. Your purchase of products and your use thereof from providers is at your sole risk and is without warranty of any kind by the author or publisher, expressed, implied or otherwise including warranties of title, fitness for a particular purpose or merchantability. The author or publisher makes no guarantee as to the results to be achieved or the safety or efficacy of such products or services. Under no circumstance shall the author or publisher be liable for any damages arising from use of third-party products or services or transactions with providers.

TRADEMARK. Fixed Pin Publishing is a trademark owned by Fixed Pin Publishing, LLC. All other product and brand names in this book are owned or licensed by their respective providers.

Nutrition for Climbers:
Fuel for the Send

Author: **Marisa Michael**
Photography: **Andrew Burr unless otherwise credited**
Illustrations: **Lynn Mandziuk**
Art Direction & Layout: **Bennett Scott**
Editing: **Matt Samet, Kate Beezley**
Associate Publisher and Project Manager: **Kate Beezley**

© 2020 Fixed Pin Publishing, LLC
All rights reserved. No part of this book may be used or reproduced in any manner without written permission from the publisher.

International Standard Book Number:
ISBN: **978-0-9992803-1-7**

Printed in China

Fixed Pin Publishing is continually expanding its guidebooks and loves to hear from locals about their home areas. If you have an idea for a book or a manuscript for a guide, or would like to find out more about our company, contact:

Ben Schneider
Fixed Pin Publishing®
P.O. Box 3481
Boulder, CO 80307
ben@fixedpin.com

Preface

Dear climber,

I've seen you in the gym, practicing until your body aches. The endless dead-hangs, the impossible pull-ups with a kettlebell tied around your waist, the burning pump that forces you to shake your arms out as you ascend. I've seen the pain from pinched toes in climbing shoes, the grimace from falling after a dyno gone wrong.

I've seen you at the crag, fingers taped, shredded, and bloody. I've seen you gleaning precious beta from fellow climbers, miming it in the air before you start your project like some hypnotized drunkard. I've seen the whippers—dramatic and heart-stopping falls—that make you grateful for the invention of helmets.

All this exhausting and exhilarating work to send the route. To climb and conquer, simply because it's there. To feel that sense of accomplishment of climbing something previously beyond your ability.

This book is for you. This is for the casual indoor climber who hits the gym after a long workday. It's for the one living in a van and climbing full-time. It's for the teen doing comps. It's for the pros hoping to make the Olympics or World Cup. It's for the weekend warriors.

You all have something in common: You need amazing, solid nutrition advice if you want to reach your goals. But currently you don't have a good nutrition resource to do so. Sure, there are a few blog posts and magazine articles about rock-climbing nutrition. But you need more.

That's where I come in. Full confession: I am not a climber. Well, not in the sense that you probably are. Sure, I climb at the gym. I've climbed outdoors but found that, at 70 feet up the crag, it was not my thing; I prefer not to dangle from sheer rock cliffs, thank you very much. I play belay-mom to my teenage kid and shuttle him to comps.

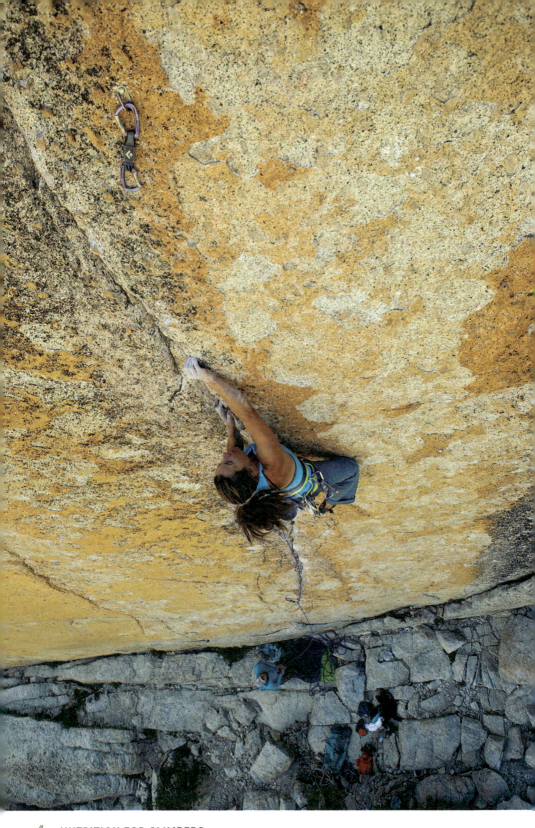

Preface (continued)

Even though I am not a hardcore climber, I have awe and respect for those of you who are. You are amazing athletes who deserve solid nutrition advice to help you achieve your goals. During my research on rock-climbing nutrition, I've discovered there is a huge void in resources for climbers who want to get next-level performance.

As a sports dietitian and personal trainer, I can fill that void. Valid, evidence-based nutrition strategies can do wonders for an athlete's performance. Implementing these in your own training, in the right way, at the right time, will help you achieve your climbing dreams.

This book has information on everything you've ever wondered about rock-climbing nutrition, plus things you didn't even know you needed to know (but once you know, you'll wonder how you got along without them).

If you understand your body, you'll know how to nourish and fuel it. This book will cover comprehensive nutrition strategies and principles for rock climbing as well as the reasoning behind them, outlining basic physiology in plain English. This book will tell you how to easily implement nutrition changes in your own life.

This book isn't the next fad diet. It's not a thinly disguised advertisement for supplements or shakes. It's not a laundry list of things you can and can't eat. It's real nutrition principles that will help you perform better, taken from sports nutrition research, and climbers like you. It's organized into discrete chapters and sections so you can easily flip to what applies to you.

Thanks for taking the time to read this book. When you send the route, or crush the project that previously eluded you, you'll be glad you did.

~Marisa Michael

Table of Contents

PART I: NUTRITION BASICS 9

Chapter 1: Nutrition Basics 11
- Energy
- Carbohydrates
- Protein
- Fat
- Fluids
- Micronutrients

Chapter 2: Climbing Physiology Basics 23

PART II: NUTRITION FOR DIFFERENT TYPES OF CLIMBING 31

Chapter 3: Nutrition for Indoor Climbing 33
- A climbing session at the end of the day (after work or school)
- All-day comp
- Multi-day comp
- Long gym session

Chapter 4: Nutrition for Outdoor Climbing 41
- Altitude
- Climbing in the cold
- Climbing in the heat
- Ultralight meal planning

Chapter 5: Nutrition for Different Types of Climbing 67
- Speed climbing
- Sport/toprope/lead climbing
- Bouldering
- Olympic platform
- Traditional (trad) climbing
- Free soloing
- Alpine climbing/ice climbing

PART III: NUTRITION FOR SPECIAL SITUATIONS 77

Chapter 6: Special Nutrition Needs 79
- Vegan/vegetarian climbers
- Living the van life
- Climbers with digestive issues
- Youth & adolescent climbers
- Nutrition for older athletes (over 55 years)
- Female athletes
- Adaptive climbers/para climbers
- Travel nutrition

Chapter 7: Injury Prevention & Recovery 133
- Nutrition for injury prevention
- Nutrition for injury recovery
- Supplements to consider
- Inflammation and antioxidants: not all inflammation is bad
- Crap, i got a cramp

Chapter 8: Supplements 143

Chapter 9: Nutrition Periodization, etc 163
- Body-composition tests
- Things to consider before losing weight
- Periodization
- The fat-loss pyramid

Chapter 10: Eating Disorders and Disordered Eating 195

Chapter 11: Recipes and Menus 209
- Mug recipes
- Recovery power bowls
- Outdoor recipes

Chapter 12: Menus and Recipes for Climbers 227

Appendix 270

Acknowledgements 273

Index 277

"For me, nutrition for climbing is mostly about the speed of recovery. What is the right nutrition? Of course, there are so many different opinions. I have experimented a lot, and what I feel is most important is eating real food."

-Adam Ondra

PART I

THE BASICS

1 - NUTRITION BASICS

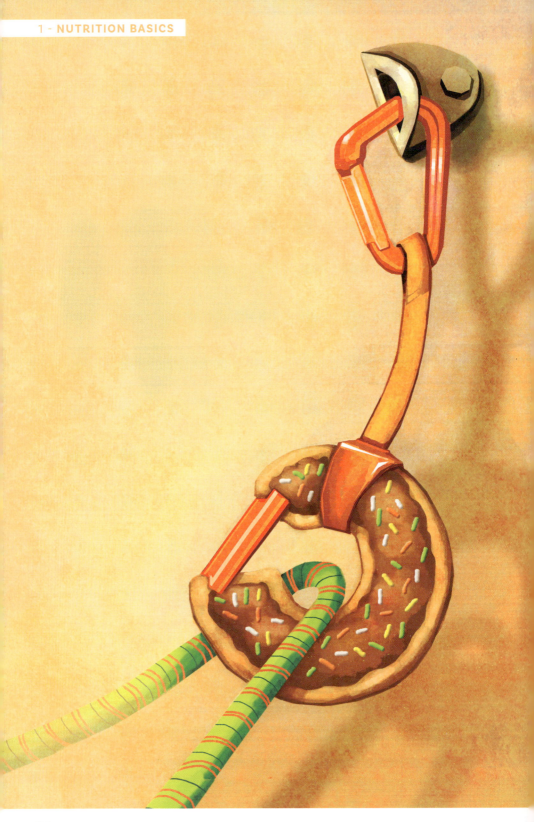

CHAPTER 1

NUTRITION BASICS
WHAT YOU NEED TO KNOW

Mont Blanc, the highest peak in Western Europe at 15,777 feet (4808 meters), rises high where Italy, France, and Switzerland converge.

In 1851, Englishman Albert Smith and his team attempted to climb it. To do so, they brought along 91 bottles of wine, two bottles of champagne, four legs of sheep, 46 birds, a bottle of raspberry syrup, and six packets of chocolate. Yes, this was a climbing expedition, not a college frat party.

In today's age of ultralight gear, freeze-dried backpacking meals, and sleek, high-end equipment, bringing 91 bottles of wine and a flock of birds might seem like the introductory line to a bad joke: Telling your climbing partner you're bringing legs of sheep along leaves them hanging for the punchline.

Modern sports nutrition science has come a long way since 1851. We have answers to a lot of our nutrition questions. Humans have achieved greater physical feats than ever before. Rock climbers are no exception. Powered by sheer grit, desire, training, and good nutrition, you can achieve next-level climbing.

To join the ranks of well-fueled athletes, you first need to know some nutrition basics. This book is your nutrition primer.

> First, there are a few terms to be familiar with when you're thinking about nutrition:
> - **Overall energy (calories)**
> - **Macronutrients:**
>   - **Carbohydrates**
>   - **Protein**
>   - **Fat**
> - **Fluids**
> - **Micronutrients**
>   (vitamins and minerals)
> - **Other substances,** such as fiber, antioxidants, and phytochemicals

All these play a role in your health and training. You need the right nutrients to fuel your lifestyle and sport. And in sports nutrition, timing is everything. Eating candy is usually frowned upon, but sugar can be your best friend during an intense training session. Fiber can cut a training session short with gastrointestinal issues, but fiber during a recovery meal can help promote good bowel health. The right protein at bedtime can help support muscle growth and repair, while too much protein during a comp can slow digestion and leave you under-fueled. Take some time to understand this chapter before moving on, because it is the foundation for understanding all the recommendations and guidelines in the rest of this book.

Something to keep in mind:

While I drew on a large body of nutrition science, current research, and nutrition recommendations to write this book, it's important to understand a couple of things about nutrition science.

First, it's always evolving. Studies are conducted regularly, with new research being published constantly. This shapes the way we understand how the body works and how nutrition recommendations should be implemented. So, something you read today in this book might be clarified in a later study down the road. That doesn't mean science is misleading or incorrect—but sometimes it's incomplete and we do the best we can with the data we currently have.

Second, there are not a lot of studies specific to rock climbers and nutrition. There are quite a few research studies on the physiology of, and energy expenditure in climbers, but only two published studies (can you believe it?!) about nutrition for climbers. In order to give sound and valid nutrition recommendations, at times I have to pull data from similar sports that also demand a high strength-to-weight ratio, such as gymnastics, or sports where leanness usually means increased performance, such as running.

Keep in mind the limited research on climbers as you read this book. My main goal is to bring you quality nutrition information based on good-quality evidence, and sometimes I need to borrow recommendations from other sports in order to do so. Let's get started!

Energy

Have you seen that meme that says, "Calories (noun): tiny, little creatures that live in your closet and sew your clothes a bit tighter every night"? Most people think of calories as a bad thing, as in, "Dang, I ate way too many calories today!" Or, "I can't eat that–it has too many calories." Do yourself a favor and scratch that thinking. A calorie is simply a unit of energy: fuel for your body's movement.

Here's a helpful analogy: Imagine a campfire. You need the right size and number of logs to keep the fire burning well. Too little wood and it goes out. Too much wood or a log that is too big, and the fire also goes out because the flames get smothered. But, if you put the right size log on the fire at a constant rate as the other logs burn, you can have an endless fire that's controlled and gives off the right amount of heat.

The campfire analogy is like your body using energy. Your body needs energy (calories) in order to do daily tasks: cooking, laundry, computer work, walking the dog, etc. You need additional calories to climb. Over the course of a week, you may take in fewer calories one day, and more on another day. (I'm looking at you, weekend binge!) But overall, your calorie intake evens out. But, if you take too much in, over time you may see unintended weight gain. Or if you are undereating, you can have unintended weight loss. This weight loss may be from lean muscle mass, or even bone, and can create dysfunction in other body systems, like your immune system and reproductive system. Taking in too few calories over a period of months or years can wreak havoc on your health.

Eating the correct amount of overall calories (energy) helps your body fuel normal body processes, such as respiration, pumping blood, and cell turnover. Calories in fact fuel all body functions, including immunity, reproduction, hormone regulation, and cognition. They also help fuel your normal daily activities, plus whatever sports, exercise, and climbing you do. All climbing you do, plus any strength training or cross training, needs additional energy (calories) to fuel that activity. If the body doesn't have enough calories, you become fatigued and lose training gains, and your health is compromised. Hence, you need to feed your "fire" with the right amount of calories at the right rate.

Energy (continued)

Macronutrients are nutrients containing energy (calories). The four main macronutrients are carbohydrates, protein, fat, and alcohol. Eating the right ratio of macronutrients (carbohydrates, protein, and fat) can take your training even farther. We will leave alcohol out for now, as chapter 9 goes into more detail on how alcohol impacts your training. For now, just file this concept away in your mind. No need to get into the nitty-gritty of how many calories you need to eat. This chapter is very, well,—it's all about the big picture and understanding basic nutrition concepts. Each subsequent chapter will give more advice and guidance on specific calorie needs. For example, you may need more calories to climb outdoors than indoors. You'll learn more details within each respective section. For now, read on for more macronutrient nutrition basics.

Carbohydrates

Ah, carbs. The often maligned, misunderstood macronutrient. If you read through popular nutrition blogs, you may think that carbohydrates are evil. But in sports performance, carbs are king.

Carbohydrates are made up of carbon, hydrogen, and oxygen atoms that create sugar units. Longer chains of sugar units linked together make up complex carbohydrates. These are found in foods like whole grains, beans, vegetables, bread, pasta, potatoes, broccoli, corn, and legumes. These foods tend to also provide fiber, which is helpful for regular digestion.

Simple carbohydrates are single- and double-sugar units. These are found in foods that have naturally occurring sugar, such as milk, fruit, and some vegetables. This category also includes refined sugar, such as table sugar and corn syrup. In general, it's best to eat less refined sugar. But there are some instances where it's actually strategic to use refined sugar as a quick fuel source. There are no "good" or "bad" carbs. It's just food; it's fuel for your body. Eating certain types of carbohydrates at certain times and in certain amounts can help you excel at your sport.

CARBOHYDRATES

Your body uses carbohydrates to fuel both your muscles and brain, along with many other organs. Without carbohydrates, performance suffers. The body stores carbohydrate (glucose) in skeletal muscles and the liver—this is called glycogen. Carbohydrates are also circulating in your blood as glucose—blood sugar. People only have a finite amount of glycogen stored up (about 1400–2000 calories-worth, which is about two to three hours of hard work). Your glycogen stores are influenced by your training and diet: It's advantageous to eat some carbohydrate after a workout or training session because it will replenish the glycogen that you just used up to fuel your workout.

You use glycogen for muscle contraction. It's on-board fuel for your muscles. Without glycogen, it's very difficult to do hard work. When your body doesn't have enough carbohydrate available for a workout, training session, or comp, it relies on other fuel sources, such as fat. Fat isn't as effective as carbohydrate for big muscle contractions, explosive movements (like dynos), and intense training. Eating enough carbohydrates will help you feel better and stronger as you climb.

Here are the main food groups that are high in carbohydrates:

Grains and grain products: quinoa, wheat, spelt, teff (an African grain high in fiber and protein), rice, oatmeal, and rye. Anything made with grains, such as cereal, bread, pasta, couscous, pancakes, waffles, tortillas, and baked goods (cookies, anyone?).

Fruit and fruit juice: these include all types of fruit, as well as any fruit juice.

Starchy vegetables: such as potatoes, sweet potatoes, yams, corn, peas, and squash.

Dairy products: milk, flavored milk, yogurt, and cottage cheese. (Note: Most other cheeses fall into the "protein" category and have much less carbohydrate than cottage cheese.)

Legumes: lentils, kidney beans, garbanzo beans (chickpeas), lima beans, black beans, black-eyed peas, pinto beans, etc.

Sweets and desserts: cookies, cake, ice cream, jelly beans, hard candies, anything with added sugar.

Protein

Perhaps no nutrient is more worshiped in the athletic world than protein. You'll find no shortage of protein powders to purchase. There are endless articles and blogs praising protein. Even whole diets are dedicated to eating more protein. What gives?

Protein is essential for a wide array of body processes. Most people think of protein when they want to build muscle. But protein's role goes way beyond muscle-building. It helps with the immune system, hormones, bone health, connective tissue like tendons and ligaments, skin health (and healing), hair, nails, and basically all your organs. So yeah, protein is a big deal.

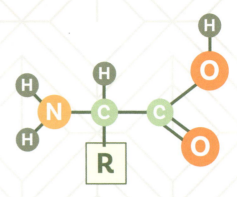

Protein is made up of amino acids. Think of these like building blocks for proteins–little Legos that can be connected to make tissues in your body. Some foods have all 20 amino acids, and some don't. Each food has a different amino acid profile with differing amounts of amino acids. Certain amino acids, like leucine, play a bigger role than others in sports performance and muscle rebuilding and repairing.

Most people get enough protein in their diet, including athletes, **but athletes do need more than less-active people.** You also need more if you are trying to heal from an injury, build muscle, or recover from a hard training session.

Here are the main food groups that are high in protein:

Meat, poultry, fish: beef, pork, chicken, tuna, salmon, tilapia, and turkey.

Eggs

Dairy products: milk, cheese, yogurt, cottage cheese, and kefir.

Legumes: dried beans listed in the carbohydrate section, along with lentils; nuts and seeds, such as peanuts, walnuts, almonds, sunflower seeds, and chia seeds. Also, products made using legumes, such as hummus, almond butter, and peanut butter.

Soy products: tofu, tempeh, and their related products.

Fat

Fat is essential for life. Many people bemoan their fat, wishing they could lose weight. Or take extreme measures to remove it. But guess what? Your body needs fat! It serves as an insulator and a protective barrier for your organs. It is an organ! It is metabolically active and secretes hormones. It makes up a big part of your brain as well. While it is true that fat in excess can raise your risk for disease, most people can be "fat" and be healthy.

For climbers, fat takes on a whole different meaning within the context of performance. If a climber is too heavy, it makes it more difficult to climb. If a climber is too thin, he/she is at risk for health concerns and injury. Some climbing organizations don't let climbers compete if they are too thin.

Fat is your friend. In addition to body fat serving a useful purpose, dietary fat (the fat in foods you eat) is useful as well: It helps contribute to a feeling of fullness, called satiety. Think about a meal you've had that left you feeling hungry. It probably wasn't a large-enough portion, and likely didn't have enough fat or protein in it. Fat helps you feel full and satisfied.

Main food groups containing fat:

Dairy: full-fat dairy products like whole milk, cheese, whole milk yogurt, and ice cream.

Meat, poultry, fish: poultry with the skin on, red meat with visible fat or marbling within the cut of meat, and fatty fish like salmon.

Nuts and seeds: peanuts, walnuts, almonds, pumpkin seeds, etc.

Some produce and their oils: avocado/avocado oil, olives/olive oil, and coconut/coconut oil.

Some fats are very healthful and should frequently be included in your diet. These are monounsaturated fats and foods containing omega-3 fats. Examples include salmon, walnuts, almonds, pine nuts, avocado, sardines, flaxseed, and chia seeds, as well as olive oil and avocado oil.

1 - NUTRITION BASICS WHAT YOU NEED TO KNOW

Fluids

Hydration is important. Dehydration can lead to mental confusion and fatigue. In a sport where a mistake can mean injury or death, being properly hydrated is key.

Fluids serve a valuable purpose in your body. They help eliminate waste, lubricate joints, regulate temperature, carry oxygen and nutrients into cells, and much more. Most people realize the importance of drinking the right amount of water each day. But if you add in a tough climbing session, altitude, or extreme weather conditions, hydration becomes even more crucial.

Did you know that you don't have to drink just water? A lot of my clients are surprised when I tell them that any fluid except alcohol can contribute toward your overall fluid intake for the day. Coffee, tea, milk, juice, sports drinks, soups, and water all hydrate you. Some fruits and vegetables with a high water content also can be hydrating (like watermelon or cucumber), but don't count on these if you're out on the crag—they aren't super convenient. Just drink! Look for more details about hydration in each section of this book.

Micronutrients

Micronutrients are vitamins, minerals, and antioxidants. Your body needs much smaller amounts of these than macronutrients (carbohydrates, protein, and fat). Examples of vitamins include the fat-soluble vitamins A, D, E, and K; vitamin B6, vitamin B12, folic acid, niacin, and vitamin C. Examples of minerals include electrolytes: sodium, potassium, calcium, and magnesium. Iron, zinc, copper, chromium, and selenium are also minerals. Examples of antioxidants include beta carotene, vitamin C, and vitamin E.

You need vitamins and minerals in your diet to live and be healthy, because your body doesn't make most of these substances. When applying this to climbing performance, vitamins and minerals help with muscle contraction, hydration, fuel metabolism, muscle rebuilding and repair, injury recovery, and respiration (breathing).

Most people who eat a wide variety of healthful foods will get adequate vitamins and minerals in their diet. You don't necessarily need more vitamins, minerals, or antioxidants than a normal person just because you are an athlete. In fact, taking extra supplements is sometimes harmful. If you suspect a deficiency, like vitamin D deficiency or iron deficiency-anemia, let your doctor advise you as to whether you need to take a supplement.

To maximize your vitamin and mineral intake, a good rule of thumb is to eat foods that are minimally processed.

Fruits and vegetables: these are chock-full of wonderful nutrients, antioxidants, and phytochemicals to help your body be strong and healthy, and adapt to all your training. B vitamins, as well as vitamin C, beta carotene, potassium, vitamin K, and many others, are found in fruits and vegetables.

Whole grains: whole-wheat pasta, whole-grain bread, brown rice, quinoa, barley, oatmeal, etc.

Dairy: depending on the dairy product, these contain vitamin D, calcium, potassium, sodium, and other minerals.

Meat, fish, and poultry: contain micronutrients such as zinc, iron, and vitamin B12 (only found naturally in animal products).

Eggs: contain biotin, choline, vitamin B12, selenium, and other micronutrients.

Nuts and seeds: contain a variety of micronutrients, such as selenium, magnesium, manganese, copper, and B vitamins.

Now you know some nutrition basics. You have a rock-solid (see what I did there?) foundation to get the best nutrition for your climbing.

SIDEBAR: Loose macronutrient recommendations—for specific targets, see a dietitian

1 pound = 2.2 kilograms; kcal=calorie

	Calories	Carbs	Protein	Fat	Fluid
PER KG BODY WEIGHT	30-45 kcal/kg fat-free mass	3-7g/kg	0.8-2.2 g/kg	1 g/kg*	30-35 mL/kg
PER POUND BODY WEIGHT	14-20.5 kcal/lb fat-free mass	2-3 g/lb	0.7-1.2 g/lb	n/a	0.5 oz/lb
PERCENTAGE OF ENERGY INTAKE	100%	50-60%	15-20%	>20% or whatever is left over	N/A

Fat-free mass: This includes muscle, organs, and bone—basically everything in your body except fat.

*One gram per kilogram of fat is a recommendation in its infancy. It has not been thoroughly studied to determine a recommended range of fat intake for athletic performance and health. This is a general guideline that is sometimes recommended in the absence of more-robust research.

THE WRAP-UP FOR NUTRITION BASICS

Macronutrients are carbohydrates, protein, and fat. **Micronutrients** are vitamins, minerals, and antioxidants. A wide variety of foods is best to provide you with all the nutrition you'll need to be a great climber. Eating more fruits, vegetables, whole grains, lean meats, eggs, and dairy rather than heavily processed foods can help you with your training and overall health. **Fluids** are important to maintain proper hydration and promote performance.

All nutrients play a role in fueling your climbing, cross training, and everyday activities. Eating enough overall calories helps fuel training adaptations and normal body processes.

CHAPTER 1 REFERENCES

Burke., L.M. 2010. "Fueling Strategies to Optimize Performance: Training High or Training Low?" *Scandinavian Journal of Medicine & Science in Sports* 20: 48-58.

Burke, Louise M., John A. Hawley, Stephen HS Wong, and Asker E. Jeukendrup. 2011. "Carbohydrates for Training and Competition." *Journal of Sports Sciences* 29, no. sup 1: S17-S27.

Cotter, James David., Simon N. Thornton, Jason KW Lee, and Paul B. Laursen. 2014. "Are We Being Drowned in Hydration Advice? Thirsty for More?" *Extreme Physiology & Medicine* 3, no. 1: 18.

Gorissen, Stefan HM, and Oliver C. Witard. 2018. "Characterizing the Muscle Anabolic Potential of Dairy, Meat and Plant-based Protein Sources in Older Adults." *Proceedings of the Nutrition Society* 77, no. 1: 20-31.

Hawley, John A. 2011. "Fat Adaptation Science: Low-Carbohydrate, High-fat Diets to Alter Fuel Utilization and Promote Training Adaptation." *Sports Nutrition: More Than Just Calories-Triggers for Adaptation,* vol. 69: 59-78.

Maughan, Ronald J., and Michael Gleeson. 2010. *The Biochemical Basis of Sports Performance.* Oxford University Press.

Maughan, Ronald J., Susan M. Shirreffs. 2015. "Physiology of Sports," *Clinical Sports Nutrition, 5th ed.,* edited by Louise Burke and Vicki Deakin, 767-786. Australia: McGraw Hill Education.

Mountjoy, Margo, Jorunn Sundgot-Borgen, Louise Burke, Susan Carter, Naama Constantini, Constance Lebrun, Nanna Meyer, et al. 2014. "The IOC Consensus Statement: Beyond the Female Athlete Triad—Relative Energy Deficiency in Sport (RED-S)." *British Journal of Sports Medicine* 48, no. 7: 491-497.

Phillips, Stuart M. 2012. "Dietary Protein Requirements and Adaptive Advantages in Athletes." *British Journal of Nutrition* 108, no. S2: S158-S167.

Position of the Academy of Nutrition and Dietetics, Dietitians of Canada, and the American College of Sports Medicine: Nutrition and Athletic Performance. 2016. *Journal of the Academy of Nutrition and Dietetics,* 116: 501-528.

Rodriguez, Nancy R., Nancy M. DiMarco, and Susie Langley. 2009. "Position of the American Dietetic Association, Dietitians of Canada, and the American College of Sports Medicine: Nutrition and Athletic Performance." *Journal of the American Dietetic Association* 109, no. 3: 509-527.

Sanzaro, Francis. "The Art of Climbing: The Untold Story" *Rock and Ice Magazine: Ascent, May 2018.* Carbondale, Colorado: Big Stone Publishing, issue 250: 104-113.

Schoenfeld, Brad Jon, and Alan Albert Aragon. 2018. "How Much Protein Can the Body Use in a Single Meal for Muscle-building? Implications for Daily Protein Distribution." *Journal of the International Society of Sports Nutrition* 15, no. 1: 10.

2 - CLIMBING PHYSIOLOGY BASICS

CHAPTER 2

CLIMBING PHYSIOLOGY BASICS

I have a son who was too skinny. For a climber, that's usually a good thing. But this was not a good thing. At age 12, he started dropping off his growth curve. In the United States, kids get annual checkups where the doctor weighs and measures them, then tracks their growth on a growth chart. My son dipped below his growth curve, meaning he wasn't gaining weight like he should have been.

He was a good climber, partially because he was so light. But if he continued on this growth (or rather, lack of growth) trajectory, he was in for some possible health issues. He might not reach his full adult stature. He might not hit key puberty milestones. His climbing, ironically, would eventually suffer, because he wasn't eating enough to fuel his sport and his growth. I always knew he was skinny, but having real data helped his doctor and me get him back on track, and it also helped us realize that there was a potential problem. Understanding physiology was key to helping my son be healthy. I knew exactly how much to feed him, what types of foods, and when. Having physiology knowledge on my side helped him shoot up six inches in one year.

If physiology isn't your forte, that's OK. Don't let this chapter scare you away. It is critical to understand how your body uses food and turns it into fuel for your climbing. If you have a solid understanding of the basics of nutrient metabolism, it will help you better understand the nutrition recommendations in this book. It can also help you troubleshoot your own nutrition situation when training and climbing. If you understand that the body uses carbohydrates for dynos and that you use protein to build and repair muscle, you'll understand what to eat to fuel your climbing.

While there aren't very many studies about nutrition for rock climbers, there are quite a few about energy expenditure and physiology in climbers. These studies looked into how many calories climbers burn and their heart rate during activity. Let's look at each study more closely.

Energy

Calories are energy. In diet and nutrition books, you'll see the term "energy" used a lot. It's easy to inherently understand that you need energy to do something. You need energy to hike to the crag, set up equipment, climb, belay, and everything else. When we are talking about energy needed for climbing, you need to eat food to get this energy. Calories from the foods you eat are digested and metabolized into energy, which powers your brain and muscles so you can perform tasks, such as sending a tough route.

> Climbing on average burns about 10–11 calories per minute of active climbing. One study showed about nine calories per minute on an easy route, and 12.6 calories per minute on a harder route. More calories are used if the route is overhung. Makes sense, right?

If you climb for a two- to three-hour session, you may burn around 600-900 calories depending on how much of that is actual climbing versus belaying, resting, sharing beta, and general goofing-off. A one-hour session at the gym may only burn about 200 calories. But a four-hour session during which you hike to the crag, carry your gear, and climb may demand up to 1200 calories. Furthermore, more energy is burned if you are climbing all day. The more familiar you are with a route, the less energy it takes to climb it.

Outdoor climbing also burns more calories than indoor climbing on average. This is because volume of maximum oxygen uptake, aka VO2 max (the oxygen your body uses during exercise), and heart rate are usually higher in outdoor climbing. Why would your oxygen uptake and heart rate be higher during outdoor climbing? Usually people spend more time in isometric contraction (this means holding one position while muscles are flexed) in outdoor climbing. This uses more calories. Also, outdoor climbs usually just take longer to send than indoor climbs. Outdoor climbs also have a certain thrill or fear factor that causes you to expend extra energy in your body's response to the climb. If the outdoor climb takes place in extreme conditions, such as high altitude, heat, wind, or cold, this also requires more energy.

At rest, your body is using energy to maintain body processes—respiration, circulation, digestion, normal cell turnover, etc. When you start to work, your body responds by increasing circulation, respiration (breathing), and heat production, contracting muscles, and so on. Thus, all body processes in action use more energy.

Everything we eat–carbohydrates, fats, proteins, and alcohol–can be used for energy to fuel these needs. To understand what kind of fuel your body needs, it's important to understand the different energy systems the body uses.

There are three main energy systems:

Creatine-phosphagen: OK, remember the Krebs Cycle from high school biology? Nope? Here's a refresher, minus the quiz: There is something called ATP, which stands for adenosine triphosphate. This is often called the "energy currency" of the cell. A molecule called creatine phosphate (CP) is used to make ATP. There is a very limited amount of both CP and ATP in the muscles. The creatine-phosphagen energy system uses CP and ATP to create energy for short bursts of intense work, lasting less than around 30 seconds–like a sprint, speed climbing, or a hard push through a crux of a route.

Anaerobic glycolysis: Anaerobic means "without oxygen". This energy system uses energy in glucose (blood sugar) to make ATP. It uses glucose by breaking it down into a molecule called pyruvate. This energy system helps muscles work intensely for around 30 seconds to 3 minutes.

In the anaerobic energy system, oxygen is not present. It's primarily used in short, explosive moves that really tax your body, like a big dyno where you can only keep up this intensity for a few seconds; breathing and heart rate are high. The main fuel for this energy system is carbohydrate. Fatigue occurs quickly when working at this intensity. You may also feel the waste product of lactate build up, which causes the burning feeling in muscles. This isn't harmful. Lactate can actually be taken up and used by the cells again for fueling exercise. But as any climber knows, it's certainly uncomfortable and can be a limiting factor in how well you climb.

Aerobic glycolysis: The aerobic energy system means oxygen is present to fuel metabolism. It uses a combination of carbohydrate and fat. You are using this system when you are climbing, walking, running, or doing any other activity at an endurance pace. It's something you could keep up for a while. Breathing and heart rate are higher than at rest, but manageable.

PHYSIOLOGY BASICS

Energy (continued)

While the different energy systems rely on different fuels, in general the body doesn't exclusively rely on one fuel. As workload increases and you start to exercise harder, the body doesn't "switch" from one system to the other. As you go from aerobic to anaerobic, the proportions of the energy systems recruited change to utilize more carbohydrate, but usually you are using a mix of carbohydrate, fat, and protein.

This is why it's important to eat regularly if you are climbing more than two hours, such as during all day, multi-pitch climbing, or all-day comps. It's also important to eat after you climb, because this helps replenish glycogen stores to get your body ready for the next climbing session.

Glycogen comes into play here. Glycogen is a stored form of sugar in your skeletal muscles. Think of it as on-board fuel for your muscles. It is used for muscle contraction while climbing, hiking, or any other exercise. You have glycogen in your liver as well. This glycogen is usually used to fuel your body overnight while you are sleeping. Overall, most people have about 1400–2000 calories worth of glycogen stored in their bodies, depending on how much carbohydrate they ate and how much exercise they did the previous day.

As you begin to climb (or hike to the crag, or warm up, or whatever), your body starts using that glycogen to fuel your activity. After about 90 minutes of work, glycogen may be used up (or, at least, it's lower than when you started) and your blood sugar can drop unless you've been fueling during that time by either eating or drinking something with carbohydrate in it. If you have to hike an hour or two just to get to the crag, you may already be out of fuel by the time you're ready to climb.

Your body can adapt over time to utilize more fat during exercise via specific training regimens. I.e., you can change your nutrition intake to strategically and purposefully eat less carbohydrate for certain training days or sessions, in order to teach your body to adapt to using fat more than carbohydrate. This has been researched in endurance athletes, but not climbers. But the gist of it is that you might not have to be so reliant on carbohydrate.

There are a couple of drawbacks to training your body to fuel via fat. First, intensity suffers because your body utilizes carbohydrate for hard, explosive moves. If your body is not able to access the carbohydrate because (1) it's depleted, (2) that energy system has been downregulated (because it's not used regularly), or (3) your diet doesn't have enough carbohydrate, your climbing performance can suffer. Dynos, jumps, pushing through a crux—basically anything that takes a significant amount of intense effort—will be harder to perform. Second, climbers are usually really lean. If you don't have a lot of fat stores to draw from, purposefully training your body to utilize fat while climbing doesn't make much sense because it's not there.

Later in the book, we'll cover what types of foods to eat, when to eat them, and how to eat for different goals, such as replenishing glycogen, losing weight, or building muscle.

Heart Rate

In terms of aerobic intensity, indoor climbing has been compared to someone running at a moderate pace of about 8 to 11 minutes per mile. Heart rate seems more elevated in climbing than one would expect given the rate of exertion. In most sports, heart rate increases proportionately with intensity–If you run faster, your heart rate goes up more than if you run slower. But in climbing, even while climbing at a slow or moderate pace without using up too much oxygen, heart rate skyrockets. The effect is even more pronounced in outdoor climbing. Why is this?

Researchers aren't sure, but they have some theories. One is that a lot of forearm-muscle contraction increases heart rate. Another is that arms raised above the head (as in common climbing positions) increases heart rate. And another is that the psychological aspect of being up high on a wall increases anxiety. A bit more freaking out, if you will, causes an elevated heart rate.

Other factors that raise heart rate include lead climbing versus toprope climbing, and climbing on routes with difficult angles or hold configurations. It seems that climbers on familiar routes have lower heart rates and less of a physiological response than climbers who are climbing a route for the first time. This means that if you want to feel calmer, familiarity with the route can help.

Heart Rate (continued)

One study showed climbers' heart rates ranging between 129 and 180 beats per minute during activity, which is a pretty normal range for someone exercising.

In an interview with Hans Florine, a world-class climber, I got a little insight that's exciting for a nutrition and exercise nerd like myself. He often wore a heart-rate monitor while climbing in Yosemite, and his heart rate was usually around 118. Contrast this with his average heart rate during a marathon, which is 140. So, climbing does elicit a lower heart rate than endurance exercise, at least for someone as trained as Hans Florine. For an exclusive interview with Hans about what he eats to fuel his climbing, see page 60.

Alex Honnold and Tommy Caldwell in 2018 set the speed record for climbing the *Nose* on El Capitan in Yosemite National Park (California, USA) at a blistering fast 1:57:07. They chatted during a podcast about their heart rates. Although they weren't wearing heart-rate monitors while climbing that day, they said they guessed their heart rate felt like it would during a slow, easy jog for most of the ascent. Only toward the end when there was a final push did Caldwell feel like he redlined (meaning his heart rate went beyond what is normal for exercising: It was very high and felt intense).

If you feel like your heart rate skyrockets while climbing (aside from speed climbing), it's a good idea to incorporate some cardiovascular training and base-level endurance climbing into your routine. This can help you better tolerate hard climbing, be more efficient with energy use, and also get into better shape for long approaches.

THE WRAP-UP FOR CLIMBING PHYSIOLOGY

The creatine-phosphagen energy system **is utilized for short bursts of intense activity lasting less than 30 seconds. The** anaerobic glycolysis energy system **is used for about 30 seconds–3 minutes of hard work. These both use carbohydrates. The** anaerobic glycolysis energy system **is used for endurance activities and uses both carbohydrate and fat.**

Heart rate **is in general higher during outdoor climbing versus indoor climbing.**

CHAPTER 2 REFERENCES

Balás, Jan Kodejška, and Nick Draper. 2014. "The Relationship Between Climbing Ability and Physiological Responses to Rock Climbing." *The Scientific World Journal* no. 2: 678387.

Billat, Veronique, Pierre Palleja, Therry Charlaix, Pierre Rizzardo, and Nicolas Janel. 2005. "Energy Specificity of Rock Climbing and Aerobic Capacity." *Journal of Sports Medicine and Physical Fitness* 35: 20-24.

Booth, John, Frank Marino, Chris Hill, and Tom Gwinn. 1999. "Energy Cost of Sport Rock Climbing in Elite Performers." *British Journal of Sports Medicine* 33, no. 1: 14-18.

de Moraes, Bertuzzi, Rômulo Cássio, Emerson Franchini, Eduardo Kokubun, and Maria Augusta Peduti Dal Molin Kiss. 2007. "Energy System Contributions in Indoor Rock Climbing." *European Journal of Applied Physiology* 101, no. 3: 293-300.

Dickson, Tabitha, Simon Fryer, Gavin Blackwell, Nick Draper, and Lee Stoner. 2012. "Effect of Style of Ascent on the Psychophysiological Demands of Rock Climbing in Elite Level Climbers." *Sports Technology* 5, no. 3-4: 111-119.

Fryer, Simon, Lee Stoner, Keeron Stone, David Giles, Joakim Sveen, Inma Garrido, and Vanesa España-Romero. 2016. "Forearm Muscle Oxidative Capacity Index Predicts Sport Rock-Climbing Performance." *European Journal of Applied Physiology* 116, no. 8: 1479-1484.

Maughan, Ronald J., and Michael Gleeson. 2010. *The Biochemical Basis of Sports Performance*. Oxford: Oxford University Press: 10-11.

Maughan, Ronald J., Susan M. Shirreffs. 2015. "Physiology of Sports," *Clinical Sports Nutrition*, 5th ed., edited by Louise Burke and Vicki Deakin, 767-786. Australia: McGraw Hill Education.

McDonald, Dougald. "Alex Honnold and Tommy Caldwell on The Nose" (Podcast). Accessed April 26, 2019. *The Cutting Edge Podcast, Episode 8. American Alpine Journal*.

Mermier, Christine M., Jeffrey M. Janot, Daryl L. Parker, and Jacob G. Swan. 2000. "Physiological and Anthropometric Determinants of Sport Climbing Performance." *British Journal of Sports Medicine* 34: 359-365.

Mermier, Christine M., Robert A. Robergs, Susie M. McMinn, and Vivian H. Heyward. 1997. "Energy Expenditure and Physiological Responses During Indoor Rock Climbing." *British Journal of Sports Medicine* 31, no. 3: 224-228.

Sheel, A. W. 2004. "Physiology of Sport Rock Climbing." 2004. *British Journal of Sports Medicine* 38, no. 3 (2004): 355-359.

Watts, P. B., M. Daggett, P. Gallagher, and B. Wilkins. 2000. "Metabolic Response During Sport Rock Climbing and the Effects of Active Versus Passive Recovery." *International Journal of Sports Medicine* 21, no. 03: 185-190.

Watts, Phillip B. 2004. "Physiology of Difficult Rock Climbing." *European Journal of Applied Physiology* 91, no. 4: 361-372.

Wimer, Gregory S., and James C. Baldi. 2012. "Limb-Specific Training Affects Exercise Hyperemia but Not Sympathetic Vasoconstriction." *European Journal of Applied Physiology* 112, no. 11: 3819-3828.

Zarattini, Josiane A., Daisy Motta-Santos, Edgardo AC Abreu, Herikson A. Costa, Guilherme L. Carvalho, Thiago T. Mendes, and André Scotti Rabelo. 2018. "Lead Climb Induces Higher Heart Rate Responses Compared to the Top Rope in Intermediate and Advanced Climbers." *Journal of Exercise Physiology Online* 21, no. 1.

"I feel like variety is very important. It's easy to get tired of the same types of foods.... People think I'm weird packing a whole green bell pepper in my pack, but it's lightweight and really refreshing up on the wall...Just think of things you enjoy eating and take them with you. There's usually a way to bring whatever food you'd like to bring."

—Hans Florine

PART II
NUTRITION FOR DIFFERENT TYPES OF CLIMBING

3 - NUTRITION FOR **INDOOR CLIMBING**

CHAPTER 3

NUTRITION FOR INDOOR CLIMBING

Joe is an accountant. He's in a rush in the morning, so he skips breakfast. He sits at his desk all day, crunching numbers and mindlessly munching on popcorn from the break room. There's no real lunch to speak of, just some trail mix and an apple at his desk. He sits some more, then drives to the climbing gym after work. At the gym, he feels frustrated that he has plateaued in his climbing. He's not getting stronger, and he hasn't climbed a harder grade in six months. He is irritable and slips off easy moves.

Joe isn't real, but he represents many clients who come through my office door–professionals by day, athletes by night. Under-fueled and overstressed, not making gains and not feeling well.

If you are a climber who trains and competes predominantly in a gym, this chapter will help you home in on specific nutrition advice that will help you progress. Even if you're a hardcore outdoor climber, you usually end up climbing indoors at some point, so the information in this chapter will be helpful as well.

> From a nutrition standpoint, there are a few things to consider about **indoor climbing** that differ from outdoor climbing:
>
> » Often, climbing sessions take place after work or school, which means you may be low on fuel if you weren't able to eat enough during the day.
>
> » Indoor climbing is in a temperate environment (no extreme heat, cold, humidity, or wind).
>
> » Indoor climbers usually have easy access to food, water, and restrooms.
>
> » Climbing competitions (comps) can be all-day or multi-day events, meaning a strategic fueling plan is necessary to avoid running out of fuel or over-fueling/-hydrating.
>
> » Weekend warriors who only hit the gym once a week, but go for a long, hard session, need to properly fuel that session and the recovery period afterwards.

3 - NUTRITION FOR INDOOR CLIMBING

This chapter outlines how to eat for all these different scenarios. Keep in mind that throughout this book, the recommendations are for adults. If you are a teen/adolescent climber, there is a separate section just for you (see chapter 6). Many of these nutrition concepts still apply to you, but teens/adolescents need to consider their growing bodies, and thus may need to fuel differently.

A Climbing Session at the End of the Day (After Work or School):

This means you've had a long day of doing other things (like sitting at a desk, thinking hard, or participating in school PE) that may drain you. To feel fresh for a climbing session, it's important to fuel right throughout the day as well as just before the climbing session.

Start the day right by eating a breakfast with both protein and carbohydrate. Eating within an hour of waking up will help your body be energized for your day. Eat according to your hunger throughout the day, usually every three to four hours. Lunch should be substantial. An afternoon snack an hour or two before you climb will help you re-fuel from your mostly digested lunch, but at the same time should be small enough as to not feel too heavy in your stomach when you start climbing.

Here is what a sample meal plan looks like for a climber who works or goes to school during the day, and climbs in the late afternoon or evening. Portion sizes will vary from person to person, based on calorie needs and current hunger level.

Meal	Time	Food
BREAKFAST	8 am	2 eggs, whole-grain toast with peanut butter, orange
SNACK	10:30 am	Apple and string cheese
LUNCH	1 pm	Tortilla wrap with black beans, avocado, shredded cheese, salsa, and spinach
SNACK	4 pm	White mini-bagel
CLIMB!	5 pm–6:30 pm	Not needed unless hungry
DINNER	7 pm	Salmon, quinoa, and asparagus
SNACK	9 pm	Chocolate milk

EXAMPLES OF QUICK-DIGESTING CARBS:

- Pretzels
- White mini-bagel
- Fruit—apples, bananas, oranges, etc.
- Dried fruit
- Sports drink
- Graham crackers
- Chocolate milk
- Animal crackers
- Waffle or pancake (not whole grain)
- Gels (like Gu)
- Sports gummies and chews
- Fruit leather

You might need to pair the carb sources above with some protein to help the food last longer in your system. You'd do this if you had the time to digest between rounds (about two to four hours). Things like string cheese, nuts, jerky, nut-butter pouches, protein bars and shakes, a tuna or chicken sandwich, and hardboiled eggs are quick, easy snacks that you can consume throughout the comp.

Be sure to test all foods and fluids before the actual comp by trying them out during practice, to make sure you tolerate them. You don't want any gastrointestinal surprises during competition! Nothing new on comp day.

All-Day Comp

For a competition that lasts all day, you want to fuel consistently to make sure you have enough energy when it's time to climb. Unpredictable comp schedules make it hard to know when, what, and how much to eat. If you're going to be in isolation for part of the time, that's an additional nutritional challenge where you don't have access to outside food or water. Conversely, you also want to avoid overeating because of boredom or nerves.

Try to eat things that have very little fiber or fat. This allows for your stomach to digest the food quickly. This is good for two reasons: (1) It makes the food available as fuel faster, and (2) Your stomach will feel lighter and not bogged down by a heavy meal when you need to climb.

Repeat after me, "Nothing new on comp day!"

For hydrating throughout the day, you can drink according to your thirst. If you tend to get distracted or forget to drink, plan a schedule to drink about eight ounces every 60–90 minutes. Drink what agrees with your stomach and makes you feel hydrated and fueled. For some, that can mean a sports drink like Gatorade. Others prefer just water. Watch your urine color. It should be light yellow. If it's too dark, like a brown tea color, drink more. If it is clear or very light and you feel like you're going to the bathroom too much, you don't need to drink as much.

All-Day Comp (CONTINUED)

Hydrating and eating enough carbohydrates will help you climb your best. If you experience any of these symptoms, it means you are not eating or drinking enough:

- **You suddenly feel very hungry during climbing (breakthrough hunger).**
- **You feel like you fade away toward the end of your session. You can't quite do a move that should be easy.**
- **You feel like your concentration and mental focus are not as sharp as the session goes on.**
- **You make dumb mistakes you don't usually make.**
- **You feel dizzy, shaky, or nauseated.**
- **You are hangry (hungry + angry) and irritable.**
- **You quit earlier than you'd like, either from mental or physical exhaustion (or both).**

While you'll learn much more about supplements in chapter 8, it's worth mentioning one here: Caffeine can be a huge help during comps. Along with ingesting carbs and hydrating, caffeine can give you an extra boost. It can improve endurance, delay fatigue, improve mood and alertness, improve reaction time, and decrease perceived pain.

An effective dose is around 100–200 milligrams. A cup of coffee has about 60–150 milligrams. Energy gummies have 20–150 milligrams (check the label). Caffeinated soda pop has about 35–115 milligrams. Avoid energy drinks that have excessive amounts of caffeine or other ingredients whose effect is unknown (like herbal additives).

Be cautious if you are not used to caffeine. Watch out for digestive issues, jitteriness, anxiety, or an elevated heart rate. Don't use caffeine if you feel these side effects. Also, make sure you are in compliance with your governing body by triple-checking to make sure caffeine is a permitted substance. It would be a terrible thing to be disqualified based on having a cup of coffee.

> **TO SUMMARIZE:** Eat foods that are easy on your stomach and quick to digest. Avoid fatty, greasy, or high-fiber foods. Hydrate properly.

This sample menu gives you an idea of what to eat for multiple climbing rounds. If they are closer together, just have quick-digesting carbs as listed on page 35. If they are farther apart and you have 2–4 hours to digest something, you can have a bit more fat and fiber in your meal. Drink about 8 ounces (250 milliliters) every hour, or so, of either water or sports drink.

SAMPLE MENU: All-Day Comp with Multiple Rounds*

Event	Time	Time Eaten	Food
BREAKFAST	8 am	Prior to event	Steel-cut oats with walnuts, berries, and milk. Orange juice as a beverage
ROUND 1 CLIMBING	10 am	After event	Pretzels and sports drink
ROUND 2 CLIMBING	12 pm	After event	Peanut butter and jam sandwich on white bread with apple slices. Chocolate milk as a beverage
ROUND 3 CLIMBING (ISOLATION)	3 pm	Eat/drink as needed in isolation	Sports gummies and sports drink.
ROUND 4 CLIMBING	5 pm	Prior to event as needed	Raisins and sports drink
DINNER	7 pm	After event	Quinoa bowl with black beans, salsa, cheese, avocado, and ground beef, with a fruit and yogurt smoothie

*Food and beverage quantities vary based on age, body weight, number of rounds, and discipline.

Multi-Day Comp:

Your nutrition needs will be similar to an all-day comp, just set on repeat.
Your body is in recovery mode for 24-48 hours after you work out, rebuilding and repairing muscles. As soon as 30-60 minutes after working out, certain body processes begin to kick in to start the recovery from your training session.

The evening meal after the comp should be heartier–and be sure to include both carbohydrates and protein. Eating both does a couple of great things for your body: First, carbohydrates help replenish glycogen, which is the stored form of glucose (sugar) in your muscles. It's the on-board fuel that helps with muscle contraction. Replenishing glycogen will set you up for a well-fueled workout the next day. Second, eating enough protein helps support muscle growth and repair. Protein before bed helps your body repair and build muscle during the night. The dose is high: Aim for 20-30 grams, which you can get from two scoops of protein powder, four eggs, or a large chicken breast. Finally, also enjoy a diet full of fruits and vegetables to provide vitamins, minerals, and antioxidants for cell function and repair.

POST-COMP MEALS

The following examples will get you well on your way to proper recovery:

» Power grain bowl: quinoa, chicken, black beans, shredded cheese, and salsa. Pair with a piece of fruit and some chocolate milk.

» Turkey sandwich with cheese and avocado. Pair with carrots and hummus.

» Veggie omelet and avocado toast. Pair with chocolate milk.

» Pasta with tofu and veggies.

» Fruit and yogurt smoothie with a PB&J sandwich.

» Veggie wrap with tofu. Pair with a fruit salad.

Long Gym Session

If you're the type of person who doesn't climb during the week, then goes all-out on the weekend, there are a couple things to keep in mind for your nutrition needs.

First, you can fuel similarly to the all-day comp strategies mentioned on page 36. Eating simple carbohydrates that are easy on your stomach and digest quickly will help you stay energized throughout the day. Couple that with some protein and healthful fats, and you're good to go.

The difference between these occasional spurts of long climbing on the weekend and climbing several times a week is that your muscles and body might feel extra sore since you're not as used to climbing and training. If you feel particularly beat-up after your weekend-warrior session, eat lean protein and healthful fats like fish, nuts, and seeds. Eat plenty of fruits and vegetables because these have antioxidants and anti-inflammatory properties, which will enable your body to recover and minimize soreness. Be sure to rest the next day by getting adequate sleep and skipping a second hard workout—this is a time for just foam rolling and light stretching.

"Food first" is a good way to eat, but some supplements may be worth considering. Muscle soreness may be helped with fish-oil supplements at 3000–4000 milligrams per day. Tart cherry juice, at least 12–24 ounces, is an anti-inflammatory and may reduce muscle damage. (Bonus: It's a food, not a supplement!) Always talk with your doctor before adding any supplements like fish oil to make sure they're right for you. For more detailed information about supplements, see chapter 8.

CHAPTER 3 REFERENCES

Beelen, Milou, Louise M. Burke, Martin J. Gibala, and Luc JC Van Loon. 2010. "Nutritional Strategies to Promote Postexercise Recovery." *International Journal of Sport Nutrition and Exercise Metabolism* 20, no. 6: 515-532.

Joubert Lanae, Larson Abigail, Weber Sarah. "Nutrition and Hydration Strategies to Enhance Sport and Multi-Pitch Climbing Performance." 2016. *Presented at the International Rock Climbing Research Association Annual Congress:* August 5-7, 2016.

Rawson, Eric S., Mary P. Miles, and D. Enette Larson-Meyer. 2018. "Dietary Supplements for Health, Adaptation, and Recovery in Athletes." *International Journal of Sport Nutrition and Exercise Metabolism* 28, no. 2: 188-199.

Sawka, Michael N., Louise M. Burke, E. Randy Eichner, Ronald J. Maughan, Scott J. Montain, and Nina S. Stachenfeld. 2007. "American College of Sports Medicine Position Stand. Exercise and Fluid Replacement." *Medicine and Science in Sports and Exercise* 39, no. 2: 377-390.

Wang, Haibo, Muraleedharan G. Nair, Gale M. Strasburg, Yu-Chen Chang, Alden M. Booren, J. Ian Gray, and David L. DeWitt. 1999. "Antioxidant and Anti Inflammatory Activities of Anthocyanins and their Aglycon, Cyanidin, from Tart Cherries." *Journal of Natural Products* 62, no. 2: 294-296.

CHAPTER 4

NUTRITION FOR OUTDOOR CLIMBING

Three exercise physiologists, one sports dietitian, and one grad student went climbing in Colorado. Through a comedy of errors, it turned out they only had about 16 ounces, or about half a liter of water, for ALL OF THEM for an entire climbing session of several hours.

How did this happen? Dr. Lanae Joubert, the dietitian in the bunch, had her trusty water bottle with her, which started out full at the airport. While driving from the airport to the climbing destination (with a traffic jam and several wrong turns), she drank about half. The other people in the party brought nothing with them. Everyone had been traveling and in a rush. No one thought ahead of time. No one volunteered to hike the mile back to the car and drive somewhere to get water because that would have cut into precious climbing time.

> When Dr. Joubert realized she was the only person with water (and an inadequate supply even for just her), she quickly added up in her head **all the fluid losses for the day:**
>
> » **4½ hours on an airplane** (flying is dehydrating)
>
> » **Climbing at a higher altitude** than she is used to: 6400 feet above see level vs. 600 feet at home (high altitude increases fluid needs)
>
> » **Exercising in the heat** (heat increases fluid needs)

The result wasn't pretty: a severe headache, a climbing session cut short, and cranky climbing companions. Fortunately, no one got injured or severely dehydrated. This example is proof that, even with abundant knowledge of nutrition, one can make mistakes in their hydration and fueling.

Another less fortunate story: Yosemite National Park, May 2015. Three climbers on their third day on the *Nose* made simple mistakes—a dropped nut, a Grigri closed but not clipped to a rope—that led to a fatality which possibly could have been avoided. The post-accident analysis concluded, among other things, that drinking and eating regularly could have prevented this tragedy. "Even the most experienced climbers are vulnerable to errors. . . Recognizing our vulnerability to these mistakes, and how exhaustion, hunger, and dehydration play into them, is the first step in preventing. . . Outdoor climbing is a serious business. Errors can result in injury and death. Fueling and hydrating properly can not only enhance performance but can help prevent tragedy by adequately fueling the brain and muscles," Alexa Flower and Miranda Oakley wrote in a feature posted at Climbing.com.

> There are some things to consider with outdoor climbing that are different from indoor climbing. For one, you are outside (duh), so you are at the mercy of Mother Nature. Weather conditions can play a role in how much you need to eat and drink. Altitude affects your carbohydrate and fluid needs. Wind, heat, snow, and humidity all play a role in how your body needs to be fueled.
>
> Think about the last time you were climbing outdoors. Did you feel hungry? Weak? Shaky? Did you fade away toward the end of the session? Make simple mistakes? Feel like your mind wasn't as sharp? Get irritable? (Your climbing buddies LOVE that!)
>
> Some of these things are natural consequences of your body just becoming fatigued from climbing. But often, they're a result of not eating and drinking enough. All these are symptoms of either dehydration, low blood sugar, or both.

So how do you prevent this? How much food and water do you need? That depends on your gender, height, weight, body composition, the type of climbing you do, whether you need to hike to/from the crag, weather, and myriad of other factors. Obviously, it's impossible for me to tell you how much to eat and drink for each situation. But by using some sports nutrition principles applied to climbing, I can give you a good idea.

First, let's talk about overall energy needs. You get energy from the food you eat, and also any beverages that have calories. Eating enough calories while climbing throughout the day is a must. Drawing from chapter 2, remember that you burn about 10–11 calories per minute of active climbing. Outdoor climbs usually involve some hiking as well. If you load your pack with gear, food, and water, you may be carrying an extra 20–40 pounds (9–18 kilograms). This means extra calories are needed to carry that load while hiking. A four-hour climbing excursion with a hike in and out can use up about 1200–1500 calories.

If you are climbing all day, you need to eat regularly. Those calories are important. Without fuel, you can become fatigued more quickly and are more prone to making mistakes, both physically and mentally. You need to be sharp in order to climb well and safely.

Carbohydrates

are necessary to help fuel your muscle contractions, fuel your brain, and keep your blood sugar up. Carbs help all energy systems in your body run. If you are low on carbohydrates, you will suffer from fatigue and irritability, not to mention your mental game will not be as sharp. Whether your route has slow moves with isometric contractions (holding still while flexing muscle[s] to pause on a route) or has dramatic dynos, you will need carbohydrates to fuel your climb.

A range that may work for you is about three to five grams of carbs per kilogram of body weight per day. Endurance athletes need a lot more carbs—their recommendation is usually around 9 to 12 grams per kilogram per day. Climbers have different needs. To find your carb requirements, first find your weight in kilograms. Take your weight in pounds, divided by 2.2. For example, a 150-pound person weighs 68 kilograms. Then multiply that by three to five. 68 x 3 = 204. 68 x 5 = 340. So, you need about 204–240 grams of carbs per day on average. You can track that in an app like MyFitnessPal, LoseIt, or Track by Nutritionix, or just read the food label and add up your grams of carbs eaten per day.

During periods of rest throughout your climbing session, eat or drink about 20-30 grams of carbs per hour. Here's a list of foods that meet that carbohydrate requirement:

- 1 oz (28 grams) pretzels (23 grams of carbs)
- 1 banana (27 grams of carbs)
- 1 white mini-bagel (23 grams of carbs)
- 14 ounces (414 milliliters) sports drink (25 grams of carbs)
- 2 oranges (22 grams of carbs)
- 1 apple (25 grams of carbs)
- 2 applesauce pouches (130 grams of carbs)
- 1-ounce (28 grams) animal crackers (21 grams of carbs)
- ½ c (170 grams) blueberries (21 grams of carbs)
- 2 graham cracker sheets (22 grams of carbs)
- ½ c (170 grams) dried apricots (40 grams of carbs)
- 30 crackers (20 grams of carbs)
- 1 box raisins (34 grams of carbs)
- 2 fruit-leather strips (22 grams of carbs)
- 2 packets honey (24 grams of carbs)
- 2 sports gummies (24 grams of carbs)
- 1 pouch fruit snacks (21 grams of carbs)
- 1 Pop Tart (34 grams of carbs)

Protein

is useful for all-day climbs as well. It helps keep you feeling full, rather than relying solely on carbs. If you are only eating carbohydrates all day long, you will feel temporarily better from a blood sugar spike, but then the spike will quickly dissipate, leaving you feeling hungry or under-fueled an hour or two later.

Pairing carbs with protein during long climbs helps stabilize blood sugar. This also contributes to satisfaction and not feeling hungry too quickly. Another great thing about protein is that it can help with muscle rebuilding, repair, and recovery. If you are already consuming protein throughout the day, you'll be much more apt to recover once you're done climbing. In general, about 10 grams of protein every two hours will be sufficient.

Here are some examples of protein-containing snacks for climbing:

- 1-ounce (28 grams) jerky (12 grams of protein)
- ½ c (170 grams) mixed nuts (14 grams of protein)
- 1 shelf-stable chocolate-milk box (9 grams of protein)
- 1 almond butter squeeze pouch (7 grams of protein)
- 1 peanut butter and jelly sandwich (20 grams of protein)
- 1 hardboiled egg (eat early in the day to avoid spoilage; 7 grams of protein)
- 1 Cheese stick (eat early to avoid spoilage; 8 grams of protein)
- 1-ounce (28 grams) pepperoni stick (6 grams of protein)
- 1/2 c (170 grams) trail mix (8 grams of protein)
- 1-ounce (28 grams) pretzels with 2 Tbsp (28 grams) hummus (7 grams of protein)

Here are some examples of mixed (carb and protein) foods that are good for outdoor climbing:

- Peanut butter and jelly sandwich
- Shelf-stable fruit cups
- Bars (KIND, Clif, Larabar, Picky Bars, Nature Valley, and Rx bars are examples of bars made with whole ingredients)
- Energy bites made from nut butters, chopped nuts, chocolate chips, coconut, honey, protein powder, etc. (see chapter 12 for sample recipes)
- Trail mix
- Pudding cups
- Canned soups, chili, ravioli
- Wraps
- Tuna pouches
- Crackers

Hydration

is critical. Even just mild dehydration can impair your thinking and judgement. As you begin exercising, you sweat. Even when it's cold outside, your body will lose water through sweat, metabolic processes, and respiration (breathing). Your mental and physical performance decline if you lose more than around two percent of your body weight as water weight during exercise. Your athletic performance (climbing ability and effectiveness) will also likely suffer even more as the day goes on as you lose water. In endurance athletes, exercising for more than 90 minutes with this 2 percent (or greater) body-weight loss results in poorer performance. We don't know what this means in climbing, but it's safe to say that hydrating properly is important to all athletes.

Hydration studies conducted in other sports show that dehydration is accompanied by a loss of endurance performance, mental sharpness and accuracy, and also increases fatigue. If you think about it, hydration is probably more important in climbing than most other sports. If someone is playing soccer, tennis, or football, or running or doing anything else, it's usually not life-threatening to be a bit dehydrated. Your performance suffers a bit, you don't feel good, but unless dehydration is severe, you'll be OK.

Contrast this with climbing, where a small mistake, sluggish reaction time, or fatigue can mean neglecting to follow safety protocols. This can translate into severe injury or death.

I don't want to scare anyone, but it's important to understand how dehydration can affect your ability to make good decisions, climb well, and stay safe.

Hydration (continued)

Most sports nutrition research studies about hydration have been done on endurance athletes, such as cyclists and runners. Although climbers aren't endurance athletes, there is usually an element of endurance on a climbing trip. Hiking to and from the crag is endurance, especially if it is a long approach. Climbing a long or multi-pitch route is also endurance. Even though most of what we understand about hydration comes from studying different types of athletes, what we know can still apply to climbers. It is certain that performance suffers with dehydration. Starting the day already hydrated better sets you up for a great climbing day.

To make things even more complicated, you can't always rely on thirst to tell you when to drink. In situations where you might not have access to water (say, 80 feet up on a crag in a desert), you might not drink regularly. Physical exertion and the environment (wind, temperature, humidity, altitude) can alter thirst sensations. This means you may need fluids even without feeling thirsty.

Now that you understand the importance of avoiding dehydration, let's take a look at how overhydration can be just as harmful. You don't want to be overhydrated. You don't want to be underhydrated. So where is the happy medium?

Overhydration

Overhydration can affect your climbing a few different ways. First, a sloshy stomach full of fluids isn't so pleasant when you are on a physically demanding route. If you have to contort your body like a master yogi, or do a heel hook or a bat hang, you don't want your stomach to feel heavy or sloshy. But beyond that, there is a state called hyponatremia (meaning the sodium in your blood is low) that can occur with too much fluid intake.

Hyponatremia happens when someone drinks so much that they actually dilute their blood sodium levels to a perilous degree. This can happen in endurance sports where the events are really long. Think about a really slow marathon runner. If it takes someone five hours to do a marathon, they are on the race course longer than a faster runner. This means more opportunities to drink at aid stations. Meandering down the race course while constantly sipping water can make a person overhydrate.

No one knows if this really happens in climbers, because it's never been studied. But if you are out there all day long exerting yourself, you might also be drinking a lot–especially if you are hot and thirsty. So, over the course of the day, you could develop hyponatremia if you don't also have some sodium with your water.

Symptoms of hyponatremia include dizziness, nausea, confusion, headache, and fatigue. This is a dangerous medical condition that needs immediate attention.

Carbohydrate Mouth Rinse

A new tactic endurance athletes use is called carbohydrate mouth rinse. Cyclists sometimes use this technique when they don't need to take on more fluid, but want an extra boost in performance. This is untested and un-researched in rock climbers, but it may be useful in certain situations. It's a specific strategy wherein you drink a bit of sports drink, swish it around in your mouth, and spit it out (don't swallow).

Why would you do this? Usually you'd do so if you feel like you're already pretty hydrated and you want to avoid a heavy stomach, but at the same time you feel like you need some fuel to keep you going.

The act of rinsing out your mouth with something sugary sends a signal to your brain that makes it think it's receiving food. In endurance athletes, this mouth rinse has helped them extend their time to exhaustion and improve their rate of perceived exertion. This could possibly translate into going longer and stronger when climbing.

Carbohydrate mouth rinse isn't for everyone, and not all situations need it. Mostly, it's best to just eat and drink. But keep the mouth rinse in mind if you are hydrated and want to avoid overhydration. (Side note: Some athletes have adopted the swish-and-spit method when fasting during Ramadan. It allows a bit of a performance boost without breaking the fast.)

Dehydration

So now a few words about dehydration. Signs and symptoms of dehydration include increased thirst, dry mouth, dark urine, dizziness, foggy mind, and fatigue. This also is a dangerous condition that needs immediate treatment.

How do you know how much to drink? A general rule of thumb is about eight ounces (250 milliliters) per hour of either sports drink or water. Choose a sports drink with carbohydrates and electrolytes in it (like Gatorade) if you're going to be climbing for hours. It's just smart. It replenishes the carbohydrates you use up while climbing, hydrates you, and gives you electrolytes all in one.

Avoid sports drinks if they cause upset stomach or gastrointestinal issues. If this is the case, just drink water and eat food. You may need to add electrolytes without sugar, such as Nuun, to your water.

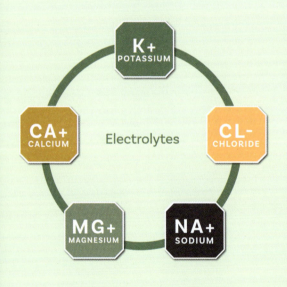

Electrolytes

And while we are on electrolytes, here's something most people don't know: "electrolytes" don't just include sodium! They're also calcium, magnesium, potassium, chloride, bicarbonate, and a few others. These are all substances in cells and blood that are necessary for normal bodily functions.

Often when people get a muscle cramp, they think they need to eat some salt. Cramps can be caused by depleted electrolytes, like sodium, but also by other things: anxiety/nervousness, dehydration, muscle fatigue, some medications, and other factors such as heat or humidity. If you are prone to cramps, talk with a sports physician and/or sports dietitian to figure out what may be causing the cramps and how to treat and prevent them.

Hydration & Urine Color

Your urine color can be a helpful tool to indicate your hydration status. Although some people may find this gross, if you can get past the ick factor, knowing all about your urine will help you be properly hydrated.

Urine color and volume can be affected by activity level, fluid intake, some medications/supplements, and diet. In general, urine should be a light yellow, like straw or lemonade. If it is darker, this may indicate dehydration. If it is very dark, like cola or tea, seek medical attention immediately. To really assess your urine color, you need to pee into a clear container, not the toilet. If you urinate into the toilet, the toilet water will dilute your urine and you won't really know the true color.

To get even more specific, you can order urine test strips. These are little plastic strips (called "urine reagent strips") that you can dip into your wonderful cup of urine you just collected. The urine then reacts to the paper and turns colors. The color corresponds with something called "urine-specific gravity." This can help you determine your hydration status.

Here's how you do it:

1. First thing in the morning, pee into a clear cup.
2. Dip your urine stick into the pee.
3. Take out the strip. Watch for the color change.
4. Compare the color change to the manufacturer's color chart to determine your urine-specific gravity.
5. Drink as needed to re-hydrate or maintain proper hydration status.

Results
Urine-specific gravity (USG) numbers interpreted:

<1.009 = Well-hydrated. Nice job.
1.009–1.020 = Hydrated. Nice job, keep it up.
1.021–1.025 = Minimally dehydrated. Drink eight ounces (240 milliliters) of water or fluid with electrolytes, and drink throughout the day.
1.026–1.030 = Dehydrated. Drink 16 ounces (480 milliliters) of water or fluid with electrolytes over the next 45 minutes. Drink throughout the day.
≥1.031 = Severely dehydrated. Drink 24 ounces (720 milliliters) of fluid with electrolytes and seek medical attention if needed.

Hydration & Urine Color (continued)

Things to remember:

» Matching the color to the manufacturer's recommendation is vital to accuracy. If the strips are old, expired, or exposed to extreme heat, they may not be accurate.

» Using strips can result in false positives or false negatives about 10-15 percent of the time. If you got a reading that seems weird, think back on the previous day—what were the circumstances? Did you drink enough? Did you have a particularly sweaty or hot workout? Do you have any signs or symptoms of dehydration or overhydration? Consider that the result may be false if it doesn't agree with what you were anticipating.

» You don't need to test your urine every day. You may only want to if you feel that your hydration is off and you need more data to figure out what to do next (i.e., drink more or seek medical attention). Testing USG can also be useful during a training or trial period where you are also measuring sweat rate and fluid consumption to really drill down into the specifics—for instance, you are planning a big climbing trip and need to know how much water to carry on the big wall, or you cramp a lot and are trying to make sure your hydration is right.

» If you are getting this specific with USG, sweat rate, and other tools, it's probably time to seek the help of a sports dietitian to guide you through the process.

Of note:

Caffeine won't dehydrate you, although some people do experience a diuretic effect—meaning it makes them have to urinate more often. Most people can tolerate up to four to five cups of coffee per day.

Urine Chart:

Color	Description
	Doing OK. You're probably well hydrated. Drink water as normal.
	You're just fine. You could stand to drink a small glass of water.
	Drink about 1/4 bottle of water, or a whole bottle if you're sweating.
	Drink about 1/2 bottle of water, or 1.5 bottles if you're sweating/exercising.
	Drink 2 bottles of water right now. If the color does not improve, go see a doctor.

Altitude

If you don't live in an area of high altitude, it's important to take precautions when climbing at higher elevations. Lower altitude is between 1000–2000 meters (3280–6561 feet), moderate is 2000–3000 meters (6561–9842 feet), high is 3000-5000 meters (9842–16,404 feet), and extreme is >5000 meters (>16,404 feet). A few different things happen in your body at high altitude.

If you're only there for a limited time for a climbing trip, your body won't really have time to adapt physiologically to the higher altitude. If you're going to be at higher altitude for weeks or months, your body will begin to adapt.

No matter what length of time you're planning on staying at high altitude, your body will react in a couple of different ways when you first arrive.

First, it is easier to become more dehydrated (which is a bad thing) because your respiratory water losses are greater, and your urinary losses are too. This means you might pee more. This translates into less overall blood volume in your body, which means your heart rate may increase, but cardiac output (the amount of blood pumped by the heart per minute) decreases. This means for each heartbeat, your muscles and other tissues aren't getting the same blood and oxygen delivered to them that they are used to. Heat regulation also becomes more difficult. According to one study, there is about a 3 percent decrease in exercise capacity for every 300 meters above 1500 meters. Imagine trying to climb a tough route at high altitude when you're not used to it. Perceived effort is increased, which means it may feel harder to do tasks you are normally used to doing without much effort. To make matters worse, usually sleep is compromised at high altitude. But proper nutrition and hydration can help with all of these negative consequences of altitude.

Altitude (continued)

Fluid needs are around three to five liters per day (that's about 13–21 eight-ounce cups!) at moderate to high altitude. This is a lot, especially if you struggle with drinking enough in general. Some studies have shown that drinking a beverage that has carbohydrates and electrolytes (like sports drinks) hydrates you better than water alone at altitude. You need extra fluids because of increased fluid loss through respiration and sweat from dry air. There's some evidence that good sleep patterns and adequate hydration can help prevent symptoms of altitude sickness.

Remember carbohydrates, the king of macronutrients for sports performance? Your body also needs more at high altitudes. Adrenaline, noradrenaline, and cortisol are all elevated with exercise at altitude. These hormones increase the use of carbohydrate for fuel. Carbohydrate is also your body's preferred energy source, especially at altitude. One study even found that using a carbohydrate sports drink instead of plain water helped mountaineers climbing Mt. Fuji reduce their heart-rate response and led to decreased body-weight loss, meaning they lost less fluid with consumption of a sports drink than with water. This could be useful information for climbers and alpinists at high altitude.

Researchers recommend at least 60 percent of your intake be from carbohydrates at high altitude.

This can be done by eating foods and drinking fluids that contain carbs. Things like bread, pasta, fruit, potatoes, rice, quinoa, tortillas, Gatorade, or other sports drinks will get the job done.

There isn't a lot of information about protein intake at altitude and how it may affect muscle growth. It's probably safe to assume that you'll need at least as much protein at a higher elevation than you would at sea level. Eating about 20-30 grams of protein after exercise and additional protein to meet your usual daily needs is probably sufficient. Daily needs are anywhere from 0.8-2 grams per kilogram of body weight.

Like protein, we don't know a lot about ideal fat intake at higher elevations either. But high-fat foods tend to be higher in calories, which is good for ensuring we eat enough overall calories to prevent weight loss. Things like jerky, chocolate, nuts, and nut butters are portable and non-perishable choices to take along to the mountain or crag.

Weight loss is a concern when spending a lot of time at high altitudes.
This is for a few reasons: You might not have access to as much food as you need at the crag or mountain, your energy expenditure (amount of energy your body uses up) increases at high altitude, you are exerting more effort because of the difficulty of the terrain, and appetite is sometimes decreased. Eating more calories can be helpful to aid your body in adapting to altitude and exercise. It can also help your immune system, which can be compromised at higher altitude. Eating adequate calories can help avoid unintended weight loss and fuel your performance.

There are a few more things to consider when you are climbing at high elevations. You want to start out with adequate iron stores. If you are planning a high-altitude climb, or climb at high altitude frequently, it's worth checking your iron. Go to a physician and ask for some blood to be drawn to test your iron stores. If you have any abnormalities, talk with your doctor and/or sports dietitian about supplementation and adding iron-rich foods into your diet. Food sources of iron include fortified grains, beef, spinach, lentils, kidney beans, organ meats, and eggs. It may also be advantageous to supplement with iron while at high altitude; using 210 milligrams of iron as a daily supplement can help prevent iron deficiency. Check with your doctor before supplementing to get the correct dose and form of iron that is right for you. You'll need to get blood work (labs) to determine this.

Climbing in the Cold

If you are climbing year-round, ice climbing, or climbing at higher elevations, you're bound to run into cold conditions. Even if it's not high altitude, but there are snow, glaciers, or rain, your body is more susceptible to becoming cold. It might be hard to maintain hydration and body temperature if you are sweating and then getting chilled. Shivering increases glucose needs and glycogen use (remember, glycogen is the storage form of sugar in your muscles). If glucose and glycogen are being used up to shiver, that makes it hard for your muscles to use them to send a route.

In general, eating adequate calories and drinking enough fluids will help in a cold environment. Warm or hot drinks and soup can help make you feel warmer.

One study looked at mountaineers climbing Denali in Alaska. They studied whether hydration status (meaning, were the climbers adequately hydrated, overhydrated, or underhydrated) affected their ability to summit. They found that over half the mountaineers were dehydrated. It didn't seem to correlate with their ability to summit, since other factors played a role, like weather, physical fitness, and if they had a guide. However, the researchers did find that mountaineers with more water bottles were able to stay hydrated better. Their suggestion was to simply carry enough water containers to stay hydrated.

Climbing in the Heat

While many climbers don't climb in the heat because sweat decreases your friction with the rock, there may be times where it's required. Some climbing competitions take place outdoors on artificial walls in hot temperatures. Similar to climbing in the cold, heat can upset your body's ability to regulate your temperature. If you are used to the heat (or purposefully go to a hot climate before climbing to get acclimatized), you will be able to tolerate it better. If you have the luxury of traveling to your hot climbing destination and getting acclimatized for about two to three weeks before you climb, your body will adapt to the heat. This results in lower heart rate, lower core temperature, lower skin temperature, better fluid balance, and higher sweat rate. All of this is good news for athletic performance. Although no specific studies have been conducted on climber performance with heat acclimatization, it's probably safe to bet that getting used to the heat before climbing a difficult route would be beneficial for your body and your performance.

If your body is not adapted to the heat, excessive sweating coupled with inadequate fluid intake can mean you fatigue more easily and you may overheat. Usually people who feel hot naturally work less. This may be the body's way of preserving itself. Pushing to an intense level of exercise when it is hot and/or humid can be dangerous, leading to heat exhaustion, heat stroke, and/or dehydration.

The biggest issue with climbing in the heat is likely staying properly hydrated.

However, being diligent about drinking enough can also lead to overhydration. Overhydration can be a problem if you drink so much as to get hyponatremia, which is a term referring to sodium dilution in your blood. For more information, see page 46.

One recommendation calls for about 13 ounces (400 milliliters) every 15 minutes for heavy sweaters (like, *you* sweat a lot, not a knit sweater). But this was in endurance athletes, and climbing is a lot different. Watch yourself to see if you think you're a salty sweater (again, not a cardigan). If you lose a lot of salt in your sweat, you will have "crusties" on your face, arms, or legs after the sweat dries. Your clothing may have crusty salt residue on it as well.

You can eat salty foods like pretzels, chips (crisps), salted nuts, or salty crackers to replenish lost salt. You can also use electrolytes or salt tabs at the dose of 20–50 milliequivalents of salt per liter, or you can do ½ teaspoon of salt per 2 liters. Using a sports drink with both glucose and sodium can help. Some good brands are Clif Shot, Skratch Labs, GU Hydration Mix, and Bonk Breaker Real Hydration.

Drinking ice-cold water (with actual ice in it) can help with performance and body-temperature regulation, as one study found. These poor study participants had to subject themselves to swallowing a pill thermometer and using a rectal thermometer. Imagine yourself as the research subject: The researcher has you not only swallow a device, but you get a thermometer placed up your buttocks as well. (Oh, the things we do in the name of science. I hope the subjects were well compensated!) This study found that the stomach and gastrointestinal region were cooler when ingesting an ice drink versus room-temperature fluids. The practicality of having ice while outdoor climbing is a bit laughable, but maybe you own a hard-core cooler, and can park really close to the crag. Alternatively, a frozen water bottle might do the trick.

Sweat Rate

Since we're on the topic of hydration and sweating, it's nice to know about your own specific sweat rate so you are not guessing whether or not you are hydrated. There is a simple way to measure how much fluid you lose during a climb. This can only be done practically if you can climb super close to a scale. It also needs to be a relatively short climbing session—one to two hours—since you can't eat before or during climbing to get accurate results. Here are the steps:

1. Weigh yourself before you climb with as little clothing on as possible. This should be in the morning after having a bowel movement, after urinating, and before eating.

2. Climb. Keep track of how much you drink. Don't eat.

3. After climbing, weigh yourself again with as little clothing as possible.

4. Figure out how much weight you lost.

5. For every pound that you lost, drink 16 ounces (480 milliliters) of fluid to replace it.

For example, let's say you woke up and weighed yourself. You were 150 pounds (68 kilograms). You climb for two hours and drink 16 ounces of fluid. It was a super-hot day and you sweated a lot. When you were done climbing, you weighed 147 pounds (66.7 kilograms).

This means you lost three pounds. But you drank 16 ounces while you were climbing. If you didn't drink that, you would actually have lost four pounds total! You need to drink 48–60 ounces (1440–1800 milliliters) over the course of the next several hours to re-hydrate.

Next time you climb, you know you can drink more than 16 ounces safely.

This sweat-rate test is worthwhile for a couple reasons. If you feel dehydrated or overhydrated often, it's worth figuring out how much to drink, rather than relying on thirst sensations, which aren't always reliable in heat, cold, or in older adults. Certain medications can also interfere with thirst sensation. If you get muscle cramps, this test is worth doing to make sure dehydration is not causing your cramps. And if you tend to over-drink and get a sloshy stomach, measuring sweat rate can help you avoid over-drinking. You can then set a schedule to drink regularly every 15–30 minutes or so.

The sweat-rate test is just a way to calculate an average amount of fluid you lose when you climb, which can help you gauge how much to drink. This is better than a generic recommended amount. (Raise your hand if you've ever heard, "Drink eight glasses of water per day!") To get a more accurate sweat rate, you can average multiple tests. For example, measure your sweat rate every Monday for three weeks in a row, then average the results.

Be safe and smart when doing a sweat-rate test, and when in doubt, consult a sports physician or sports dietitian for guidance.

Ultralight Meal Planning

Finally, a word about meal planning. It's tough enough to carry gear while hiking, plus think about carrying food (and potentially fluid if you're not near a water source). Don't let poor planning or your desire to carry less compromise your nutrition. If you don't have a good nutrition plan, all the time and money you've spent on climbing will be wasted. You could possibly end up in a medically dangerous situation from dehydration, overhydration, or fatigue from being under-fueled. This can open you, and your climbing partners, up to making dangerous or even fatal mistakes.

On a one-day climbing trip, it's easy to bring food like pre-packaged salads, jerky, trail mix, and sandwiches. It gets trickier on multi-day trips or adventures that involve both hiking long distances and climbing.

This section will be brief, but it could really take an entire book to discuss: recipes, meal planning, brands of dehydrated food, cooking methods, and so on. Here are a couple of critical nutrition-related things to consider regarding meal planning:

- » **Bring a variety of foods.** This will allow you to have a wide range of nutrients and prevent you from becoming tired of the same thing. Living off of rice, ramen, and tuna for days is boring and doesn't offer the wide variety of nutrients your body needs to climb well.

- » **Test the foods at home first.** This will make sure that you like them, and that you tolerate them. It can also work out any kinks in food preparation—like the beef stroganoff package says to boil it for three minutes, but it really takes eight minutes to be tender enough. By testing at home first, you'll also make sure your gut can tolerate the food. No one needs diarrhea, or cramping and gas, on a climbing trip.

- » **Keep it light.** Mountain House, Backpacker's Pantry, AlpineAire, and Good To-Go dehydrated and freeze-dried meals are popular. MREs (meals ready-to-eat) are a great option, too.

- » **Stock staples.** Powdered eggs, hot cereal, powdered milk, granola, pasta, and jerky are easy to prepare and offer good nutrient additions to most meals.

Ultralight Meal Planning (continued)

One other option is to dehydrate your own food. A dietitian, Aaron Owens Mayhew, runs a website called Backcountryfoodie.com. She is a thru-hiker who has all sorts of amazing recipes, tips, and tricks for preparing your own ultra-light meals. She also consults if you want to hire her to figure out all your calorie, carbohydrate, and protein needs, and create meal plans for your backcountry adventure.

Another great website with recipes and meal tips is called Gourmet Hiking. This is also run by a dietitian, Genevieve Masson. She is active in hiking, backpacking, and other backcountry adventures. This website has great blog articles about nutrition for various sports, as well as recipes and meal plans.

With all this information, I hope you've been able to understand how vital it is to fuel and hydrate properly while climbing. It can make the difference between sending or not. It can also help you feel better and more powerful, recover more quickly, build and maintain muscle, and fuel your brain and muscles.

It cannot be overstated: Eating and drinking adequately can prevent injury and death. Alexa Flower and Miranda Oakley in Climbing Magazine wrote this sage advice about the Yosemite accident mentioned at the beginning of the chapter: "Bring ample food and water. Remember, short tempers and sluggishness can be signs of hunger and dehydration. Left untreated, these can lead to mistakes... force yourself to eat and drink regularly. If you've developed good habits, a red flag will appear if you stray." I couldn't have said it better myself.

Sample all-day climbing meal plan

Meal	Time	Food
BREAKFAST (AT HOME)	7 am	Eggs, toast with peanut butter, and fruit and yogurt smoothie
SNACK	9 am	Pretzels and energy bar with water or sports drink
LUNCH	12 pm	Bagel sandwich with almond butter and jam. Dried apricots, trail mix with water or sports drink
SNACK	3 pm	Crackers and jerky with water or sports drink
DINNER (AT HOME OR RESTAURANT)	6 pm	Spaghetti and meatballs, green beans, fruit salad, and chocolate milk and water
RECOVERY SNACK AT HOME	Before bed	Protein shake, cottage cheese, or chocolate milk
SNACK	9 pm	Chocolate milk

THE WRAP-UP FOR OUTDOOR CLIMBING

Proper hydration, consuming enough overall calories (energy), and eating carbohydrates and protein **are crucial to climbing successfully. Dehydration, over-hydration, and under-fueling can lead to mistakes, injury, and death.**

Eat about 20-30 grams carbs **per hour of active climbing.** Eat about 10 grams of protein **every 2 hours of active climbing.** Drink about eight ounces of fluid **every hour of climbing. You may need more if it is hot, dry, windy, humid, or at higher elevations.**

Author's note: While it's fascinating to learn what top-performing climbers eat, you are a unique individual with your own personalized nutrition needs. Keep in mind that you do not need to eat, fuel, hydrate, and supplement your diet like Hans Florine and Adam Ondra. These interviews represent their own dietary beliefs and practices. Always consult a physician and dietitian before making any dietary or supplemental changes to your routine.

An Interview with Hans Florine

Hans Florine, an internationally known climber, has set and broken the speed record for the *Nose* of El Capitan in Yosemite National Park. He has climbed the *Nose* more than 100 times, and has won several formalized climbing competitions. I was lucky enough to pick his brain about what he likes to eat and how he fuels his body for climbing. He was so courteous to take time out of his busy schedule to talk nutrition with me over the phone as I scribbled copious notes.

What do you like to eat before a big climb?

Hans: I love eating steak or spaghetti or something substantial like that the night before, something with some carbs and protein in it. In the morning, I do a sweet potato or potato. Honey Stinger is one of my sponsors, so I like eating the Honey Stinger chews. I take Nuun or Gatorade with me on the climb. Sometimes I use GU as well.

Before a comp, I like to eat something with sugar in it along with some caffeine about 45 minutes before I'm going to climb. Always some carbs before a comp.

For the fastest ascent on the *Nose* in 2012 in 2:23, I just took two GUs and one liter of water.

What do you like to eat during climbing?

Hans: If it is a long climb, I make sure to eat every 90 minutes or so. I've climbed with others that forget to eat or aren't as diligent about eating regularly, and it slows us down. They don't have the energy they need to climb well. I try to make sure I fuel myself regularly.

I feel like variety is very important. It's easy to get tired of the same types of foods. I take things like trail mix, energy bars, and bagels. Hard cheeses like Parmesan and some pepperoni sticks are good too. Some other things I like that are a bit different are pickles and bell peppers. I think it's good to take something that is both savory and sweet to mix it up. People think I'm weird packing a whole green bell pepper in my pack, but it's lightweight and really refreshing up on the wall. A pickle is great too—you can buy one individually packaged at a gas station and just take it in your pack. Just think of things you enjoy eating and take them with you. There's usually a way to bring whatever food you'd like to bring.

I also love dried cranberries. They are different than raisins and help bring variety. It's a great food for an alpinist.

What do you like to eat on a day-to-day basis?

Hans: I usually like eggs, sausage, or cereal in the morning. I love beets. I just eat anything, lots of normal foods. And I love ice cream. Like REALLY love it. I eat stuff like cucumbers, fermented stuff, just anything that I enjoy and that I think will help my body be healthy.

Any special tricks or hacks you'd like to share?

Hans: I know a lot of people like Camelbacks, but I personally don't use them. I feel like the straw and tubing get gross, and I've heard of mold growing in there. I also feel like it's hard to tell how much you have had to drink if the bladder is enclosed in a bag like that. I've climbed with people using Camelbacks, and they run out of water halfway through the climb because they didn't realize they needed to spread out their water rations. I've also climbed with people that get to the top and realize they have two liters of water left, and they should have drunk more while climbing. And if the bladder leaks, you are screwed.

For me, it works well to just take liter water bottles that are clear. I have two liters in my pack and one on my waist. I just hook it on and take it out when I need to drink. That way the water stays clean, there is no hose that gets dirty, and I can see how much I have drunk and how much I have left. It helps me keep track of my water inventory.

I did hear of one guy that threw his Camelback in the freezer after each time he used it. That was one way to keep mold from growing, which I thought was pretty smart.

Do you use any supplements?

Hans: For cramps, I always have some Tums on hand. If I start to get a cramp in my forearms, I just take the Tums. Since it has calcium in it, which is an electrolyte, it seems to really work well. I used this when going up the *Nose* years ago. My forearms were cramping really badly, and I had really bad "claw hands", like I couldn't even straighten out my fingers. Using Tums really helped take away the cramp. I also use Nuun tablets in my water for my electrolytes, which I really like.

Some people use ibuprofen a lot, but I feel like it's not really good to make it a habit. If you are in so much pain that you need it constantly, you are doing something wrong.

Right now, with my injury (Hans had an accident in Yosemite in 2018 and broke both his legs), I am taking calcium supplements, vitamin D, and collagen protein. I am also taking probiotics to help out my gut since I had to take antibiotics for my injury.

When I am strength training, I use creatine*. It's really been helpful for my training sessions. I feel more powerful and can lift more. I wouldn't use it right before a comp, just because I wouldn't want to carry any extra water weight, but for training it's been great.

*For more information on creatine, see chapter 8.

4 - NUTRITION FOR OUTDOOR CLIMBING

An Interview with Adam Ondra

Pavel Blazek

I was fortunate to have Adam Ondra, widely considered one of the world's best climbers, send me an audio file answering some nutrition questions I posed to him via email. He was kind enough to take time out of his busy training and competing schedule to answer a few questions for this book. Here are his selected responses. Enjoy!

Have you found that nutrition and hydration play an important role in your climbing and training?

Adam: Yes, definitely. I do feel that the right nutrition helps me to climb harder, most notably in making the recovery much faster. So actually, when I am training, I feel that nutrition is even more important than when I am about to give a performance. Hydration: That's something that's pretty obvious–I need to drink a lot, and I mostly drink just water. For Chinese medicine, I drink a lot of warm water. It is easier to digest for my constitution and I drink a lot of herbal tea and black tea, especially in the morning.

What do you consider important for your nutrition?

Adam: I feel it is mostly about the speed of recovery. What is the right nutrition? Of course, there are so many different opinions. I have experimented a lot, and what I feel is most important is eating real food. I believe in Chinese medicine. It is something that helps me.

What do you enjoy eating for training and competing?

Adam: I mean, for training, it's important to eat real food, and the diet has to be complex, so, more or less eating everything, as long as it's real food. For breakfast I usually have something warm, so I usually have some oatmeal with some spices, usually cinnamon, that is easier to digest, with some sort of proteins and fat, like seeds and nuts, with maybe honey or some homemade marmalade. And if the training day is going to be hard, I increase the volume of protein by using some vegan protein powder. I use vegan protein because it is the best to digest for my stomach.

In between breakfast and lunch, and in between lunch and dinner, I usually have some really small snacks. Usually consisting of dried fruits, and maybe a little bit of nuts and seeds. Lunch, even if I'm at the crag (which is sometimes complicated), I would cook at home usually some kind of cereal or lentils, or chickpeas with some vegetables. Vegetables, especially in the wintertime, I eat vegetables that are cooked or baked. As for my constitution, it definitely makes me feel better. And for dinner I would usually have some animal protein, mostly fish, with a little bit of cereal such as quinoa or brown rice, and some vegetables again.

And if the training is very hard, right after training I would eat some sort of protein and carbohydrate, so I would have a little bit of protein powder mixed with oats and eat it as fast as possible. So that's what I do on a regular day.

Do you use any supplements?

Adam: Yes, I use BCAA [branched chain amino acids] and protein powder,* nothing more. All the rest that I am trying to eat is 100 percent natural.

Is there anything else you would like to share about nutrition and hydration? Do you have any stories about a time when you felt like it really helped? Or if you had poor nutrition and you felt a difference?

Adam: For example, if I am not really following the instructions for Chinese medicine in winter, I definitely feel much colder. Of course, if I train super hard and I don't eat very well, I don't recover—but that's pretty logical. It's the whole complex really: If you train hard, you should eat well, you should recover well, you should sleep enough. There are all these kinds of things that help you recover faster, and eating well is one of them. Overall it is something that will help you to feel healthy. But as I said, what is eating well? That is very individual. Everybody has a different point of view. I think, looking at it from the most complex point of view with the most years of experience, and for me that's traditional Chinese medicine. Hydration is a very important part of Chinese medicine. There are many people that don't drink enough because they don't feel thirsty. I drink a lot. I feel it's most important to drink during the morning, so I always start the day with almost half a liter of warm water before I eat anything. That is a nice start of the day and all of a sudden you feel much better.

Author's note: Hans Florine and Adam Ondra are following individualized nutrition and supplement plans based on their own health needs and preferences. If you are thinking about including any of their tips in your own climbing routine, check with your doctor before adding supplements or changing any part of your diet to make sure it is right for you.

*For more information on supplements and protein powder, see chapter 8.

SIDEBAR

Do you need to eat like Alex Honnold?

The nutrition world is chockful of people telling you what and how to eat. Tom Brady, the quarterback for the New England Patriots, eats a restrictive diet cutting out normal salt (only pink Himalayan salt will do, apparently), sugar, white flour, coffee, dairy, tomatoes, and peppers. Michael Phelps, the Olympic swimmer, eats seemingly endless calories in the form of eggs, pizza, French toast, pancakes, and more. Novak Djokovic, the famous tennis player, avoids gluten. Venus Williams, another famous tennis player, is vegan. The list is endless. Celebrity athletes tout one diet or another, claiming that their particular diet is the one you should follow. You may see these athletes and wonder if you should eat like them; too. If they found so much success by eating a certain way, could you, too?

Here's the thing: while nutrition is important for athletic success, celebrity athletes are not successful solely because of their diet. They have good genetics. They train incessantly. They have probably been in their sport since childhood. They have an entourage of coaches, trainers, physical therapists, massage therapists, sports physicians, sports psychologists, and more all helping them achieve better performance. If all you had to do all day long was perfect your body and your sport (and you had an entourage of professionals to help you on your journey), you could be amazing, too! Don't fall for celebrity athlete diets. Most of them are rife with pseudoscience and misinformation. And you are a different person with different nutrition needs. You don't need to demonize meat, shun gluten, or forego tomatoes to be a great climber. Instead, find a sports dietitian who can personalize a nutrition plan based on your health history, current training status, food preferences, lifestyle, needs, and goals.

You'll be so much better off.

CHAPTER 4 REFERENCES

Burdon, Catriona A., Matthew W. Hoon, Nathan A. Johnson, Phillip G. Chapman, and Helen T. O'Connor. 2013. "The Effect of Ice Slushy Ingestion and Mouthwash on Thermoregulation and Endurance Performance in The Heat." *International Journal of Sport Nutrition and Exercise Metabolism* 23, no. 5: 458-469.

Backountryfoodie. Accessed April 19, 2019. **http://www.Backcountryfoodie.com**

Cheuvront, Samuel N., and Michael N. Sawka. 2005. "Hydration Assessment of Athletes." *Sports Science Exchange* 18, no. 2: 1-6.

Cotter, James David, Simon N. Thornton, Jason KW Lee, and Paul B. Laursen. 2014. "Are We Being Drowned in Hydration Advice? Thirsty for More?" *Extreme Physiology & Medicine* 3, no. 1: 18.

Flower, Alexa, and Miranda Oakley. December 18, 2017. "The Deadly Valley: An Inside Analysis of Five Recent Yosemite Accidents." Accessed April 19, 2019. **https://www.climbing.com/skills/the-deadly-valley-an-inside-analysis-of-five-recent-yosemite-accidents/**.

Gourmethiking.com. Accessed April 19, 2019. **http://www.Gourmethiking.com**.

Govus, Andrew D., Laura A. Garvican-Lewis, Chris R. Abbiss, Peter Peeling, and Christopher J. Gore. 2015. "Pre-altitude Serum Ferritin Levels and Daily Oral Iron Supplement Dose Mediate Iron Parameter and Hemoglobin Mass Responses to Altitude Exposure." *PLoS One* 10, no. 8: e0135120.

Horiuchi, Masahiro, Junko Endo, Koichi Kondo, Tadashi Uno, Mayuko Morikawa, and Hiroshi Nose. 2015. "Impact of Carbohydrate-Electrolyte Beverage Ingestion on Heart Rate Response While Climbing Mountain Fuji at~ 3000 m." *BioMed Research International*, no. 8:1-7.

Joubert, Lanae, Abigail Larson, Sarah Weber. 2016. Nutrition and Hydration Strategies to Enhance Sport and Multi-Pitch Climbing Performance." *Presented at the International Rock Climbing Research Association Annual Congress:* August 5-7, 2016.

Kechijan, D. 2011. "Optimizing Nutrition for Performance at Altitude: A Literature Review." *Journal of Special Operations Medicine: A Peer Reviewed Journal for SOF Medical Professionals* 11, no. 1: 12-17.

Kenefick, Robert W., and Samuel N. Cheuvront. 2012. "Hydration for Recreational Sport and Physical Activity." *Nutrition Reviews* 70, no. suppl_2: S137-S142.

Ladd, Eric, Katherine M. Shea, Patrick Bagley, Paul S. Auerbach, Elizabeth A. Pirrotta, Ewen Wang, and Grant Lipman. 2016. "Hydration Status as a Predictor of High-altitude Mountaineering Performance." *Cureus* 8, no. 12: e918.

Maughan, Ronald J., and Susan M. Shirreffs. 2008. "Development of Individual Hydration Strategies for Athletes." *International Journal of Sport Nutrition and Exercise Metabolism* 18, no. 5: 457-472.

McDermott, Brendon P., Scott A. Anderson, Lawrence E. Armstrong, Douglas J. Casa, Samuel N. Cheuvront, Larry Cooper, W. Larry Kenney, Francis G. O'Connor, and William O. Roberts. 2017. "National Athletic Trainers' Association Position Statement: Fluid Replacement for The Physically Active." *Journal of Athletic Training* 52, no. 9: 877-895.

Ross, Megan, and Martin David. 2015. "Altitude, Cold and Heat," *Clinical Sports Nutrition, 5th ed.*, edited by Louise Burke and Vicki Deakin, 767-786. Australia: McGraw Hill Education.

Sawka, Michael N., Louise M. Burke, E. Randy Eichner, Ronald J. Maughan, Scott J. Montain, and Nina S. Stachenfeld. 2007. "American College of Sports Medicine Position Stand. Exercise and Fluid Replacement." *Medicine and Science in Sports and Exercise* 39, no. 2: 377-390.

Sawka, Michael N., Julien D. Périard, and Sébastien Racinais. 2015. "Heat Acclimatization to Improve Athletic Performance in Warm-Hot Environments." *Sports Science Exchange* 28: 1-6.

Sims, Stacy. 2016. *Roar: How to Match Your Food and Fitness to Your Female Physiology for Optimum Performance, Great Health, and a Strong, Lean Body for Life.* New York, New York: Rodale Books.

Stuempfle, Kristin J., and Daniel G. Drury. "Comparison of 3 Methods to Assess Urine Specific Gravity in Collegiate Wrestlers." *Journal of Athletic Training* 38, no. 4 (2003): 315.

USDA National Nutrient Database for Standard Reference Legacy Release. Accessed April 10, 2018. **https://ndb.nal.usda.gov/ndb/**

Yanagisawa, Kae, Osamu Ito, Satsuki Nagai, and Shohei Onishi. 2012. "Electrolyte-carbohydrate Beverage Prevents Water Loss in the Early Stage of High Altitude Training." *The Journal of Medical Investigation* 59, no. 1, 2: 102-110.

5 - NUTRITION FOR DIFFERENT TYPES OF CLIMBING

CHAPTER 5

NUTRITION FOR DIFFERENT TYPES OF CLIMBING

A boulderer isn't the same as a sport climber, and a speed climber pursues perhaps the most unique of all climbing disciplines. If you've climbed various styles, you know that different types of climbing demand different styles of movement. And a speed climber on comp day isn't going to eat the same as an outdoor climber with a long approach and a multi-pitch route in their sights, and shouldn't. Eat according to your discipline and planned session. Here's how to do it.

Speed Climbing

Speed climbing for the purpose of this section is specifically talking about the official event in comps. This is not "speed climbing" in the sense of Alex Honnold and the likes trying to set speed records in Yosemite. I'm talking about two climbers side-by-side on artificial routes who are racing to the top on autobelays. These explosive, high-energy movements call for mainly, or perhaps even exclusively, carbohydrate burning. Other climbing disciplines use both carbohydrate and fat while you are climbing, but speed climbing is a whole different animal. Eating around five to seven grams of carbs per kilogram of body weight is a good bet. If you attempt speed climbing with depleted glycogen, your speed and performance will suffer. Stay hydrated, but don't over-hydrate, as it will just make you heavier and fuller.

Creatine may or may not be useful. Creatine causes water retention, and even small amounts of extra body weight at the highest levels of competition could mean the difference between winning and losing. Test for tolerance and performance during training to see if you notice a difference (either negative or positive) with creatine.

It may be tempting to strive for thinness in speed climbing–if you drop a few pounds, you may be faster in theory, but being too thin is a health concern. See chapter 10 for more information.

Sport / Toprope / Lead Climbing

All these styles of climbing are lumped together, even though they are unique disciplines, because they are similar enough as far as body movement and energy demands. Also—you might get tired of me saying this—there is not a lot of research on nutrition for these types of climbers! One study had 20 elite climbers record their food intake for one week, and the researchers then analyzed the data. They found that these climbers only ate about 40 percent of their energy-intake needs and under-consumed fat and vegetables. About 50 percent of the participants in this study did not meet their nutrient (aka vitamin) needs. That's of concern because not eating enough can compromise your training, your climbing, and your health.

Sport, toprope, and lead climbing are all different than bouldering in that the routes are usually longer. Routes take on average 2-7 minutes to climb, compared to the 30–40 seconds that short boulder problems take. In the competition arena, the International Federation of Sport Climbing (IFSC) competition rules state that a climber has 6 minutes to complete a lead route indoors, and at least 50 minutes of rest between their first and second routes. This means competitive climbers have to build up endurance and stamina in order to climb well. Fueling properly will help with this.

If you're lead climbing, you have to also clip draws as you go, which means a bit more finger and forearm action (and perhaps a bit more forearm burning). However, carbohydrate, hydration, and overall calorie needs are likely similar to those needed for bouldering and toprope climbing because they have similar movement patterns and use similar energy systems.

Bouldering

Climbers use a lot of forearm strength combined with isometric holding patterns, and boulderers are no exception. Bouldering is a bit different than trad or sport/lead/toprope climbing because you aren't using ropes, harnesses, or protection. While roped climbers try not to rely on the rope or rest on protection during their ascent, sometimes this happens. With bouldering, there is less potential to rest since there's no rope! If you're on the wall, even in a rest position, you're still working.

Indoor bouldering-comp problems take on average 40 seconds to complete. World Cup boulderers have four minutes to complete each boulder problem. Contrast this with a long outdoor trad route or multi-pitch route, measured in hours, and you can see there is a difference in energy expended and likely a difference in nutritional needs. **One small study found that boulderers took about 30 seconds of climbing activity to send a problem, compared to two to seven minutes of climbing activity for a sport climb.**

Bouldering movement requires enough carbohydrates to fuel this type of muscle contraction, but it's not necessary to overthink it. A modest intake of carbs, about five grams per kilogram per day, will likely be sufficient. If you are doing a long comp with multiple rounds of problems, eating carbs throughout the day will help. Too much carbohydrate intake can actually add more body weight, which might be undesirable. Remember how a molecule of glycogen is stored with three molecules of water? If you are carb-loading, the glycogen will go into skeletal muscles. Please note that there's no actual research on this to determine if carb-loading or the minor weight gain that accompanies it would be detrimental to your climbing performance. It's just a theory. Again, don't overthink it! Carbs, in general, are your friends.

OLYMPIC PLATFORM: LEAD/SPEED/BOULDERING

Keeping in mind everything you just read about speed, lead, and bouldering, use this information to translate nutrition recommendations nicely to the Olympic platform.

The Olympic platform for Tokyo 2020 includes bouldering, lead, and speed. All climbers must compete in all disciplines, and they are ranked according to a combined point system from all three. A climber can't get the gold medal by just being excellent at bouldering or lead climbing–they must climb all three and rank in the top three spots per gender in order to medal.

Proper fueling before, during, and after such a multi-discipline competition will help you stay on top of your game. Recovery meals with a mix of carbs, protein, and fat are important. Adequate hydration is key to staying in peak-performance mode. Don't eat anything you have never eaten on comp day (or for a few days leading up to it). I'll say it again: "Nothing new on comp day!"

To help avoid any under-fueling surprises, plan ahead by asking yourself a series of questions: Where is the competition taking place? What will the temperature and humidity be like inside the competition space? How long am I allowed to warm up? What is the timing of the rounds? How many rounds? How long will I be in isolation? Be familiar with your comp schedule in order to time your fueling and hydration appropriately. The IFSC lists the rules and format for the combined schedule on their website; use these to optimize when you eat. The qualification round and final rounds are held on separate days, which means you can get a nice recovery meal and plenty of rest before finals.

Current rules for Tokyo 2020 state that for the qualifying round, you get at least 30 minutes of recovery between the speed and bouldering rounds, and at least 120 minutes of recovery between the bouldering and lead rounds. For the final round, you get at least 15 minutes between speed and bouldering, and at least 15 minutes between bouldering and lead. Note that this may change in subsequent Olympics.

Understand where you are seeded, when you will start each round, and how much time you have in between each round. If you are fortunate enough to be competing for a country with a sports dietitian on the support staff, meet with them ahead of time to plan out your fueling strategy. Take note of any foods you may need to bring with you for proper hydration and nutrition (checking all travel regulations both within countries you are traveling to and from). Explore which foods you can purchase when you arrive in the country. Have a game plan for how to obtain and prepare foods that are ideal for you: A smart food strategy will give you an edge when it's time for competition.

Traditional (Trad) Climbing

Trad climbing is a bit different than the other types of climbing in that you have more weight as you ascend because of your rack. It may thus take a bit more energy (calories) than other types of climbing because of the added weight. Take this into account as you eat before, during, and after your climbing session. Eat and drink enough to prevent feeling irritable, hungry, dizzy, weak, or mentally fuzzy. You may need to eat around 1.2–1.8 g/kg/day of protein in order to maintain, build, and repair muscles.

Trad climbing will likely land you in some higher-elevation areas. Make sure you hydrate and eat enough for the higher altitude. See page 51 in chapter 4 for more nutrition information about high-altitude situations.

Free Soloing

What can I say? Free soloing is extremely risky. Yet it is a part of climbing culture and history, and probably always will be. We are not advocating that anyone take up free soloing.

If you are going to free solo, I have a few thoughts.

First, never eat anything new to you within about three days of your solo climb. This is not a hard fact; this is just my opinion. Why might this be a good idea? This is enough time for your body to digest any food that may upset your stomach. You don't want to feel crampy, gassy, bloated, or have constipation or diarrhea while trying to free solo.

Second, be sure to start the climb hydrated and fueled. It would be dangerous, even more so than usual, to feel dehydrated, or experience a drop in blood sugar while climbing. This can lead to stupid mistakes, lost strength, and decreased mental clarity.

Third, be sure to acclimatize to the climate and altitude for at least three weeks. It's a good idea to get a thorough physical with a sports physician at least six months ahead of time. Check labs as well, such as complete blood count, complete metabolic panel, lipid panel, iron, vitamin D, and vitamin B12. Any nutrient deficiencies can be corrected before the big climb, allowing you to climb your best and be as healthy as possible.

Finally, thoroughly test any new supplements for weeks or months before you climb to be sure how you respond to them. Check with your doctor before adding supplements to your routine to make sure they are safe and appropriate for you.

Alex Honnold, famous for his free-solo ascent of El Capitan, said this about his diet the day of the climb:

"I'd pre-rigged my breakfast bowl—muesli with fruit, hemp milk, and chia seeds—and my bag was already packed. Everything was done, so in the morning I could roll out of bed and just execute. . . . I'd cached a liter of water and a couple of energy bars on the route in two places. Over the whole route, for four hours, I stopped maybe six times total for a couple minutes each."
(Sohn 2017)

So, there you have it. A sample breakfast idea from one of the world's best free soloists.

Alpine Climbing - Ice Climbing

If you're going to be out for hours in a cold environment, one nutrition challenge is how to keep your food from freezing. Things like cheese, shortbread, freeze-dried and dehydrated meals, peanut butter, and nuts are great. High-calorie foods are perfect for ice climbing, since you need a lot of calories to climb, hike, and maintain body temperature. The *Feed Zone Portables Cookbook* has some good recipes for climber-friendly portable food as well. A thermos filled with hot drinks or soups is also useful to keeping your core temperature warm.

Along with considering cold conditions, ice climbing presents its own unique challenges. Usually ice climbing is part of a longer, more involved day: hiking or skiing to reach the base of the climb, taking longer to gear up and get ready, taking longer to place a piece of gear, longer to lead a pitch, managing heat loss by frequently adding and removing layers, managing hydration and nutrition, and to top it all off, your pack weighs even more than when carrying trad gear. Ice climbers usually have additional gear and clothing beyond what a rock climber might wear. The gear and weather demands of ice climbing make it a lot more logistically complicated than other climbing disciplines. Given the full-body nature of ice climbing, it can also possibly take more energy and forearm and shoulder strength, as well as leg strength for front pointing, than rock climbing.

Alpine Climbing - Ice Climbing (continued)

A logical strategy is to eat enough to avoid drops in blood sugar, and drink enough to stay hydrated. This will allow your muscles and brain to be well-fueled for ice climbing. Also, don't be tempted to under-drink to avoid having to urinate. Even though it's likely inconvenient to urinate in the cold with all your gear on, it's not worth risking dehydration from altitude, decreased fluid intake, and increased respiration. Adequate fluids will also help you maintain body temperature. **For more information on climbing in the cold, see page 54.**

And now, let's talk about screaming barfies, AKA hot aches. Winter climbers report feeling sensations of pain, numbness, tingling, and throbbing when climbing in the winter—usually after completing a pitch. This is sometimes accompanied by nausea, irritability, dizziness, and temporary loss of vision and hearing. This usually lasts one to five minutes, and 96 percent of climbers in one survey reported experiencing hot aches at some point in their career. No one is quite sure why it happens, but the current theory is that blood flowing to cold limbs makes blood vessels dilate, causing these symptoms.

For more insight into hot aches, I reached out to **Josh Wharton,** who is a climber and alpinist known for his bold ascents. He writes via email:

> I've had the barfies way too many times! Generally I get them while rock climbing in very cold conditions (like under 40 degrees Fahrenheit). When you get them warm once, your hands generally stay warm for the rest of the day assuming you do a good job of staying well dressed between climbs.... I imagine being hydrated would be a positive.

The authors who studied hot aches wondered if diet and nutrition can play a role in treatment or prevention, postulating that maybe caffeine, coffee, or tea can help. No one really knows for sure, but adequate hydration can help with blood flow. Adequate food intake helps keep blood sugar stable. Guess what some symptoms of low blood sugar are? Nausea, irritability, and dizziness. Hmmm...perhaps just eating and drinking enough will help with the hot aches?

THE WRAP-UP FOR DIFFERENT TYPES OF CLIMBING

For all types of climbing, adequate fueling and hydration are key to having enough energy and staying safe.

Alpine and ice climbing involve the possibility of swinging body temperatures. Staying hydrated will help regulate body temperature. Warm or hot drinks can also help.

CHAPTER 5 REFERENCES

International Federation of Sport Climbing. nd. 2019. "International Federation of Sport Climbing, Rules 2019." **https://www.ifsc-climbing.org/index.php/world-competition/rules**

Melvin, Andrew, and Jacob George. 2016. "A Descriptive Study of Hot Aches: A Previously Unreported Winter Climbing Phenomenon." *Sports Medicine* no. 2:36.

Smith, Edward J, Ryan Storey, and Mayur K. Ranchordas. 2017. "Nutritional Considerations for Bouldering." *International Journal of Sports Nutrition and Exercise Metabolism* 27 no. 4:314-324.

Sohn, Tim. 2017. "Rock God: How Alex Honnold Climbed El Capitan." GQ Magazine. **https://www.gq.com/story/alex-honnold-el-capitan-as-told-to. Accessed May 1, 2018.**

Thomas, Biju, and Allen Lim. 2013. *Feed Zone Portables: A Cookbook of On-the-Go-Food for Athletes.* Boulder, Colorado: Velo Press.

White, Dominic and Peter Olsen. 2010. "A Time Motion Analysis of Bouldering Style Competitive Rock Climbing." *The Journal of Strength and Conditioning Research* 24 no. 5:1356-1360.

Zapf, J., B. Fichtl, S. Wielgoss, and W. Schmidt. 2001. "Macronutrient Intake and Eating Habits in Elite Rock Climbers." *Medicine & Science in Sports & Exercise* 33, no. 5: S72.

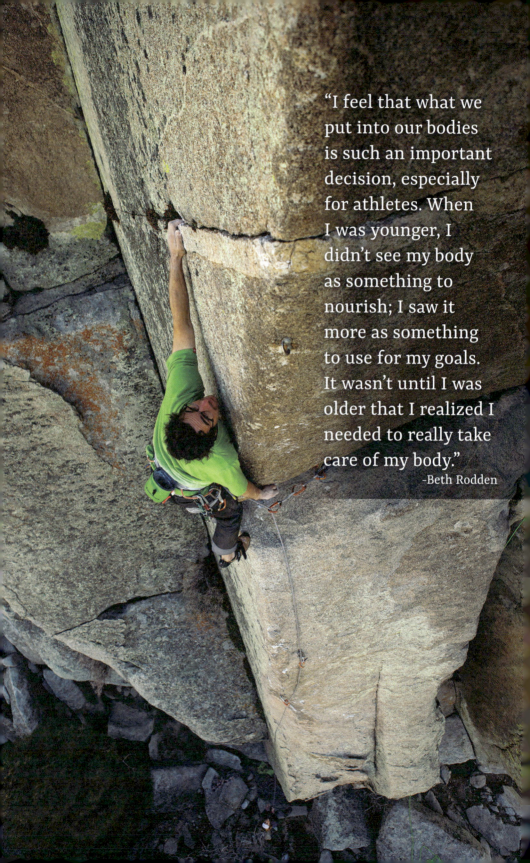

"I feel that what we put into our bodies is such an important decision, especially for athletes. When I was younger, I didn't see my body as something to nourish; I saw it more as something to use for my goals. It wasn't until I was older that I realized I needed to really take care of my body."

-Beth Rodden

PART III

NUTRITION FOR
SPECIAL SITUATIONS

6 - **SPECIAL NUTRITION NEEDS**

CHAPTER 6

SPECIAL NUTRITION NEEDS

Aika Yoshida sustained a C6 (sixth cervical vertebrae) incomplete spinal cord injury while practicing acrobatic yoga. Today a competitive adaptive climber, she uses nutrition to her advantage. Since many movements in para climbing are inefficient (thus requiring more calories), she eats enough calories in order to fuel her specific climbing needs. This is just one example of a special situation where bespoke nutrition can help you be a better climber. This chapter will cover myriad of special nutrition needs.

Vegan/Vegetarian Climbers

First, a word about going vegan or vegetarian. Living this lifestyle can be really healthy, but for some reason it has become a charged and polarizing issue in the nutrition world. There is no right or wrong way to eat. There are ways to eat better to support health and performance, but you are not a bad person if you have a cupcake or a hamburger. We need to remove the "morality" attached to food. If you are a person who believes that animals should not be harmed or used for food, I honor and respect that. However, it is OK for another person to eat meat if that is a part of their value system. Meat offers many nutrients that can be a key part of one's diet. Being vegan, vegetarian, pescatarian, flexitarian, or any other "-tarian" you choose to be is OK. All of these patterns of eating can be healthful or harmful depending on how they're executed.

My purpose in writing this section is to support those climbers who have chosen to live vegan or vegetarian. If you are not already doing so and would like to consider trying it, first please be sure you are doing it for the right reasons. There are many pseudo-experts and an abundance of misinformation about veganism and vegetarianism. Some books, websites, blogs, and documentaries can be very persuasive about convincing people that eating animal products is bad for your health. Please be assured that many animal products are healthful and offer a variety of nutrients that are beneficial for overall health.

If you are already living the vegan or vegetarian lifestyle, you've probably done a lot of research as to how to get all the nutrients you need.

Vegan/Vegetarian Climbers (continued)

Here are two main things to consider with these two lifestyles.

Fiber Makes You Feel Full

Vegans and vegetarians may get a lot of fiber in their diet: fruits, vegetables, grains, legumes, nuts, and seeds. While all these things are nourishing and healthful, they also make you feel full. This could potentially be a negative if you are getting too full too quickly at a meal, and thereby eating less than you actually need. Some people may need to eat more refined grains in order to combat this feeling of fullness and to allow for enough calorie intake. It's important to get enough overall calories to support your muscles, immune system, reproductive system, bone health, brain, and digestive system. More on that is coming in chapter 9. But file this in the back of your mind: You need enough calories to be healthy and be a good climber.

You Need to Plan Carefully So You Don't **Miss Out on Nutrients**

Certain nutrients are more easily absorbed in your body and are more abundant in animal foods than plant foods. This means you have to plan your diet accordingly so you don't become deficient in one or more nutrients. Let's take a closer look at each one.

Iron

Iron is important to athletes for a number of reasons. It transports oxygen to the blood and muscles. And you need oxygen to climb. Ever been pumped? Burning forearms? Yeah, I thought so. Oxygen helps with both of these things. Oxygen also helps with energy metabolism. It is involved with helping the cells turn fuel into energy for your working muscles. Iron status is especially important if climbing at higher elevations. (See chapter 4 for more information about nutrition for high altitude.)

There are two types of iron: heme and non-heme. Heme iron is better absorbed by the body and is found in red meat, seafood, and poultry–all no-nos for vegans and vegetarians. Non-heme iron is not absorbed as well in the body, and is mostly found in grains, spinach, kidney beans, lentils, and almonds. If you're vegetarian, eating eggs provides you with a good source of heme iron.

Iron (continued)

Coupling an iron-containing food with vitamin C helps with absorption. You could have orange juice, bell peppers, or strawberries with your iron-rich meal or snack to help your body absorb the iron better.

Cooking with a cast-iron skillet also imparts extra iron in the food you cook in the skillet.

How much iron you need per day varies based on a number of factors including how old you are; menstruating females need more iron, and endurance athletes, particularly runners, also need more iron than most people. The general guideline in the United States is 8 milligrams per day for males and 18 milligrams per day for females.

If you suspect you have iron-deficiency anemia, get comprehensive blood work from your physician. Symptoms include fatigue, weakness, shortness of breath, inability to regulate body temperature (feeling cold easily), headaches, dizziness, and lightheadedness. Talk with your physician and dietitian about proper supplementation, dosing, what form of iron you need to take, and what foods you can include to make sure you are eating enough iron.

Phytate is a substance found in soy products, nuts, legumes, and grains. It actually can bind to iron so the iron isn't absorbed in your body. Sometimes called "anti-nutrients," phytates don't allow your body to use as much iron as you are eating. This is why, for vegans and vegetarians, the recommended daily iron intake is actually higher—at 33 milligrams per day. Fermenting, sprouting, and soaking legumes and grains, such as eating bread made with sprouted grains or soaking dried beans before using them in a recipe, can decrease the phytate content.

Vegan/Vegetarian Climbers (continued)

Vitamin B12

This vitamin is involved with red-blood-cell formation, DNA synthesis, and neurological function. It's really important to get enough vitamin B12. This helps with heart health, brain function, and nerve health. It's found in meat, fish, poultry, eggs, nutritional yeast, and dairy products. Unfortunately for vegans, it is not found in plant foods. Vegans can get vitamin B12 by supplementing and by eating fortified breakfast cereal, fortified non-dairy milk, and fortified meat substitutes. Vegetarians also may need to supplement B12, depending on what foods they allow in their diet.

Certain medications, such as those for acid reflux and metformin (a common diabetes medication), can affect the absorption of vitamin B12. Absorption also decreases as you age. It's a good idea to get your B12 status checked annually by your physician, along with vitamin D and iron.

Symptoms of vitamin B12 deficiency include fatigue, weakness, weight loss and loss of appetite, poor digestion, tingling in the fingers and toes, and anemia. This condition is serious and needs medical attention. If you have any concerns about your vitamin B12 status or intake, talk to your doctor. The recommended intake of vitamin B12 in the United States is 2.4 micrograms per day for most adults.

Calcium

Calcium is needed for a ton of different body processes, including bone health, heart health, and blood-pressure regulation. Climbers might be most interested in the fact that calcium is involved with muscle contraction. It also helps with nerve conduction and blood-vessel dilation. Could this be the answer to alleviating your pump? Who knows. But you need calcium regardless. While most vegetarians can get enough calcium if they eat dairy products, vegans may be challenged to get enough.

Calcium is found in dairy products like milk, cheese, and yogurt. It's also in green vegetables such as bok choy, kale, and broccoli. Vegans can choose tofu, which naturally is a good source of calcium, as well as fortified soy or nut milks, orange juice, and breakfast cereal. The recommendation for daily intake in the United States is 1000–1200 milligrams for most adults.

As with iron, there are substances in foods that bind to calcium to prevent its absorption. Oxalic and phytic acids are found in green vegetables and grains. So, even though food such as spinach, seeds, and whole grains may contain calcium, it may not be absorbed in your body very well. Supplementation is easy. Again, as with all supplements, check with your doctor first.

Vitamin D

Vitamin D has emerged in recent years as the new nutrient of interest among nutrition researchers and professionals. Vitamin D is involved with many aspects of your body's functioning, including bone health, muscle function, mood, calcium absorption, immune function, cell growth, and inflammation.

Often called the "sunshine vitamin," vitamin D can be synthesized in your body by exposure to sunshine.
For people who don't see much sun (say, indoor climbers with a desk job) or people living in areas of the world where the sun isn't out much (Seattle) or at a low angle (Iceland), it can be difficult to get enough vitamin D. In addition, using sunscreen decreases your body's ability to make vitamin D.

Vitamin D isn't actually found in many foods either. Mushrooms and eggs have some. And dairy products do if they have been fortified with vitamin D (many are in the United States). It's usually a good idea to take a supplement of vitamin D, especially for vegans. But before adding a supplement, check with your doctor and get your vitamin D status tested. The results will determine if and how much vitamin D you need to take. In the United States, the recommended daily amount is 600 International Units for most adults.

There is some debate among sports nutrition professionals as to whether athletes might need more vitamin D than the average person. There is a level of vitamin D in your blood where it is considered "sufficient," and then there may be a level that is optimal for athletic performance. We just don't have enough information right now to definitely say whether your vitamin D needs to be at certain levels for athletic performance.

Vitamin D may help with preventing illness. It may also prevent and/or treat stress fractures and soft-tissue injuries (muscle, tendon, and ligaments). That would be big news for climbers, who often suffer from these injuries. *For more on nutrition for injury prevention and recovery, see chapter 7.*

As with all supplements, check with your doctor before adding it into your routine. It is simple to test vitamin D levels, so visit your doctor and get yourself checked before guessing at your actual needs. Too much vitamin D can lead to elevated blood calcium and heart arrhythmias.

6 - SPECIAL NUTRITION NEEDS

Vegan/Vegetarian Climbers (continued)

Zinc

Zinc is a mineral that supports immunity and protein synthesis. It's also involved with aiding numerous enzymes that help with cell metabolism. It also helps with DNA synthesis, and growth and development from fetus all the way through adolescence.

Zinc is found in oysters, red meat, poultry, crab, lobster, beans, cashews, almonds, whole grains, fortified grains, and dairy. As you can see, the list of zinc foods that vegans can eat is pretty small. And as with other minerals such as calcium and iron, zinc is not absorbed in your body very well because of the phytates, which bind to the zinc and prevent it from being absorbed as well.

In the United States, the daily recommended intake of zinc is 8 to 11 milligrams. Zinc deficiency is actually not that common, but vegans and vegetarians may need to eat more zinc-containing foods than omnivores in order to get enough. Soaking beans or letting grains sprout enhances the bioavailability of zinc (meaning your body can absorb it better).

Iodine

Iodine is often overlooked, but is a crucial nutrient to the work of thyroid hormones. If you've ever had your thyroid out of whack (or known someone with this condition), you know that proper thyroid balance is important for weight regulation. Symptoms of low thyroid hormones include weight gain, hair loss, and fatigue. Iodine deficiency itself can cause stunted growth, mental retardation, and goiter.

Iodine is found in very few foods. Unless the food was made with iodized salt (salt where iodine is added) or seaweed, it likely doesn't have iodine in it. Eggs and milk do have some iodine in them. Vegans and vegetarians can get iodine in their diet by simply using iodized salt. This is super common and also very cheap. If you are using fancy Himalayan pink salt or sea salt, just switch. Good ol' iodized salt is actually a better way to go. In the United States, the recommended intake for most adults is 150 micrograms daily. If you are concerned about your iodine intake, you can get your thyroid function and iodine status checked by a doctor.

Omega 3 fats

These types of fats are important for brain and heart health. These are commonly found in fish. Since vegans and vegetarians don't eat fish (unless you're a pescatarian), you need to find them in other sources, such as flax and chia seeds, walnuts, and if you're vegetarian, eggs from chickens fed with special feeds that contain EPA and DHA (two types of omega 3s).

Often, it's hard to eat enough seeds and walnuts to get a meaningful amount of omega 3s in your diet. This means you need to supplement with either fish oil (vegetarians) or algae oil (vegans). Check with your doctor first before supplementing.

Creatine

Creatine is not a nutrient, but it is important to know about if you are a vegan or vegetarian athlete. Remember back in chapter 2 when I talked about the energy systems in your body? Creatine is a part of the phosphagen energy system. Here is a refresher: Energy in your muscles is powered by a molecule called adenosine triphosphate (ATP). This is the "energy currency" of the muscle. ATP is used to power a muscle contraction. It happens like this:

» ATP gets broken down into ADP (adenosine diphosphate) and a Pi (inorganic phosphate).

» Phosphocreatine (PCr) is broken down into creatine and phosphate. This lone phosphate gets hooked onto the ADP to make ATP. The ATP powers the muscle, and the phosphocreatine helps to regenerate that ATP.

Did you notice that creatine hanging out? If you have sufficient creatine, it can help power a muscle contraction, such as the hard work you do when climbing. Creatine helps with short, high-intensity exercise and your ability to perform these types of moves repeatedly. So, it would be useful for a dyno, a strong lockoff, or basically any other climbing move where you need intense effort.

Most people get some creatine in their diet from meat, and your body also makes creatine. But if you don't eat meat, you won't be getting creatine in your diet. Research shows that vegans and vegetarian athletes have less creatine stores than omnivores. Strength and power athletes, like rock climbers, may benefit from having adequate creatine. There's also some evidence that it can help with muscle soreness. Creatine can also potentially help with pump in your forearms, since it helps to increase blood flow.

If you don't eat meat, luckily it is easy and safe to supplement with creatine. This is one of the most well-researched sports supplements (albeit not in climbers), and one that has little to no negative side-effects. The recommended schedule is to use creatine monohydrate 10–20 grams per day divided into four equal daily doses for five to seven days, then go to a maintenance dose of 3–5 grams per day.

One caveat with creatine: When taking this supplement, you may gain water weight. Some reports are up to two to five pounds (around one to two kgs). This isn't permanent body mass; it's just water weight that will shed off when you use your muscles and/or sweat. However, if you're wanting to be as light as possible in order to have a high strength-to-weight ratio (or just feel light when you send a route), having five pounds of fluid on you might not feel the best.

You can experiment with using creatine to see if it helps you. It is a safe supplement and one worth considering, especially if you're vegan or vegetarian. And, are you tired of me saying to check with your doctor before supplementing? No? Great. Be sure to do that! Also, as with all supplements, it may contain contaminants. Select supplements that are third-party tested, and don't take them if you are a competition climber and this is an impermissible substance as defined by your governing body. *See chapter 8 for more supplement information.*

Vegan/Vegetarian Climbers (continued)

Protein

Protein might be one of the most misunderstood and talked-about macronutrients among vegans and vegetarians. Omnivores often mistakenly think that vegans don't get enough protein (or any!). Rest assured, you can get enough protein if you are vegan or vegetarian.

Amino acids are the building blocks of protein. Leucine is a particular amino acid that builds muscle. 20–30 grams of complete protein, spaced regularly throughout the day with three to four meals, is ideal timing for protein intake.

Good sources of leucine include beef, pork, poultry, seafood, eggs, and milk. Vegans, did you just read this list and feel your heart sink? While it's true that animal sources of protein are very well absorbed and utilized in the body to build muscle, you can still get enough protein through plant sources. You may have to eat more protein than an omnivore to get an adequate amount, as plant proteins are often not as digestible. Plant sources of leucine include soybeans, white beans, kidney beans, lentils, soy, and peanuts.

Here are some non-meat sources of protein:

- Legumes/dried beans (like peas, kidney beans, chickpeas, and black beans)
- Nuts and seeds
- Vegetables
- Whole grains
- Eggs (vegetarians)
- Soy products
- Dairy products (vegetarians)

Plant-based protein-powder blends are usually better than a single source of protein, such as hemp or soy protein. If you are looking to purchase a protein powder as a vegan, go for one that includes a variety of protein sources, such as pea, soy, corn, and rice. If you are vegetarian, whey is the way to go, as it is high in leucine.

Vegan climbers may need more protein overall than other climbers in order to ingest enough overall amino acids and protein that are digestible and bioavailable. Current recommendations range depending on how active a person is, how much weight training they are doing, and if they have any injuries to heal from. A good range is likely 1.0–1.8 grams per kilogram of body weight per day. *(To calculate your weight in kilograms, see page 43)*

Last Thoughts about Vegan/Vegetarian Climbers

Maybe you are thinking of making the switch to being vegan or vegetarian. Maybe you already have but are unsure how to do it right. Maybe you've done it for years. One caution I would add is to please, please do it for the right reasons. If you feel strongly that it is good for the environment, good for your health, or any other reason, go for it. If you feel pressured to do it based on a book you've read, a friend or family member, or any other outside source, think twice. Make sure you're ready for it. It can be a challenging lifestyle to implement, but a bit easier with the help of a dietitian.

Also, please examine yourself and make sure you are healthy. Some people switch to veganism only to discover that they lose muscle mass, lack energy, and have other negative health effects. Others may find that they have increased anxiety and stress around food, and they miss out on the social and emotional components of food enjoyment. Still others use veganism and vegetarianism as a way toward disordered eating/eating disorders. If you feel anxious, stressed, or less healthy after switching to a vegan or vegetarian lifestyle, please seek help from a qualified registered dietitian.

6 - SPECIAL NUTRITION NEEDS

Living the Van Life

Ok, I need to tell you, I have never lived in a van. Sometimes it feels like I do since I have three kids in sports and activities–the minivan is our home on wheels. But I have never live-lived in a van. My idea of van cuisine is Goldfish crackers that fell on the floor. Despite the unglamorous introduction, this section will give you suggestions and ideas about how to eat well while living the van life and climbing full-time.

There are a few things to think about while living in a van. First, do you have refrigeration? Do you have a way to heat food? How much storage space for food do you have? How much access to grocery stores and restaurants do you have? If you're in the middle of nowhere on your epic climbing trip and run out of pancake mix, there is no grocery store down the road. Planning ahead and having staples at all times will make sure you can be well-fueled despite living in cramped quarters.

I reached out to Lori Nedescu, MS, RDN, CSSD to help me write this section. She is a sports dietitian and cyclist. She runs a consulting business called Hungry for Results, and she lives in a van for a huge chunk of her life, traveling to different bike races throughout the country. She has some amazing suggestions for what to pack in your van, as well as great meal ideas that can be prepared in a van. Here are Lori's lists of suggestions for van nutrition "essentials:"

VAN LIFE

EQUIPMENT BASICS:

- Cutting board
- Knife
- Whisk
- Can opener
- Plastic/glass food-storage containers
- Sandwich bags
- Camp stove
- Two-cup rice cooker
- French press
- Kettle
- Sponge
- Dish soap
- Portable sink/tub
- Plates, cups, bowls, utensils
- Hotplate ("hob" for all you British readers)
- Travel mug that plugs into your car to boil water

FOOD BASICS:

- Hardboiled eggs
- Tuna in a can or pouch
- Shelf-stable milk or nut milks
- Bread
- Bagels
- Mixed greens
- Carrots
- Hummus
- Peanut butter
- Rice
- Granola/muesli/cereal
- Oatmeal/porridge
- Coffee and tea
- Bananas
- Drinkable soup cartons
- Seasonings/spices/herbs
- Protein and granola bars
- Sport-specific foods you like (gummies, chews, protein powders, etc.)
- Ranch dressing/mustard/hot sauce/ketchup (condiment packets instead of full bottles)
- Olive oil
- Jerky
- Trail mix
- Shelf-stable tofu
- Dehydrated/freeze-dried backpacking meals and MREs (meals ready-to-eat)

VAN LIFE

MEAL IDEAS:

Breakfast:
- Oatmeal with granola, fruit, nuts, and milk
- Omelet with veggies
- Overnight oats
- Yogurt with granola and fruit
- Toast with peanut or almond butter
- Avocado and egg toast
- Flat bread with cheese, ham, and egg
- Pancakes from a mix with peanut butter and bananas

Lunch/Dinner:
- Stir fry with rice, canned chicken, and veggies
- Wrap with deli meat, veggies, and cheese
- Salad with canned tuna, veggies, and nuts
- Pasta with canned chicken and veggies
- Fajitas with veggies and cheese
- Savory egg sandwich on an English muffin

Lori recommends keeping things simple. Limited storage and prep space mean streamlining foods, making meals with simple ingredients, and rotating through staples. You may find that your variety becomes limited. When you just can't bring yourself to eat another rice bowl, have things on hand that you'd saved for a special occasion, like a good chocolate bar. If you are in civilization, visit a local market or café to add variety and fun. This will help keep your food interesting and add more variety and nutrients to your overall intake.

Awkward Van Life Facts:

Even though you are living in a van, you still need to use the restroom. It's important to stay hydrated no matter where you are living. One option is to use a bottle or portable plastic urinal (label this well, obviously!) so you're not going in and out of the van constantly at all hours. Resist the urge to not drink so you can urinate less often. Just drink as you need to in order to stay hydrated, and urinate as needed. Watch for light-yellow urine, like straw or lemonade. If it is too dark, this probably means you are not drinking enough. Plan ahead by using a composting toilet and/or digging a hole for your solid waste at least 6–8 inches deep, and at least 200 feet from bodies of water. Pack out your toilet paper and follow Leave No Trace principles.

Climbers with Digestive Issues

The last thing any climber wants is to be high up on a wall and have diarrhea. A bivy is not so fun if you are trying to manage your digestive system. Trying to hang upside down or squeeze into an offwidth is tough if you are bloated. If you feel your stomach revolt after eating certain foods, you may want to pay attention to which foods are causing you problems.

An allergic reaction is different than intolerance. Common food allergies include milk, eggs, nuts, soy, wheat, and fish/shellfish. Symptoms include diarrhea, rash, itchy throat, and difficulty breathing. If you have true food allergies, please always avoid the foods you are allergic to and seek immediate medical attention if you have an allergic reaction. This is life-threatening. See an allergist or doctor specializing in food allergies if you aren't sure whether you're allergic to a food.

For this section, I reached out to **Niki Strealy, RDN, LD**. She is a registered dietitian specializing in digestive health. She calls herself the Diarrhea Dietitian and has written a book by the same name. She is a great resource for anyone experiencing digestive problems. Here are some solutions for you if you are seeking nutrition help for your digestive issues.

First and foremost, test all foods on a small, easy climb before you embark on a comp, multi-pitch, or multi-day climb. This way you will know what you can tolerate and what to avoid. Don't rely on other people to bring food for you. What works for your climbing partner may spell disaster for you. Be self-sufficient and bring foods you know you can tolerate. And bring enough of them to last the trip and avoid hunger or fatigue.

Be aware of the way your body digests certain foods. If you find yourself with chronic bowel problems, you may need to cut down on fiber or other fermentable carbohydrates (called FODMAPS) that may give you problems. These are a group of small-chain carbohydrates that can ferment in your intestines, causing gas, bloating, cramping, and diarrhea.

FODMAP stands for Fermentable Oligosaccharides, Disaccharides, Monosaccharides, and Polyols. Say that three times fast. Bonus points for working it casually into a conversation at the crag.

Climbers with Digestive Issues (continued)

There have been whole books written about the low-FODMAP diet for those with digestive issues (*The Low FODMAP Diet Step by Step* by Kate Scarlata is a great one), so this section is only a very brief summary.

Basically, fibrous foods and foods containing FODMAPS can cause stomach and bowel upset. You can eliminate these foods, but it's only recommended to do so for a short period of time. This allows you to explore what foods you don't tolerate, and slowly add back in foods you do tolerate. As with any diet that eliminates foods, you are at risk for missing out on nutrients. Be sure to ask a dietitian and your physician for help with eliminating foods that give you troublesome symptoms. If you feel you need to eliminate some high-FODMAP foods, there is a two-week elimination-diet protocol. Only undertake this with guidance from a registered dietitian specializing in digestive health.

Examples of foods high in FODMAPS include:
- » Lactose-containing foods, such as milk, cream, ice cream, yogurt, and cottage cheese.
- » Fructose-containing foods, such as apples, mangos, pears, watermelon, asparagus, snap peas, high fructose corn syrup, and honey.
- » Fructan-containing foods, such as dried fruits, onion, garlic, wheat, watermelon, and nectarines.
- » Polyol-containing foods, such as apples, apricots, nectarines, peaches, pears, mushrooms, cauliflower, and sugar alcohols.
- » Legumes (dried beans), pistachios, and cashews.
- » Some grains, like wheat, rye, and barley.
- » Some added fiber sources, like inulin and chicory root.

Even if you tolerate FODMAP-containing foods, you might still experience diarrhea or stomach upset. If this is the case, about two days before a big climbing day, eat foods with less fiber in them. This will give your body a chance to digest and (hopefully) get rid of all of it before the big climb. Trade out whole-wheat bread for white bread and bagels. Use white rice instead of brown rice. Eat fewer fruits and vegetables, and only those ones you know you tolerate.

Also, caffeine and alcohol can speed up digestion, so steer clear of these if you're experiencing trouble.

Sometimes sheer nerves can exacerbate the digestive system.
If you find yourself feeling nervous or anxious before or during climbs, and you get diarrhea, make sure you are eating very little fiber and sugar. You might want to consider talking to a sports psychologist as well, to get solid strategies on how to calm yourself and be mentally ready for your climb.

Often females have digestive issues in the week or so leading up to their period—usually it is loose stools and bloating. If this is an issue, it doesn't mean you need to eliminate foods forever. Just eliminate fibrous foods for a few days to see if that helps improve your symptoms.

Diarrhea can be dehydrating, so be sure to drink fluids, replace lost electrolytes, and pay attention to how your body feels. Be on the alert for symptoms of dehydration, such as dizziness, headaches, mental fogginess, dry mouth, and excessive thirst. Abort your climb and take care of your hydration status before trying to push yourself. Being dehydrated or having gastrointestinal upset can be a recipe for injury or accident.

If you know your route is going to involve some contorting, folding, or twisting of your body, it's a good idea to forgo fiber and greasy, fatty foods for a day or two beforehand. This will allow you to feel light enough and not bogged down by intestinal upset when you have to bend like a master yogi to send the route. If bloating is a problem, try lower-FODMAP foods and lower-fiber foods. Many sports drinks and trail foods (like dehydrated foods, jerky, and nuts) have added salt that can lead to water retention. If you feel bloated or swollen from these, don't use these types of foods if you know you'll be trying a route that involves some contorting.

The evidence in endurance athletes suggests Ibuprofen and aspirin increase gastrointestinal upset as well.
It's not known if these affect climbers as much, but if you are having stomach and intestinal problems and have been routinely taking ibuprofen, stop for a bit and see if it helps you. Of course, ask your doctor for other pain-relieving options that would be appropriate for you.

If you need more help, call your physician, see a gastroenterologist, and talk to a dietitian specializing in bowel health. Bowel problems may be a sign of underlying issues, such as celiac disease, irritable bowel syndrome, ulcerative colitis, colon cancer, or ovarian cancer. A good medical provider can be invaluable in helping you find a good treatment plan for your bowel health.

Youth & Adolescent Climbers

In one study, researchers described how a male adolescent climber reportedly gained weight due to the onset of puberty. As a result, his finger strength decreased—his fingers could no longer support his heavier body the same way. He ramped up his finger-strength training to compensate for this, but the additional campus-board training deformed his fingers and decreased his range of motion. This could have been prevented had he or his coach known that campus-board training isn't recommended for adolescents. Being familiar with adolescent physiology and nutrition needs can help make sure these kids stay safe while training.

Taking the time to really understand how adolescent and youth bodies are different from adult bodies will help you be armed with good information for kids nutrition, hydration, and sport-specific fueling. This section will focus on youth climbers, defined as teen or pre-teen going through puberty, and under the age of 18.

With many adolescent athletes emerging in the international field of competitive climbers, it's easy to forget that they are not adults. Many youth athletes can send difficult routes just like adults can; some even surpass adults in their ability.

Youth & Adolescent Climbers (continued)

There are not a lot of nutrition studies involving young athletes. This means that we don't have a lot of good, hard evidence as to how to fuel their bodies. Children are not just tiny adults: Their bodies work a bit differently.

For example, children who haven't begun puberty have increased fat oxidation and decreased glycolysis when compared to adults. In simple terms, that means that children likely use more fat for energy than carbohydrates during exercise. Another example of their differences: Youth may be at more risk for ligament tears than adults. In climbing, there is a high risk for soft-tissue damage such as ligament tears, so training needs to be adapted to prevent injury. Children who haven't undergone puberty also may not be as developed in their thirst and pain mechanisms. This means if they need water they might not realize it, or if they are in pain they might not be able to recognize and stop the movement that is causing pain before an injury can occur.

Children and teens are also growing, and their bodies are changing constantly. If a youth is participating in climbing, and oftentimes another sport as well, they need to eat to fuel both their growth and extra physical activities. Couple this with the fact that they often have physical education during school (and recess!), and it becomes clear that they need to eat a lot of food to power all those movements.

If you have kids, you know that sometimes you buy them a pair of shoes and then literally two weeks later they have outgrown them. Climbing shoes, as you may know, are often "supposed" to fit tightly in order to offer better control and grip. But when they fit too tightly, and a kid has rapidly growing feet, it can cause damage to the foot. Along with the feet, other body parts are growing as well. And all this growth needs calories (food!).

Pre-teens and teens going through puberty have the added challenge of gaining weight, sometimes very rapidly, and coping with adapting to a new-to-them body. For climbers, this can be a special challenge, particularly if the youth is gaining both weight and height at the same time. Routes and moves that once seemed easy and natural may be more difficult in a heavier, longer body. In addition, children are at greater risk for injury because of a lack of developed coordination and skills, because they are just less experienced than adults. There is a reason kids don't use campus boards—the risk of injury is too high until their growth plates close. According to researchers, too many dynos, too much crimping, and too much bouldering also seem to increase the risk of injury because of kids' bodily need for longer recovery times and their underdeveloped coordination.

Youth & Adolescent Climbers (continued)

Girls can gain up to 40 pounds (18 kg) during puberty. Sometimes much of this weight is gained rather quickly, and parents, coaches, and girls alike may become alarmed, worried that the girl is becoming "too fat" or gaining too much weight to be a good athlete. Rest assured, this weight gain is normal and desirable as a predictable part of puberty. But for a very thin, light female climber, it can feel unsettling. You can teach your teen to trust her body and resist comparing her body to others' (or her own former body).

With both boys and girls, there is evidence in the literature that normal puberty growth can have a socioemotional component, sometimes perceived as a bad thing by the athlete. In a sport where a high strength-to-weight ratio is crucial for success, it's difficult to suddenly gain weight and feel like you are an inferior climber simply because you're going through puberty.

I hope with all these examples you can see that it's clear we need to be careful with the way we train and fuel our kids. We need to support the puberty process, help them eat enough to do well in school, and help them develop a healthy relationship with food and their bodies.

Parents observing children's eating habits may notice that it seems sporadic. One day a kid may eat everything in the house and be begging for more. A couple of days later, the same kid may eat what parents view as not enough food. This is normal. Kids eat according to their hunger and growth. They are living in bodies that demand constant change. It's natural to eat more one day than the next.

Nutrition plays a role in all of this. Although there is a definite lack of research on climbing and adolescent nutrition, we can take what we know about adolescent sports nutrition and make some pretty good educated guesses.

Here are some things to consider:

Track Your Youth Athlete's Growth
This can be done by your pediatrician with regular checkups. If your child's growth slows or plateaus, it is a warning sign that your child may not be getting the right nutrition.

Track Your Youth Athlete's Puberty Stages
These are called the Tanner stages or Tanner scale. Again, this can be done with regular pediatrician checkups. Having regular check-ins with the doctor can help you make sure your child is on track to hit their "right" size.

Have an Open Dialog with Your Child
Educating your children on puberty, growth, fueling, and nutrition needs can help them understand how to take care of their bodies and excel in climbing.

Picky Eating May Be Normal. Or Maybe It's Not.
Picky eating at young ages is normal, but as a child gets into elementary- and middle-school years (around ages 7 to 12), he or she should be mostly beyond this. If you feel your child is continuing to be picky or restrictive, seek the help of a pediatric registered dietitian. This type of dietitian is well-qualified to gently lead you and your child toward a healthy relationship with food and increased food acceptance.

A parent or caregiver can also be an influence on a child's relationship with food and perception of their body. If you have a child struggling with normal eating patterns, but know that you yourself also struggle, it's worth exploring this with professional guidance from a dietitian and therapist to heal these relationships with food and body image.

Dieting and Food Restrictions, Unless Medically Necessary as in the Case of Food Allergies, Are Usually Contraindicated in Children.
Kids need a wide variety of food and nutrients to grow and develop. Limiting nutrients or food groups is not recommended.

Youth & Adolescent Climbers (continued)

Here are some general guidelines about nutrition needs for adolescents:

Energy: Energy in this sense isn't the boundless energy a two-year-old has, running around and driving her parents crazy. This is calories—energy from food that the body uses for exercise, growth, and normal body processes. Your body needs enough energy (or calories) to support respiration, your heart beating, cell and tissue turnover, bone health, reproductive health, immunity, growth of new tissues (such as building muscle or healing from an injury), and more. Even your brain needs energy!

Taking all this into consideration, think about this in the context of a child or adolescent. They need energy for all of the above—just the same as an adult—but then they need extra energy to support a growing body and puberty. If kids don't get enough overall calories, negative health consequences can occur. These include stunted stature (meaning they won't grow as tall as they could have), delayed puberty, poor bone health and bone density, increased risk of injury, and mood disorders. Think about the last time you were hungry to the point of being irritable. Have you been hangry (hungry + angry) lately? Now think about a growing kid. They can be permanently hangry if they are not getting enough food to support all that is going on in their body.

A kid who has gone to school all day, possibly with recess and PE within that school day, and then goes to climbing practice after school needs a lot of calories to support all that learning, growth, and exercise. Feed your kid enough and they will do better in school and sports (and probably home life too)!

Side note: This happened with my growing teenage boy the other day. He had 30 minutes between school and climbing. He came home and was upset and irritable, to the point of almost being irrational. After I tried to talk with him, the little lightbulb went off above my head, *ding!*

ME: When was the last time you ate?
HIM: I dunno, like lunchtime?
ME: So, five hours ago?
HIM: Yeah.
ME: Here, have some cereal.
HIM (10 minutes later): Much, much happier son with functioning reason restored. He was able to hold a conversation and was ready to climb.

So how much energy (calories) does your kid need each day? The answer is...who knows?! There actually is no really good equation or method to determine calorie needs. Frustrating as that is, we do have one study that examined how many calories kids burn when they are climbing.

The study strapped kids into a device

Youth & Adolescent Climbers (continued)

that measures their VO2 (volume of oxygen uptake) and energy expenditure (calories burned) while climbing. The average age of these kids was about 11 years old. The researchers had the kids climb for five minutes of sustained climbing followed by a five-minute rest period. They again had the kids climb, but this time for intervals of one minute five times, with rest periods in between. They found that the kids burned on average 22–85 calories during these climbing + rest periods. The interval climbing burned more calories.

The kids varied vastly in the amount of calories burned. The take-home message here is probably that we don't really know how many calories kids need, but it is safe to say that they need enough to fuel growth and sporting activities. A good measure to track if they are getting enough calories is to follow their growth patterns with a pediatrician.

Protein: As with energy (calories), we don't have good information or research on how much protein a child needs. Dietitians usually set an estimated target range for their clients based on the available data. Some studies in kids have shown that 1.35–1.6 grams per kilogram per day is a good number for youth athletes. A kilogram is 2.2 pounds. To determine a kid's protein needs, first divide their weight in pounds by 2.2. Then multiply by 1.35 and 1.6. This will give you a range.

For example, a kid who weighs 80 pounds is 36 kilograms (80 ÷ 2.2 = 36). Then take 36 x 1.35 (equals 49) and 36 x 1.6 (equals 58). An 80-pound kid likely needs 49–58 grams of protein daily.

In adult studies, protein intake has been shown to be most beneficial if it is spread out evenly over the day. For instance, eating about 20–30 grams of protein at each regular meal interval is better than eating only 10 grams of protein at breakfast, 10 grams at lunch, then 50 grams at dinner. For kids, the assumption is the same. Spreading out protein evenly over the day is probably better for their recovery, growth, muscle repair, and muscle building than having a lopsided intake.

To make sure protein is spread evenly throughout the day, a typical breakfast might include cereal with milk, a boiled egg, and a piece of fruit. Lunch could be a peanut butter and jelly sandwich on whole-wheat bread, a string cheese, and some carrots and hummus. Dinner could be chicken with veggies and quinoa. And an evening snack could be cottage cheese with fruit. In these examples, each meal or snack includes protein.

CHAPTER 6 - SPECIAL NUTRITION NEEDS 99

Youth & Adolescent Climbers (continued)

Carbohydrates: You'll start to notice a theme here: We don't have good information on how much carbohydrates kids need either. After reviewing the literature, it seems reasonable to recommend about three to five grams per kilogram per day for youth climbers. Endurance athletes such as cyclists and runners need more, but climbing is a bit different. Climbing involves different moves, more rests, and isometric contractions. Soccer, running, basketball, and other similar sports involve more constant running.

Climbers do need carbohydrates, though!

Remember in chapter 2, you learned that muscles need carbohydrates to contract. Your brain also uses carbohydrates to think. Climbing is a mental sport just as much as a physical sport: Consider a kid encountering a new and difficult bouldering problem–lots of brain power is needed to figure out the climb in addition to the physical demands of getting up it. Trying to figure out the right moves, problem-solving a project, staying mentally engaged with the task at hand, and thinking through safe falling all take fuel in the form of carbohydrates. Kids seem to oxidize fat more than carbohydrates when compared to adults, but kids still need carbs.

A kid would need more carbs on a heavy practice or comp day, and fewer carbs on rest days. A kid would need more carbs if they are also involved in other activities, especially running-dominant sports. And keep in mind that overall intake varies from day to day, but will average out over time. A kid may eat less one day (or one week), and then the next day or week eat everything in sight. This is totally normal! Just encourage your kid to eat according to hunger levels and remind them to eat if they are forgetful or tend to get too busy to eat.

A snack or meal of both protein and carbs is recommended immediately (or as close as possible) after exercising. This will help the body start to recover and restock fuel stores. This is especially important if there are two practices in a single day, or a long weekend comp.

Youth & Adolescent Climbers (continued)

Fats: Again, there are no set recommendations for fat intake in youth athletes. It is generally recommended that fat intake should come from healthy sources, such as fish, nuts, seeds, olives, and avocados. Fried foods and baked products have saturated fat, which is considered to be less desirable for heart health, although small amounts of saturated fat in the diet are OK. Female adolescents in particular need enough body-fat stores in order to experience puberty and begin and maintain menses (normal menstruation). If a female climber is restricting fat intake, she may not be able to have enough energy available to support growth and puberty. Males also need enough fat to support puberty and reproduction. Fat isn't the enemy people once thought it was. Fat is in fact necessary for optimal body functioning.

Fluids: Smile, because we actually have some research on kids and fluid needs with exercise. When compared with adults, kids are not as good at regulating their body temperature and can't tolerate heat as well. They can't sweat as much as adults, which means they may be more prone to overheating. In addition, children's thirst mechanisms seem to not be as attuned as adults'.

Most sports nutrition authorities recommend that children use water instead of sports drinks such as Gatorade. Sports drinks contain carbohydrates (sugar for quick energy to fuel the workout) plus electrolytes. The reason kids may not need a sports drink is that they may have lesser sweat rates and do not lose as many electrolytes and as much fluid as adults. But if we are talking about an adolescent who has been through puberty and is really close to an adult in terms of physical maturity, sports drinks may be very appropriate, especially in hot, humid conditions or prolonged climbing—like an all-day outing at the crag or an all-day comp.

A child who is more childlike and less developed, such as an eight-year-old, would likely perform and train optimally with plain water.

During training or competing, for kids ages 12 and under, drinking 3–8 ounces (100–240 milliliters) every 20 minutes should be sufficient. For older kids, they may need up to 34–50 ounces (1–1.5 liters). This recommendation is for a climbing session that takes place under normal temperatures. Heat or humidity may mean increased fluid needs.

Dehydration can negatively affect how well a kid can climb, and it is a serious and potentially life-threatening situation. Symptoms include dizziness, lightheadedness, fatigue, confusion, nausea, and dark urine.

On the flip side, overhydration is a problem too. Drinking too much can lead to a condition called hyponatremia, which is also dangerous and potentially life-threatening. Symptoms include nausea, vomiting, confusion, headaches, muscle spasms, and fatigue.

Youth & Adolescent Climbers (continued)

Supplements: The rule of thumb for any athlete of any age is foods first! This means that a well-balanced diet can and should include all the nutrients you need, without having to use supplements. Particularly with children and adolescents, it's important to preach a food-first philosophy. This can help them develop a good relationship with food and not think that relying on supplements will help them excel in their climbing.

Supplements are a slippery slope, as they are not well-regulated and often contain contaminants, fillers, ineffective ingredients, and sometimes even banned substances (substances that are illegal for competition climbers or illegal to distribute). In addition, supplements often lull people into the thought that if their diet isn't that great, at least they can use supplements as "insurance." Supplements are also usually expensive. It's not a good idea to have children taking supplements.

The exception would be if a child or adolescent has a true medical need and is taking supplements to increase a particular nutrient, or overall calories, under the supervision of a pediatrician and pediatric dietitian. Otherwise, using powders, pills, oils, or any other supplement is usually inappropriate for children and adolescents.

Truthfully, any gains that a kid would receive from supplement use may be obtained more easily, safely, cheaply, and effectively with a good nutrition plan and proper training.

For anyone looking for more in-depth information, I recommend the book *Fueling Young Athletes* by Heather R. Mangieri. It goes into depth about fueling, meal plans, macro- and micronutrients, and more. It is a thorough and excellent resource for any parent or coach of children and adolescents.

Nutrition for Older Athletes

Older adults are often very active. Especially in the climbing community, it's not hard to find people who have been climbing for years and continue to climb into later adulthood. There have been a number of studies conducted on older endurance athletes, but fewer on strength athletes. Climbing moves are more closely linked to the way a strength athlete (weightlifters, throwers in track and field, strongman competitors, etc.) moves than an endurance athlete. However, often climbing does involve endurance, like hiking to the crag or backpacking into an alpine route, for example.

We do know something about the way the body changes as it ages. Lean body mass (muscle) declines (called sarcopenia) even with regular exercise. Bone mass decreases as well. Aerobic capacity, or the ability to uptake oxygen, decreases. Remember glycogen? That's the storage form of sugar in your skeletal muscles and liver. It's the main energy source for climbing.

That decreases too. Interestingly, other changes occur that we don't normally think about, like decreased thirst recognition, decreased kidney function, decreased gastric (stomach) acid—which is involved with vitamin B12 absorption. All these declining body functions have implications for climbing performance.

Exercise can help the aging process in a number of ways. It can help retain muscle mass, help retain aerobic capacity, help preserve bone density, decrease the risk of disease, improve mood, improve glucose tolerance, preserve cognitive functioning, and decrease anxiety and depression.

Most studies refer to age 40 and older as the "older" athletes. I know, 40 is not old. But this is when the body does start to change. Fortunately, there are some nutrition interventions these climbers can implement that may help them perform better and/or retain health.

Nutrition For Older Athletes (continued)

Energy (calories): Recommendations vary based on what is going on with the individual. If you are an older athlete, you may have lost muscle mass and body mass over time, and your calorie needs decrease. You might need fewer calories at age 60 than you did at age 30, especially if your training and climbing volume have decreased. However, active older adults need more calories than their sedentary counterparts. If you are an active climber (and maybe also participate in other sports), you'll need to eat more overall than someone who doesn't do as many activities as you do. It is important to eat enough overall calories to support your climbing and other body processes. If you find yourself losing weight without meaning to, that is a good indication that you're not eating enough. It could also be a sign of a more serious illness, so be sure to visit a doctor if you have unintended weight loss. Ask a sports dietitian for a consultation to get more personalized guidance.

Carbohydrates: As with younger climbers, older climbers still need carbs! Remember, this is the main source of energy that your body uses for most climbing moves. The recommendations for older athletes are currently the same as for younger athletes. You probably need around three to five grams per kilogram per day of carbs to support climbing activities. Eating carbohydrates that are rich in nutrients and fiber–such as whole grains, fruits, vegetables, and legumes—will provide you with the vitamins and minerals you need to stay healthy.

Protein: Protein intake is important for bone density and lean muscle mass. Older adults sometimes have decreased kidney function, so a high protein intake may be even more harmful in this population. But in general, the recommendation remains around 1.0–1.7 grams per kilogram per day for active older adults with normal kidney function.

Timing is important. A regular protein intake of at least 20 grams every four hours or so, particularly after a hard workout day, is helpful to maintain and repair muscle. Whey protein is definitely a good protein for muscle mass and may be more beneficial than casein (another milk protein), soy, or other plant proteins. If you get most (or all) of your protein from plant-based sources, you need to increase the overall protein amount that you eat. This is because plant-based protein sources do not have as much leucine (that key amino acid that helps with muscle synthesis). Thus, you need to eat more plant protein than whey protein to get the same amount of leucine. Quinoa and corn (maize) are good plant-based sources of leucine.

Nutrition For Older Athletes (continued)

Fat: There isn't much difference between older and younger adult athletes and the way they metabolize fat. Dietary fat needs are the same for both.

Fluids/hydration: As people age, their thirst mechanism decreases. This means older climbers may be at risk for dehydration because they may not detect when they are thirsty. Combine that with the fact that older athletes also experience a decrease in total body water, increased urination, and decreased ability to sweat and regulate body temperature, and you may have a recipe for disaster.

If you are an older climber and have noticed these changes in your own body, be vigilant about actively hydrating. Especially if you are climbing outdoors when it is hot, humid, or windy, you may be more prone to dehydration. Starting your climb (and/or hike) already hydrated is a smart strategy. You can do this by drinking 12-20 ounces (400-600 milliliters) about two to three hours before climbing. Drinking a sports drink while climbing will help replenish lost carbohydrates and electrolytes, as well as prompt you to drink more often. Flavored drinks have been shown to be effective at helping people drink enough versus plain water. Try to avoid losing more than 2 percent of your body weight during a climbing session. A general rule of thumb is drinking about 8 ounces (240 milliliters) every hour of climbing. Alternately, you can test your sweat rate and drink accordingly. (See page 56 for more hydration information.)

CHAPTER 6 - SPECIAL NUTRITION NEEDS

Nutrition For Older Athletes (continued)

Micronutrients: A decrease in stomach acid as you age means that you won't be able to absorb some key nutrients as well: Vitamin B12, folic acid, calcium, iron, and zinc are all affected. Vegans need to supplement vitamin B12 in order to avoid becoming deficient in it, and/or consume fortified foods, such as plant-based milks and fortified breakfast cereals. A routine blood test done by your doctor can detect any deficiency.

Older adults can also lose more vitamin B6 through urinary excretion than younger people. You can get vitamin B6 in your diet by eating whole grains, fortified grains (like breakfast cereals), potatoes, meat, fish, poultry, and many fruits.

Vitamin D supports bone health, cell growth, improved immunity, reduced inflammation, and muscle-protein synthesis. Older adults may be prone to vitamin D deficiency. Fatigue, muscle pain, and muscle weakness are signs of deficiency. If you have any of these symptoms or live in a climate where sunshine exposure is limited, it's worth getting your vitamin D levels checked by your doctor. Food sources of vitamin D are fortified milk, mushrooms, tuna, mackerel, salmon, and organ meats. Vitamin D is one nutrient that is often hard to eat sufficient quantities of to prevent deficiency. A supplement may be needed—but again, check with your doctor first.

Calcium is involved with a lot of different body processes that athletes should care about: bone health, muscle contraction, nerve conduction, glycogenolysis (the breakdown of glycogen into glucose for use as fuel), wound healing, and blood clotting. Females in particular are susceptible to decreased bone density later in life, and calcium supplementation may be needed. Talk with your doctor or dietitian to see if this makes sense for you.

Older athletes may become zinc deficient if they are vegan or vegetarian, heavy sweaters (zinc is lost in sweat), or take calcium or iron supplements together at the same time (since the calcium and iron bind to zinc). Zinc is important for immune function, wound healing, tissue repair, and metabolism of carbohydrates, fats, and proteins. It's definitely important to get enough zinc. Good food sources include poultry, beef, seafood, beans, nuts, whole grains, dairy products, and fortified grains.

The take-home message here is that older climbers can still continue to crush it. **Chase your GOAT (Greatest of All Time),** climb a grade harder, climb to your heart's desire. If you have a good nutrition plan and are properly fueled, you can climb just as well (or better) as when you were younger. Talk with your doctor and sports dietitian to make sure you are fueling right, avoiding nutrient deficiencies, and are aware of any medication/nutrient interactions.

Female Athletes

There are a lot of active females out there, but unfortunately much more research is done on male athletes than females. Even so, we do have some good information on what female athletes need, how female needs differ from male needs, and what female climbers might want to consider to make sure they are fueling right and taking care of their bodies. To complicate things a little bit, the studies done on female athletes are mostly conducted on endurance athletes like runners and cyclists. A climber is a much different type of athlete, so it's hard to state definitively what a female climber's nutrition needs are. But we have some well-educated guesses.

There are some conflicting studies and not a lot of consensus around differences between males' and females' nutrition needs. But we do know a few things for sure. For instance, a female's ability to regulate body temperature, metabolize glucose and fat for fuel, regulate hydration status, and blood pressure are affected by female hormones and menstrual status. However, these same things also seem to be affected by some things within the athlete's control: how much overall energy (calories) a female is eating, if she is using oral contraceptives, and what she recently ate or what she ate after she exercised.

Everything you've read so far about climber athletes is true for females as well as males—you need carbohydrates in order to climb well. You need to hydrate in order to climb well. You need enough calories to be healthy and climb well. You need fat, protein, vitamins, and minerals...you get the idea.

These are just a few extra things to keep in mind as a female climber.

6 - SPECIAL NUTRITION NEEDS

Female Athletes (continued)

You Might Experience Differences in Your Exercise Capacity Based on Your **Menstrual Cycle**

OK, you need to understand something about your menstrual cycle. It is divided into two phases: the follicular phase and the luteal phase. A normal menstrual cycle averages 28 days, with variation between women. Day one of your cycle is the first day of your period (actual flow, not just spotting). The follicular phase is the first part of your cycle—days 1–15. The luteal phase is the second part of your cycle—days 16–28. Each phase has different hormones involved, as well as implications for your sports performance.

Day	Phase	What Happens	Performance Implications
1	Follicular	First day of flow. Increase in follicular-stimulating hormone	Strength training may feel easier.
5 OR 6	Follicular	Period is done. Increase in estrogen	N/A
12-15	Follicular	Luteinizing hormone increases and an egg is released (ovulation)	Cardio exercise may feel easier.
16-28	Luteal	Increase in progesterone. Increase in estrogen. Premenstrual period around day 23	Reaction time, coordination, blood sugar, thermoregulation, and dexterity may be lower during premenstrual days. Exercise capacity may be decreased in hot, humid conditions. Cardio may feel harder.

Those few days before your period can mean performance changes. You may need more carbohydrates, especially for really long exercise (all day at the crag plus hiking to/from) or intense bursts of power. Bloating is often a problem with women at this time of their cycle. This may not be super comfortable, especially if you feel heavier than usual, or not quite as nimble and flexible. Along with bloating, women often experience more gastrointestinal issues, such as loose stools and gas. Women with endometriosis, polycystic ovarian syndrome, or other similar diagnoses may find that gastrointestinal problems are much worse around their period. Headaches may result as well (be sure to stay hydrated to alleviate headaches).

Female Athletes (continued)

All of this may mean that you don't want to climb for a day or two, depending on the severity of your symptoms. But most women can climb before, during, and after their period just fine. You can keep a record in your calendar, get an app on your phone, or journal about your cycle, symptoms, and on which days they occur. This will help you track and understand your cycle better. If you can anticipate when you'll have severe PMS symptoms, you can plan redpoint efforts on other days if needed.

Contraceptives May Alter Hormone Levels

If you use these, have changed which kind you use, or notice symptoms that are hard for you to manage, talk with your doctor or obstetrician/gynecologist to see what can be done. There is a wide variety of birth-control options out there, and they shouldn't have to interfere with your climbing.

If you are not on birth control that stops your period, but you miss a period, your periods become irregular, or they stop altogether, sit up and take note. This is significant. You could be pregnant. If you're not, usually it is because you are not getting enough overall calories. This is a big red flag. More on that in a bit. First, I want to discuss micronutrient needs for women.

You Probably Need More Micronutrients

Females in general usually eat fewer calories than males, so it is sometimes difficult to eat all the micronutrients needed in a tight calorie budget. Specifically, calcium, vitamin D, iron, zinc, and B vitamins can be lacking, especially if you don't eat enough calories. But it is really, really important to get enough calories. (That's up for discussion in the next section.) Further, you are at more risk for not getting enough vitamins and minerals if you are vegan or vegetarian, follow any diet or fad diet that restricts certain foods or food groups, are a dieter or trying to lose weight, or have any diagnosis that interferes with nutrient absorption (like a bowel disease).

Females need adequate iron, since it's lost during menses. The Institute of Medicine has suggested that female athletes may need up to 30–70 percent more iron than non-athletes. A vegan or vegetarian may need up to 80 percent more iron than non-athletes. Recommended intake in the US for a female with normal menstrual cycles is 18 milligrams per day. Eighteen milligrams per day multiplied by 30–70 percent more is 23–30 grams per day.

Female Athletes (continued)

Here are a few foods that are good sources of iron:

Food	Portion Size	Iron Content
SHELLFISH	3.5 ounces (100 g)	28 mg
SPINACH	3.5 ounces (100 g)	3.6 mg
LENTILS (COOKED)	1 cup (198 g)	6.6 mg
BEEF	3.5 ounces (100 g)	2.7 mg
PUMPKIN SEEDS	1 ounce (28 g)	4.2 mg
QUINOA	1 cup (185 g)	2.5 mg
TURKEY	3.5 ounces (100 g)	3.5 mg
TOFU	½ c (126 g)	3.6 mg
DARK CHOCOLATE	1 ounce (28 g)	3.3 mg
FORTIFIED BREAKFAST CEREAL	1 ounce (100 g)	3.6–18 mg

You Definitely Need Enough Calories

Climbing is similar to other sports where thinness is desirable. Running, ice skating, rowing, cycling, gymnastics, dancing, and other sports all have a commonality: You see thin athletes competing. Thinness is sometimes equated with better performance. In some cases, this may be true. Climbing in particular is a sport where thinner often seems to be better, because if you are lighter it's definitely easier to climb. Climbing is a tough sport. Add in 10–20 extra pounds of body weight and it's even tougher. For that reason, some climbers try to actively lose weight in order to improve performance.

This is a slippery slope, especially if you are already at an appropriate weight for your height. There are a few reasons losing weight or a drive for thinness may be counterproductive:

» **Some sport-climbing governing bodies don't allow climbers under a certain Body Mass Index (BMI) to compete.** The Austrian Sportclimbing Organization doesn't allow females with a BMI under 17 and males under 18 to compete. The IFSC measures BMI of all competitors as well. (For reference, BMI is a ratio of your height to weight. The formula is weight in kilograms divided by height in meters squared.)

$$\text{BMI (Body Mass Index)} = \frac{\text{weight (kg)}}{\text{height (m}^2\text{)}}$$

» **Cutting back calories to lose weight can result in decreased performance and compromised training.** You don't have enough fuel to climb well. You may not see the training adaptations you expected.

» **Cutting calories to lose weight can result in decreased muscle mass.** You can't build more muscle if you're in a calorie deficit. And your body often taps into lean muscle mass to use as fuel if you're in a calorie deficit. It's a lose-lose situation.

» **Dieting is a predictor of future weight gain. Yes, you read that right.** Dieting over time may lead to weight gain. Dieting decreases a person's resting metabolism to be lower than it was pre-diet, meaning you burn fewer calories after you stop dieting than you did before starting the diet. Weight gain may also occur because bingeing is common with diets, leading to eating more calories overall than before. And finally, dieting can disrupt hunger and satiety hormones.

» **Dieting—whether by decreasing calories, cutting out certain food groups, restricting portion sizes, or following a specific regimen—leads to decreased overall nutrient intake.**

Throughout this book, I've often pointed out that there is not a lot of research in one area or another. However, in the case of female athletes, there is one area where there is actually a lot of research: the concept of low energy availability.

6 - SPECIAL NUTRITION NEEDS

Female Athletes (continued)

Low Energy Availability:

To understand low energy availability, think of it as the energy (calories) your body has left over after exercise. Your body needs a certain amount of energy to exist. Heart rate, respiration (breathing), normal cell turnover, temperature regulation, and more demand calories. This is your basal metabolic rate (BMR). Then, on top of that, your body needs more energy to digest food, move around, think, and complete normal daily activities.

The energy-availability equation looks like this:

$$\frac{\text{Energy intake (calories eaten)} - \text{Energy Expenditure (calories used)}}{\text{Lean body mass (kg)}}$$

Let's run through an example. Our sample female climber weighs 130 pounds and has 20 percent body fat. First, find the lean mass. 130 x 0.2 (20%) = 26 pounds of fat. So 130−26 pounds of fat = 104 pounds of lean body mass. 104 ÷ 2.2 = 47 kg.

If a female climber eats 2000 calories, then burns 500 calories during a climbing session, and she has 47 kg of lean body mass, we can plug it into this equation to see if she has high-enough energy availability. It looks like this:

$$\frac{2000 \text{ calories eaten} - 500 \text{ calories expended while climbing}}{47 \text{ kg lean body mass}} = 32 \text{ calories/kg leftover}$$

You can see your "energy availability" is what you eat, minus whatever calories you burned in your workout. That is the rest of the energy left over, or "available," for your body's other necessary functions like breathing, heartbeat, immune system support, bone turnover, cell rebuilding and repair, reproduction, and more. If you don't eat enough calories, but you are still exercising, your body will be short-changed. You won't have enough calories for other normal body functions.

Female Athletes (continued)

People who suffer from low energy availability have various signs and symptoms. These may include one or more of the following:

» Fatigue
» Irritability, mood disturbances, and depression
» Decreased alertness
» Sleep disturbances
» Missed or irregular periods
» Decreased resting metabolism
» Decreased muscle strength
» Decreased endurance capacity
» Increased risk of injury
» Decreased glycogen stores
» Decreased coordination
» Frequent illnesses due to decreased immunity
» Hormone disruption
» Decreased growth in adolescents
» Gastrointestinal upset

An ideal energy availability is 30–45 calories per kilogram of lean body mass. In the example above, this climber is eating enough. Most female athletes need to eat at least 1800 calories daily. Depending on their discipline, training schedule, and body composition, they may need up to 5000 calories per day. Female climbers usually demand a lower calorie intake than endurance athletes. So, if you are a climber with no other sport involvement (like running), you probably need around 1800–2500 calories daily. That calorie need goes up on days when you may be hiking to the crag, climbing all day long, or do another workout in addition to climbing (like strength training).

OK, so look at the list above. There are many items on there that will have a profound impact on your ability to climb well: **loss of coordination and muscle strength, decreased glycogen stores, and also increased fatigue and injury.** The other ones, such as a missed period, may not seem like such a big deal, but they are: A missed period is a red flag that something is wrong.

You might be wondering why this is included in the female-climber section of this book. While it is true that low energy availability affects men (and has serious health consequences), this concept of low energy availability actually evolved from researching women.

Female Athletes (continued)

Formerly known as the Female Athlete Triad,
the syndrome has evolved as a growing body of research has revealed that it is much, much more than a "triad." The Female Athlete Triad was first identified in females who had three things: 1) an eating disorder, 2) amenorrhea (missing periods for more than three months, or never starting to menstruate when you should have already), and 3) compromised bone density.

These women with eating disorders were restricting their calorie intake so much that they lost their period (or never started it) and had bone-density problems, often resulting in fractures. Since the Female Athlete Triad was first identified, much more research has added to our understanding of the grave consequences of restricting energy (calorie) intake.

Luckily, there is a solution: Eat more calories!

Those athletes, male and female alike, who suffer from low energy availability or Relative Energy Deficiency in Sport (RED-S) can address the issue if they simply eat enough.

Many athletes don't purposefully eat less than they should. They may be unaware that they are not getting enough calories, until a bothersome symptom surfaces, like a stress fracture, depression, missed period, or inability to heal quickly from an injury. Even a stable weight does not indicate that you are getting enough calories. The body is smart: It can keep your weight as stable as possible even if you're not eating enough by cutting out other "nonessential" functions like reproduction, bone health, or climbing performance.

If you suspect you're not eating enough or have experienced a missed period or irregular periods or any other symptoms, please see a doctor immediately. A qualified sports physician and sports dietitian can guide you on the best path to get healthier and improve climbing performance. If you feel yourself in a disordered eating pattern, such as restricting specific foods, bingeing through laxatives, vomiting, or excessive exercise, becoming obsessive about what you eat or what your body looks like, having a negative body image, or anything that doesn't seem quite right, please seek treatment. Early intervention is best for a full recovery.

For more about disordered eating and eating disorders, flip to chapter 10.

Pregnant Climbers

When you are pregnant, a number of different things happen to your body. You have increased blood volume, altered glycogen and glucose use, altered ability to thermoregulate body temperature, and increased flexibility. You need enough nutrients to support a growing baby, namely: iron, calcium, folic acid, vitamins A, C, D, B6, and B12, as well as increased protein and calorie needs. The old saying "Eat for two" doesn't fully apply. You are technically eating for two humans, but one of those humans is very, very tiny. The first trimester only demands about 90 extra calories per day. That's as much as a slice of bread. The second trimester you'll need about 300 extra calories per day, and the third trimester is about 450 extra calories per day. You don't need to literally double your calorie intake, but you do need some extra food.

As always, a good way to know how much to eat is to just eat when you are hungry. Also pay attention to how you feel. Pregnancy can cause fatigue. Take a nap and get extra sleep. Cravings are common as well—maybe even for food you don't normally eat. It's OK to eat according to cravings. Allowing yourself to eat the particular food you are craving will alleviate the craving and allow you to move on with your day. When I was pregnant with my first child, I craved fast-food chicken nuggets. With my next child it was asparagus. My third child was all different foods from one day to the next. I just rolled with it!

During pregnancy, you might be able to climb during the first trimester, depending on how well you feel, **but be smart.** Don't put yourself at undue risk by climbing a sketchy route, overexerting yourself, or ignoring symptoms like fatigue, nausea, or lightheadedness. Be sure to fuel and hydrate well while doing any activity. Get cleared by your doctor for all activities. Stop taking any supplements except micronutrients (vitamins and minerals) approved by your doctor. Beyond the first trimester, you may continue to climb depending on how well you feel, or if you have any medical complications or contraindications.

> If you are looking for additional resources to find community and insight for pregnant climbers, **Beth Rodden's** blog is great. In 2014, two doctors teamed up with Beth Rodden (professional climber and mom) to implement a survey about climbers' experiences with pregnancy, nursing, and return to climbing. Beth's blog has a great summary of the survey.

If you are experiencing severe nausea or any other uncomfortable symptoms, seek help from a doctor and dietitian to get personalized advice to help you feel better, and keep you and your baby safe and healthy.

Female Athletes (continued)

Nursing Climbers

This is the time where many women are excited to "get their bodies back." (But where did it go?) The baby is born, you are no longer pregnant, and it's exciting to think about your body going back to normal. If you choose to nurse, the calorie demand is actually higher than when you were pregnant. Nursing mothers need about 500 more calories per day, as well as plenty of fluids. Carry around a water bottle wherever you go, and drink often.

You will likely still feel fatigued—not because you're growing a human inside you, but because that human now wakes you up at night and literally sucks (nurses) energy out of your body at all hours.

Pay attention to how you feel—don't feel rushed or heed any outside pressure to be more active or get back into climbing before you're ready. Your body needs a chance to heal. It can take 9 to 12 months before you feel normal again. Talk with a doctor before climbing or training again to make sure you're ready for it, both mentally and physically.

If you have any trouble with nursing—whether your baby isn't latching on, your breasts are uncomfortable or it's painful to nurse, your baby seems fussy or has digestive issues, or anything else—seek out a doctor and a certified lactation specialist. These medical providers can guide you through this to make sure you and your baby get the support you need.

Female Athletes (continued)

An Interview with Sasha DiGiulian

Marv Watson

Sasha DiGiulian is well-known for her stunning climbing achievements, including winning competitions and making multiple first female ascents. She was gracious enough to answer some questions via email (June 17, 2019) regarding her take on nutrition, body image, and more.

Can you tell me about your typical training day–what do you like to eat and drink?

Sasha DiGiulian: I wake up, have a warm glass of water with lemon. I follow a quick meditation regime for about 10 minutes. Then, I have green tea and breakfast. Typically for breakfast I have greek yogurt with chia seeds, flax, granola, and fruit. Then I have a coffee, usually oat milk latte. I do some emails in the AM, then head to training or climbing outside. If I am doing a 2/day training, I will train for about 2-3 hours, then have a snack; this typically consists of a homemade protein bar or a bag of Perky Jerky (lean protein) and fruit. I always have trail mix on me, normally raw nuts, unsalted, and no-sugar-added dried fruit that I typically make myself in my dehydrator. If I am climbing outside, my lunch becomes a bit less of a meal and more a composition of snacks, focusing on a macro balance of carbs-protein-fats. For dinner, the most typical dinner I have is rice, salmon, and vegetables. I also have red wine more often than not with my meal. Throughout the day, I carry around a water bottle, which I refill. Before my second workout of the day, I will also have a Red Bull with me.

Tell about a typical multi-day or multi-pitch outdoor climbing trip–what do you bring for food and fluids? Any tips or tricks you've found that work really well for you?

DiGiulian: I make my own bars–that is the most unique thing that I bring with me on my big-wall climbs. These bars can have a myriad of ingredients and hit different macro ratios depending what I'm going for... I have a green powder I will use sometimes that ensures that I have all of my daily greens in my bar (powder form of kale/spirulina/spinach, probiotics, etc).

How have you learned to have more body acceptance for yourself and/or teach others about it? Do you think it is important to talk about this topic in the climbing community?

DiGiulian: You don't wake up every day feeling the same about your body. Some days I wake up and I feel great and confident and proud of my muscles. Other days I wake up and feel like somehow in a day I've become out of shape and whatever I had the night before didn't settle. It's not really about the day-to-day is what I've learned. Acceptance is about the overall – how do

6 - SPECIAL NUTRITION NEEDS

Female Athletes (continued)

An Interview with Sasha DiGiulian

you feel, how are your relationships with your friends and family being positively impacted by how you are feeling from a workout to refueling (food incredibly affects my mood), and where are you in comparison to where you want to be? I certainly am not perfect when it comes to body acceptance, but I can definitely say that my awareness and my acceptance of what my body needs and of what makes it feel best have improved as I've grown more comfortable in my own skin. I think that this growth is a lifelong journey, for me. I've gone through ups and downs with my own body acceptance, especially pertaining to climbing and the sheer fact that it is a strength-to-weight-ratio sport. What I have learned, though, is that gaining strength and confidence significantly bolsters athletic performance as well as enhances my confidence. When I feel good climbing, I feel good about myself. I think that this subject is incredibly important to talk about.

What do you recommend to a climber (or any athlete) who is struggling with disordered eating or body image?

DiGiulian: I recommend trying to see the larger picture. When you obsess over losing or gaining 5-10 lbs, remember, life is momentary, we shouldn't take anything for granted, so loosen up, enjoy your day, respect where you're at, and try to be as good of a person as you can be. When you have a lot of love, acceptance, and friendship in your life, the little particulars like gaining or losing a few pounds become less relevant. Remember, having the "perfect" or "thinnest" weight is totally subjective, and a couple extra pounds is just not as big of a deal as you are letting it be.

What challenges or triumphs have you experienced with trying to redefine conversations about body image and/or accept your own (or others') appearance?

DiGiulian: A challenge is that there is truth in the fact that short-term weight loss can produce short-term performance growth in climbing. Though, this is not a healthy approach nor is it sustainable. If you want to be a well-rounded, long-term athlete, with longevity and performance over time, fuel your body appropriately.

Anything else on the topic of nutrition and climbing you'd like to share?

DiGiulian: As a sport, we still have a lot of growth left when it comes to exercise science and nutrition. As a professional climber and someone who is appearing in front of young girls and boys, as well as people of all ages, I consider my appearance important; I want to represent what a "healthy" athlete looks like, barring the fact that this is very individual and subjective to genetics, your sport, and your goals.

Female Athletes (continued)

An Interview with Beth Rodden

I was fortunate enough to interview Beth Rodden via email (June 17, 2019) regarding her take on climbing, nutrition, and climbing during and beyond pregnancy into motherhood. She is well-known as one of the world's top female climbers.

What role has nutrition played in your climbing performance and overall health?

Beth Rodden: I feel like the two go hand in hand. Because of climbing, I started to research nutrition more and more. I feel that what we put into our bodies is such an important decision, especially for athletes. When I was younger, I didn't see my body as something to nourish; I saw it more as something to use for my goals. It wasn't until I was older that I realized I needed to really take care of my body.

Any specific instances you would like to share regarding a time nutrition/hydration really helped (or lack of nutrition/hydration hindered) a climb?

Rodden: I remember climbing El Cap one time and really starting to cramp until I ate some salty snacks and drank water.

Do you have any special insights regarding female-climber nutrition, especially across the phases of your own life? You've been climbing since you were very young, went through adolescence as an accomplished climber, and continued to climb through adulthood and childbearing years. How have being a female climber and/or being pregnant/giving birth impacted your climbing and your nutrition?

Rodden: When I was younger, I struggled with severe calorie limitation, and an eating disorder. I thought to climb hard you needed to be light. As I got older, I still had food issues and didn't see the need to eat "real" food as long as I was getting enough protein, etc. So I ate a lot of bars, etc. It wasn't until I was pregnant that I saw my body as being for something other than athletic performance. I was growing a human, and I realized how important eating real, nourishing food was. That's where I really feel I started to understand healthy eating. And now eating as a family, I want to show our son good eating habits, eating real food that takes time to prepare and cook, and food that has come from places that respect the earth and was grown/raised in a way that is good for the environment.

What are your favorite crag snacks/meals?

Rodden: I love fruit, and then I always bring "real" food nowadays. Cut-up veggies, good meat, fresh bread, etc.

Has nutrition played a role in pushing your body to achieve greater climbing goals and/or healing from injuries?

Rodden: Absolutely. I cook with turmeric a lot if I'm injured, and have eliminated sugar and inflammatory things from my diet.

6 - SPECIAL NUTRITION NEEDS

Andrew Chao

Adaptive Climbers/Para Climbers

Adaptive climbers fall into a special category of toughness and grit. It's difficult enough to climb for an able-bodied individual, but to take on climbing as an adaptive climber takes the sport to a whole different level.

I talked with four adaptive climbers to get a better perspective on adaptive-climbing nutrition. I chatted on the phone with Whitney Pesek of the Adaptive Climbing Group; Pesek lives in Salt Lake City, Utah (USA). She is visually impaired and climbs competitively. She is the 2018 United States Adaptive Climbing Visual Impaired Champion, as well as silver medalist in the Women's B2 (visual impairment) category at the Paraclimbing World Championships in 2018.

Enock Glidden of Paradox Sports was born with spina bifida. He has climbed *Zodiac* on El Capitan in Yosemite, and also enjoys skiing, tennis, and basketball. He has also completed the Maine Marathon—all of this in his wheelchair! He was kind enough to answer interview questions via email.

Aika Yoshida, who also answered questions via email, is an adaptive climber who is a registered yoga instructor, as well as holds a doctorate in physical therapy, so she has some really great insights on how to be a great adaptive climber and work within any physical limitations. Her deep educational background and clinical experience help her understand how to train and climb within an adaptive framework. She sustained a C6 incomplete spinal-cord injury while practicing acrobatic yoga. She has won adaptive climbing nationals in Japan and the US, as well as placed second and third at the Paraclimbing World Championships.

Ronnie Dickson has been climbing for 11 years with an above-the-knee amputation. He's a three-time national champion and two-time silver medalist at world competitions.

Adaptive Climbers/Para Climbers (continued)

These four climbers, along with my summary and application of current nutrition research on adaptive athletes, will help you get a better idea of how to alter your nutrition to fuel your climb if you're an adaptive athlete.

Depending on your particular body, adaptive climbers might climb a bit differently than able-bodied climbers. Whitney has noticed that adaptive climbers usually climb more via lockoffs and static, sustained movement with full tension and isometric holds. Dynos—not so much.

As far as nutrition implications, this might mean that you potentially use more calories than a non-adaptive climber if it takes longer to climb a similar route. Slower, sustained movements also use the aerobic energy system, meaning you will likely use a mixture of fat and carbohydrate to fuel your climb. If you do long sessions, Ronnie recommends taking regular breaks to eat and drink. Eat something with both protein and carbohydrates for sustained energy. A peanut butter and jelly sandwich, some trail mix, chocolate milk and apple, or crackers and cheese will do the job.

Enock recommends bringing both high-carb and high-protein foods when climbing for long periods. When he climbed El Capitan, he brought along bagels, oatmeal, dehydrated/freeze-dried backpacking meals, cheese, sport-energy gummies, and meat. He aimed for about 800 calories per meal. He also brought powdered Gatorade to mix into his water.

Whitney recommends listening to your body and personalizing your nutrition and training plans. Since each adaptive climber has different impairments, goals, and abilities, really creating a training and nutrition strategy that takes into account all your needs is better than implementing generic recommendations. Seek the help of a good coach, registered sports dietitian, a fellow adaptive climber, and a physician familiar with your situation to help craft a plan that works for you. What makes sense for one adaptive climber might not make sense for you.

Depending on what type of impairment you are living with, your needs may be different from those of other climbers. Those with spinal-cord injuries may have decreased muscle mass below the level of lesion, decreased stroke volume (volume of blood your heart pumps with each beat), decreased maximum heart rate, and decreased anaerobic capacity (the ability to perform explosive, short, and/or intense tasks). You may also have lower resting energy expenditure, and hence may need fewer calories on non-climbing days.

Adaptive Climbers/Para Climbers (continued)

Energy: During climbing, you may need MORE calories than an able-bodied climber, because you may have less efficient movements, and overall approach and climbing time may be increased. To summarize, you may need more energy to send the route. Aika says she eats a high-fat, high-protein diet because, "I am not an efficient hiker, so it takes more energy to get to the crag." She likes eating bacon, sausage, or eggs before the climb.

Carbohydrate: The guidelines for carbohydrate intake in those with spinal-cord injuries are the same as for other athletic populations. So, go ahead and enjoy those carbs, because you use them for fueling climbing.

Fluids: Fluid-intake guidelines may be different. Some with spinal-cord injuries have a decreased ability to sweat and regulate their body temperature, so paying attention to urine color can be a helpful gauge to your own hydration status. Keep cool by climbing indoors or in the shade, drinking regularly, and cooling your skin with water. On the flip side, if it is a cold day, you are at more risk for becoming too cool since people with a spinal-cord injuries can lose heat rapidly. Stay warm by dressing in layers and always climb with someone who is available to help you in case you become too cold or too hot. By keeping your body at a comfortable temperature, you can climb more effectively and safely.

As an adaptive athlete with a spinal-cord injury (a "sit" climber), Enock says it is sometimes hard to find a place to urinate while climbing, so he is careful to only drink as much as he needs. He tries to not over-drink since it's a challenge to have to go too often. Instead, he pays attention to how his body and temperature feel rather than drinking a certain number of ounces each hour.

Aika takes hot tea with butter and coconut oil with her in a Thermos, which is especially beneficial in winter to help regulate her body temperature. In summer, she brings ice water for the same reason.

Sometimes digestion is slowed in climbers with spinal injuries, which may affect what you decide to eat. As with other climbers, it's best to eat foods low in fiber and fat if you are within 30–60 minutes of climbing. This way, your food will be quickly digested and ready to be used as fuel in your body. If you find it takes longer to digest food or have a bowel movement, you can experiment and keep track of different foods to see how they affect you. That will help you avoid either bonking from low blood sugar (running out of fuel because you didn't eat enough) or having gastrointestinal symptoms like constipation, diarrhea, or bloating. A dietitian can be invaluable in helping you figure out which foods are best and which you may need to decrease or avoid for certain situations.

Adaptive Climbers/Para Climbers (continued)

Based on current research, climbers missing all or part of one limb seem to have similar energy expenditure as climbers with all their limbs. It can vary from person to person depending on how active they are and the location and degree of their amputation.

If pressure wounds are an issue where a prosthesis comes into contact with skin, or from prolonged wheelchair use, seek help from a dietitian to make sure you are getting enough calories, fluids, protein, and micronutrients to help the wound heal. And, of course, seek help from a doctor, wheelchair specialist, occupational therapist, and/or prosthetist to prevent future wounds. Ronnie has personal experience with this, as he told me via email:

"I can't state this enough: This device is now yours, and you have to own it. When I went to do my first triathlon, I was having trouble completing the training because I was in pain with my prosthesis. I didn't stop looking for a professional who could help me accomplish the task until I found the right one. It is a process, but you have to see it through in order to succeed. I've been with that professional now for the last 10 years, and they have been huge in all of my successes."

Ronnie sought out professional help for his prosthesis fitting, and was able to find athletic success as a result.

Enock Glidden

As a sit climber, Enock has also had experience with pressure sores. He says he checks his skin every so often during climbing to make sure there aren't signs of breakdown. Look for red areas. Press on the skin—make sure it returns to its normal color. Adjust your harness and gear as needed to make sure the skin doesn't develop a wound.

Recruiting a good team can help you climb harder and healthier. Enock recommends surrounding yourself with other able-bodied and adaptive climbers. Using these people can give you the best information because they already have experience climbing in various settings. It took 15 people to help Enock climb El Capitan. His motto: "If you try, things will happen." That is pretty inspiring. What can you try? Seeking help from fellow climbers, a sports physician, sports dietitian, and other specialists can also help you train and compete at your highest level.

Adaptive Climbers/Para Climbers (continued)

Aika recommends getting hooked up with an adaptive climbing organization such as Paradox Sports (she is an ambassador). You can find community, friends, coaches, and support that will help you meet your climbing goals.

Ronnie agreed with Aika, saying that friends, family, and other climbers are a "huge influence on my success and my general state of mind and mental health. We are more likely than not going to have to work harder to get the same results as an able-bodied athlete. Don't let this discourage you. Instead, stack the deck in your favor by making sure your sleep, nutrition, and hydration are all working in your favor and they align with your goals, not against them."

Aika also has some inspiring words for adaptive climbers: "Do not let your beliefs stop you from trying something new! When you have the opportunity to try something that typically intimidates you, try it before you say 'no.' Say, 'Let me try...' because you may surprise yourself!" This is great advice not just for adaptive climbers, but for all climbers.

The take-home message is this: While we don't have any climbing-nutrition studies in adaptive athletes, personalizing your nutrition and hydration strategy is the best way to go. Knowing your own bowel schedule, sweat rate, and specific needs and challenges will help you tailor your fueling and hydration for success. Utilize the advice on the previous pages, and reach out to a dietitian for your own individualized nutrition questions. There is no one-size-fits-all approach for any athlete.

TRAVELING

Climbers often travel to different destinations in search of new routes to explore. If you're traveling to climb, whether it be for a comp or for fun, your climbing performance could be affected. A different time zone can throw off your sleep habits. Flying in a plane can be dehydrating. Often there are new foods at new destinations. Sometimes it's hard to find familiar foods; new foods and local water can wreak havoc on your digestive system.

There are a few nutritional strategies you can implement to make traveling a little easier on your body. Being prepared to adapt to the new locale will help you perform better when climbing.

» If You Are Traveling to a Different Time Zone

Sleep is a big deal, and lack of sleep can result in a decreased ability to perform out climbing because of decreased mental capacity and physical strength. Your body may feel tired. This may mean your brain may not feel as sharp and may not be able to recover from, and adapt to, training as quickly as you are used to.

Bringing earplugs and a sleep mask can help you catch up on sleep in an unfamiliar sleep environment or on the plane. Matching your sleep schedule to your new time zone as much as possible will help, too. If you arrive at your destination during the day, but in your home time zone it is nighttime, don't fall asleep just yet. Try to fall asleep when it's night in your new time zone. After a few days, your body will adapt. Naps can be really helpful, especially if your training is particularly grueling, but take care not to let a nap extend into a long sleeping session that would disrupt your nighttime sleep schedule. Usually this means around 20–30 minutes of nap time. Avoiding caffeine at least five hours before you are supposed to sleep for the night will also help. You can conquer jet lag by taking two to eight milligrams of melatonin about one to two hours before you need to fall asleep for the night, and by making sure that your "night" is the night of your new time zone, not the one you are used to. In the morning, you can use about 200–300 milligrams of caffeine to wake you up. If you are a competition climber, stay within all guidelines of permissible substances for any supplements—including caffeine and melatonin.

TRAVELING (CONTINUED)

» Traveling to a New Country with New Foods

If you know you have a sensitive digestive system, exploring new foods in a new country (especially if you have a big comp) is not a good idea. Bring foods with you that you know you can easily tolerate. Stick with those until the critical climbing is done. Then you can let yourself loose and enjoy all the new foods with abandon.

Even if you don't have a sensitive stomach, if you are in a country that is high-risk for water and food contamination (like parts of Asia, South America, Africa, the Middle East, and Eastern Europe), there are a few precautions you can take to avoid getting a stomach bug. The Centers for Disease Control (CDC) catalogs information about food and hydration for travelers.

• Don't drink water out of the tap or faucet. Instead, drink only bottled water or canned/bottled drinks.

• Don't use ice that is made from the local water. Brush your teeth with bottled water.

• Don't eat from street carts, and don't eat raw foods.

• Eat fruits and vegetables that you can peel, like an orange or banana, rather than berries or salads that have been washed in the local water.

• You can bring a filtration device or water-purification tablets, especially if you are going on an extended climbing trip with limited access to water.

You can eat prebiotic and probiotic foods (foods that help your gut health), such as bananas, Kimchi, sauerkraut, yogurt with live cultures, kefir, onions, leeks, garlic, oats, asparagus, and apples. If you are eating local produce, be sure it was cleaned in bottled or purified water. You can also take a probiotic supplement a few weeks before you travel. Check for purity and check with your doctor (and governing body if you're a competitive climber) first. This may help get a little boost to your gut and immune system before traveling.

TRAVELING (CONTINUED)

Bringing your own food may be a good idea, especially if you have spent months training for a huge comp or planning a big climbing trip. Bringing your own food and preparing it in your hotel room can help eliminate the chance of getting food poisoning. Consider this option if you are traveling to a country that has different sanitation standards than your own or if the country or region has very little food-safety regulations in place. If you can't bring your own food, allow yourself time to get used to the local food. Test for tolerance and how it affects your performance. It may be difficult to get used to new foods. Make sure to check all travel regulations to make sure you can bring the food in your luggage or ship it.

Here's what you can eat in a hotel if you have a microwave, hot plate, or electric tea kettle and mini-fridge (if there's no mini-fridge, a cooler may work if you have access to clean ice):

- Instant oatmeal
- Soup
- Instant-noodle cups
- Energy bars
- Protein shakes
- Frozen microwaveable dinners
- Sandwiches
- Pasta
- Dried fruit
- Frozen or canned vegetables
- Eggs cooked in the microwave
- Frozen microwavable burritos
- Yogurt
- Microwave popcorn
- Cereal, granola, muesli
- Cheese
- Hummus
- Single-serve microwavable rice or quinoa
- Peanut butter, almond butter, and other nut butters
- Panini sandwiches
- Pancakes
- Grilled chicken and vegetables
- Salads
- Tuna in a pouch or can
- Jerky

See chapter 11 for recipes you can make in a mug with just a microwave and simple cooking utensils.

If you do end up getting diarrhea, vomiting, or both, be sure to hydrate as much as possible. Losing large amounts of fluid from illness can be dangerous. Use Imodium and/or seek medical care to get diagnosed and get on antibiotics if needed. If the diarrhea lasts longer than 24 hours or is severe enough to cause dehydration, seek medical help. Eat simple, bland foods as tolerated, like crackers, pretzels, plain rice, plain noodles, and white bread. Avoid fiber or fatty/greasy foods, milk, caffeine, and sugary drinks like fruit juice. If you have digestive problems even when you're back in your own country, seek medical care to rule out the possibility of a parasite or viral or bacterial infection.

TRAVELING (CONTINUED)

When consulting with a travel doctor about travel vaccines, be transparent about what you will be doing and how far you will be from medical services in case there are any additional items you'll need to carry in case of extreme situations, such as salmonella way out in the backcountry.

Be sure to get all appropriate vaccines well before your travels. Check local regulations or the CDC website for recommended vaccination schedules.

Flying Nutrition

Everyone knows that airplanes pressurize their cabins. But did you know that it is not pressurized to resemble sea-level air pressure? When flying at cruising altitudes of 36,000–40,000 feet (11,000–12,200 m), the air inside the cabin is equivalent to being at 6000–8000 feet (1800–2400 m). That is pretty high! This means that you can become pretty dehydrated just from breathing thinner air. For every hour on the plane, your body can lose 3 to 10 ounces of water from respiration.

Arriving at your destination dehydrated, especially if your destination is at a higher altitude than you are used to, could mean you experience headaches, fatigue, and poor climbing performance. It can also lead to poor adaptation to a new time zone and sleep schedule.

Sip fluids regularly throughout your flight. Adding electrolytes or using a sports drink will help you be properly hydrated when you arrive. It's tempting to skip drinking to avoid having to use the restroom, but it's better to just drink and stay hydrated. Avoid alcohol on the plane. If you feel swelling in your legs and feet, wear compression socks and get up and take little walks around the cabin as much as possible.

For food intake, bring snacks with you on the plane in case what is offered is something you don't like or don't tolerate. Traveling is often unpredictable, with canceled or late flights, long layovers, and other logistical issues. Be prepared by bringing your own non-perishable snacks on board–these can prevent hassle and keep you well-fueled. You can call the airline beforehand to order any special meals or check what will be served on the flight. Check your arrival country's rules about bringing food through customs.

TRAVELING (CONTINUED)

Some snack ideas for the plane ride include:

- Trail mix
- Energy and nut bars
- Shelf-stable chocolate milk (purchase after going through security)
- Sports drinks (purchase after going through security)
- Dried fruit or fruit leather
- Instant oatmeal packets (ask the flight attendant for hot water and a bowl or cup with spoon)
- Dried soup mixes
- Crackers
- Freeze-dried fruits and vegetables
- Sports gels and gummies
- Powdered sports or recovery drink mixes (fill water bottle after going through security and then mix packet in when ready to consume)
- Nut-butter packets or pouches

THE WRAP-UP FOR SPECIAL NUTRITION NEEDS

Special nutrition needs call for tailored nutrition recommendations. If you fall into any of these special categories, do yourself a favor and get a sports dietitian on board to make sure you are meeting your nutrition needs. Ensuring you have the right nutrients can help you achieve next-level performance. Seek the help of a sports dietitian to help you plan a nutrition strategy for your individual needs.

CHAPTER 6 REFERENCES

Academy of Nutrition and Dietetics. 2016. "Position of the Academy of Nutrition and Dietetics: Vegetarian Diets." *Journal Academy of Nutrition and Dietetics*, 116: 1970-1980.

Ackland, Timothy R., Timothy G. Lohman, Jorunn Sundgot-Borgen, Ronald J. Maughan, Nanna L. Meyer, Arthur D. Steward, Wolfram Müller. 2012. "Current Status of Body Composition Assessment in Sport." *Sports Medicine* 42 no. 3: 227-249.

Bø, Kari, Raul Artal, Ruben Barakat, Wendy Brown, Gregory A.L. Davies, et al. 2016. "Exercise and Pregnancy in Recreational and Elite Athletes: 2016 Evidence Summary from the IOC Expert Group Meeting, Lausanne. Part 1-Exercise in Women Planning Pregnancy and Those Who Are Pregnant." *British Journal of Sports Medicine* 50 no. 10: 571-589.

Borrione, Paolo, Loredana Grasso, Federico Quaranta, Attilio Parisi. 2009. "FIMS Position Statement: Vegetarian Diet and Athletes." *International Sports Medicine Journal* 10 no. 1: 53-60.

Broad, Elizabeth. 2015. "Special Needs: the Paralympic Athlete." In *Clinical Sports Nutrition*, edited by Louise Burke and Vicki Deakin, 767-791. Sydney, Australia: McGraw Hill Education.

Burke, Louise M., Bronwen Lundy, Ida L. Fahrenholtz, and Anna K. Melin. 2018. "Pitfalls of Conducting and Interpreting Estimates of Energy Availability in Free-Living Athletes." *International Journal of Sports Nutrition and Exercise Metabolism* 28: 350-363.

Campbell, Wayne W., Angela M Venderly. 2006. "Vegetarian Diets: Nutritional Considerations for Athletes." *Sports Med*, 36(4): 293-305.

CHAPTER 6 REFERENCES

Carter, Susan. 2018. "Female Athlete Triad/Relative Energy Deficiency in Sport: A Perspective Interview with Professor Barbara Drinkwater." *International Journal of Sports Nutrition and Exercise Metabolism* 28, no. 4: 332-334.

Centers for Disease Control. January 8, 2018 (last updated) "Food and Water Safety." Centers for Disease Control and Prevention. **https://wwwnc.cdc.gov/travel/page/food-water-safety**

Chodzko-Zajko, Wojtek J., David N. Proctor, Maria A. Fiatarone Singh, Christopher T. Minson, Claudio R. Nigg, George J. Salem, and James S. Skinner. 2009. "Exercise and Physical Activity for Older Adults." *Medicine & Science in Sports & Exercise*, 41(7): 1510-1530.

Deakin, Vicki, Peter Peeling. 2015. "Prevention, Detection and Treatment of Iron Depletion and Deficiency in Athletes." In *Clinical Sports Nutrition*, edited by Louise Burke and Vicki Deakin, 266-293. Sydney, Australia: McGraw Hill Education.

Desbrow, Ben, Joanna McCormack, Louise M. Burke, Gregory R. Cox, Kieran Fallon, Matthew Hislop, Ruth Logan et al. 2014. "Sports Dietitians of Australia Position Statement: Sports Nutrition for the Adolescent Athlete." *International Journal of Sports Nutrition and Exercise Metabolism* 24: 570-584.

Di Girolamo, Filippo Giorgio, Roberta Situlin, Nicola Fiotti, Marcello Tence, Paolo De Colle, Filippo Mearelli, Marco Alessandro Minetto et al. 2017. "Higher Protein Intake is Associated with Improved Muscle Strength in Elite Senior Athletes." *Nutrition* 42: 82-86.

Elliott-Sale, Kirsty J., Adam S. Tenforde, Allyson L. Parziale, Bryan Holtzman, and Kathryn E. Ackerman. 2018. "Endocrine Effects of Relative Energy Deficiency in Sport." *International Journal of Sports Nutrition and Exercise Metabolism* 28: 335-349.

Fien, Samantha, Mike Climstein, Clodagh Quilter, Georgina Buckley, Timothy Henwood, Josie Grigg, and Justin WL Keogh. 2017. "Anthropometric, Physical Function, and General Health Markers of Masters Athletes: A Cross-Sectional Study." *Peer Journal*, 5: e3768.

Gorrisen, Stefan H.M. and Oliver C. Witard. 2017. "Characterising the Muscle Anabolic Potential of Dairy, Meat and Plant-Based Protein Sources in Older Adults." *Proceedings of the Nutrition Society Scottish Section held at the University of Stirling*, Stirling on March 28-29, 2017.

Hamilton, Bruce. 2011. "Vitamin D and Athletic Performance: The Potential Role of Muscle." *Asian Journal of Sports Medicine* 2 no. 4: 211-219.

Hausswirth, Christophe and Yann Le Meur. 2011. "Physiological and Nutritional Aspects of Post-Exercise Recovery: Specific Recommendations for Female Athletes." *Sports Medicine* 41 no. 10: 861-882.

Heikura IA, Uusitalo ALT, Stellingwerff T, Bergland D, Mero AA, Burke LM. 2018. "Low Energy Availability Is Difficult to Assess but Outcomes Have Large Impact on Bone Injury Rates in Elite Distance Athletes." *International Journal of Sports Nutrition and Exercise Metabolism*, 28, 403-411.

Hunter, Sandra K., Jennie M. Schletty, Kristine M. Schlachter, Erin E. Griffith, Aaron J. Polichnowski, and Alexander V. Ng. 2006. "Active Hyperemia and Vascular Conductance Differ Between Men and Women for an Isometric Fatiguing Contraction." *Journal of Applied Physiology*, no. 1: 140-150

Jäger, Ralf, Martin Purpura, Andrew Shao, Toshitada Inoue, and Richard B. Kreider. 2011. "Analysis of the Efficacy, Safety, and Regulatory Status of Novel Forms of Creatine." *Amino Acids* 40 no. 5: 1369-1383.

Janse, XA DE Jonge, Martin W. Thompson, Vivienne H. Chuter, Leslie N. Silk, and Jeanette M. Thom. 2012. "Exercise Performance Over the Menstrual Cycle in Temperate and Hot, Humid Conditions." *Medicine & Science in Sports & Exercise* 44 no. 11: 2190-2198.

Kohler, Ryan. "Medical and Nutritional Issues for the Traveling Athlete." 2015. In *Clinical Sports Nutrition*, edited by Louise Burke and Vicki Deakin, 756-761. Sydney, Australia: McGraw Hill Education.

Lambert, G. Patrick. 2009. "Stress-Induced Gastrointestinal Barrier Dysfunction and its Inflammatory Effects." *Journal of Animal Science* 87 no. suppl_14: E101-E108.

Larson A, Joubert L, Blundt-Gonzalez G. 2018, July 9. "Training Behaviors Among a Heterogeneous Sample of Female Climbers and Boulderers." Poster presented at the 4th Research Congress of the International Rock Climbing Research Association; Chamonix, France.

Leave No Trace. "Seven Principles." Date of Access: June 5, 2019. **www.lnt.org**

Lowe, Michael R., Sapana D. Doshi, Shawn N. Katterman, and Emily H. Feig. 2013. "Dieting and Restrained Eating as Prospective Predictors of Weight Gain." *Frontiers in Psychology* 4: 577.

Madden RF, Shearer J, Parnell JA. 2017. "Evaluation of Dietary Intakes and Supplement Use in Paralympic Athletes." *Nutrients*, 9, 1266.

CHAPTER 6 REFERENCES

Mangieri, Heather R. 2017. *Fueling Young Athletes.* Champaign, Illinois: Human Kinetics.
Manore, Melinda. 2017. "The Female Athlete: Energy and Nutrition Issues." *Sports Science Exchange* 28 no. 175: 1-5.
Maughan, Ronald J., and Michael Gleeson. 2010. *The Biochemical Basis of Sports Performance.* Oxford: Oxford University Press, 10-11.
Maughan, Ronald J., Louise M. Burke, Jiri Dvorak, D. Enette Larson-Meyer, Peter Peeling, Stuart M. Phillips, Eric S. Rawson, et al. 2018. "IOC Consensus Statement: Dietary Supplements and the High-Performance Athlete." *British Journal of Sports Medicine* 28, no. 2: 104-125.
Morrison, Audry Birute, Volker Rainer Schöffl. 2007. "Physiological Responses to Rock Climbing in Young Climbers." *British Journal of Sports Medicine* 41 no. 12: 852-861.
Mountjoy, Margo, Jorunn Sundgot-Borgen, Louise Burke, Susan Carter, Naama Constantini, Constance Lebrun, Nanna Meyer, et al. 2014. "The IOC Consensus Statement: Beyond the Female Athlete Triad—Relative Energy Deficiency in Sport (RED-S)." *British Journal of Sports Medicine* 48, no. 7: 491-497.
Mountjoy, Margo, Jorunn Sundgot-Borgen, Louise Burke, Susan Carter, Naama Constantini, Constance Lebrun, Nanna Meyer, et al. 2015. "Authors' 2015 Additions to the IOC Consensus Statement: Relative Energy Deficiency in Sport (RED-S)." *British Journal of Sports Medicine* 49 no. 7: 417-420.
Mountjoy, Margo, Jorunn Kaiander Sundgot-Borgen, Louise M. Burke, Kathryn E. Ackerman, Cheri Blauwet, Naama Constantini, Constance Lebrun, et al. 2018. "International Olympic Committee (IOC) Consensus Statement on Relative Energy Deficiency in Sport (RED-S): 2018 Update." *British Journal of Sports Medicine* 52 no. 11: 678-697.
Mountjoy, Margo, Louise M. Burke, Trent Stellingwerff, Jorunn Sundgot-Borgen. 2108. "Relative Energy Deficiency in Sport: The Tip of an Iceberg." *International Journal of Sports Nutrition and Exercise Metabolism* 28: 313-315.
Pearce Jeni and Stephanie Gaskill. 2015. "Athletes with Gastrointestinal Disorders, Food Allergies, and Food Intolerance." In *Clinical Sports Nutrition,* edited by Louise Burke and Vicki Deakin, 669-689. Sydney, Australia: McGraw Hill Education.
Prado de Oliveria, Eric, Roberto C. Burini, Asker Jeukendrup. 2014. "Gastrointestinal Complaints During Exercise: Prevalence, Etiology, and Nutritional Recommendations." *Sports Medicine* 44 no. 1: S79-S85.
Reaburn, Peter, Thomas Doering, Nattai Borges. 2015. "Nutrition Issues for the Masters Athlete." In *Clinical Sports Nutrition,* 5th ed. Louise Burke and Vicki Deakin (Sydney, Australia, McGraw Hill Education Pty Ltd, 2015), 767-791.
Rodden, Beth. 2016, "Climbing Pregnant: Medical Study Results." Beth Rodden (Blog) May 10, 2019. http://bethrodden.com/2016/03/climbing-pregnant-medical-study-results/
Rogerson, David. 2017. "Vegan Diets: Practical Advice for Athletes and Exercisers." *Journal of the International Society of Sports Nutrition* 14, No. 1: 36.
Scarlata, Kate. 2017. *The Low-FODMAP Diet Step by Step.* New York, NY: Da Capo Press.
Schöffl ,Volker, Christoph Lutter, Kaikanani Woollings, Isabelle Schöffl. 2018. "Pediatric and Adolescent Injury in Rock Climbing." *Research in Sports Medicine* 26, no. sup 1: 91-113.
Schofield, W.N. 1985. "Predicting Basal Metabolic Rate, New Standards and Review of Previous Work." *Human Nutrition Clinical Nutrition* 39C (Suppl): 5-41.
Scragg, Robert. 2018. "Emerging Evidence of Thresholds for Beneficial Effects from Vitamin D Supplementation." *Nutrients* 10, no. 5: 561.
Shipton, Michael J., Jecko Thachil. 2015. "Vitamin B12 Deficiency-a 21st Century Perspective." *Clinical Medicine* 15 no. 2: 145-50.
Smith, JohnEric, Megan E. Holmes, Matthew J. McAllister. 2015. "Nutritional Considerations for Performance in Young Athletes." *Journal of Sports Medicine* 2015: 7346-49.
Vitamin B12: Fact Sheet for Health Professionals. National Institutes of Health Office of Dietary Supplements.
Vitamin D: Fact Sheet for Health Professionals. National Institutes of Health Office of Dietary Supplements.
Watts, Phillip B., Megan L. Ostrowski. 2014. "Oxygen Uptake and Energy Expenditure for Children During Rock Climbing Activity." *Pediatric Exercise Science* 26, no. 1: 49-55.

7 - INJURY PREVENTION & RECOVERY

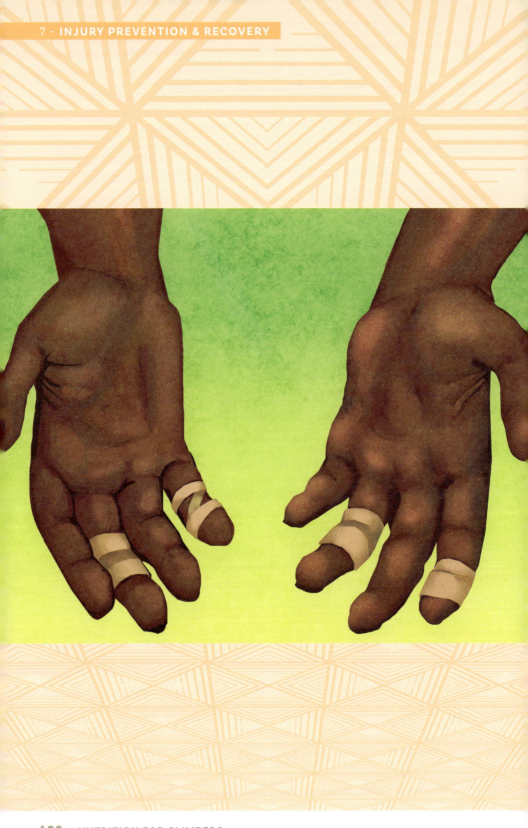

CHAPTER 7

INJURY PREVENTION & RECOVERY

The thought of getting an injury makes people shudder: the pain, the down time, the visits to the doctor, tests, x-rays, physical therapy, and so much more. Whatever your injury is, it is surely inconvenient, but nutrition can play a critical role in the recovery process.

Most injuries in climbing are upper-body injuries, such as rotator cuff tears, subluxation (partial dislocation) of the shoulders, finger pulley tears, or tendonitis. Acute sprains, strains, and fractures are most common among climbers–for instance falling and breaking your legs. Some injuries are from over-use and require rest, ice, and other medical treatments.

In children, injuries can be especially concerning if they involve a growth plate. Tight-fitting climbing shoes can lead to foot disorders in kids with growing feet. Risk of injury increases in children during puberty as well. Researcher Volker Schöffl and his team recommend taking proper care to train children correctly, and avoid inappropriate training (like campus boards or pull-ups with weights). These steps can help decrease injury risk. Children who undereat (whether on purpose to diet or unintentionally) are also at greater risk for injury. Having safe training practices, getting regular medical exams, tracking growth and puberty, and ensuring adequate nutrition can all help prevent injuries in children and adolescents. A coach specially trained in children and adolescent climbers can be a valuable resource. Children have unique physiologies that need special training techniques. They aren't just tiny adults!

In one analysis, researchers found that sport climbing tends to have overuse injuries from strenuous moves, and falls are the most common cause of acute injuries like broken bones and blunt-force trauma. Indoor climbing more commonly has overuse injuries. Falling indoors does not result in acute injury or death as much as in outdoor climbing. An interesting study by researcher Gudmund Groønhaug showed that the highest rate of injury was among males, and the most common injury was a finger injury.

Focusing on strength training, proper climbing technique, proper warm-up, stretching, massage, foam rolling, physical therapy, and cross-training will help you prevent, or heal from, an injury. But don't overlook nutrition–it is an important part of the healing process as well!

Nutrition can help heal or prevent injury in a variety of ways. First let's look at prevention, then recovery.

Nutrition for Injury **Prevention**

Being well-hydrated and well-fueled can prevent injury. How? Fueling your brain and muscles, as well as being properly hydrated, can help you stay mentally alert. This will aid in making good decisions that keep you safe. Avoiding dumb mistakes with both yourself and your equipment helps keep you injury-free. Also, if you feel fatigued, you might rush through safety checks or fail to take proper precautions, thereby leaving yourself vulnerable to injury (or death). To wit, an analysis of five climbing accidents in Yosemite, featured in a climbing.com article by Alexa Flower and Miranda Oakley, concluded that some of these accidents would likely have been prevented with adequate fueling and hydration.

A second way nutrition can help you avoid injury is by providing much-needed fuel for your training and climbing. If you are eating enough calories, your body has the fuel to adapt to increased training loads. It will reward you with muscle growth, strong bones, and healthy joints, tendons, and ligaments. This can translate into increasing maximum hang time, increased proficiency when campusing, or climbing a higher grade.

Nutrition for Injury **Recovery**

There are a lot of things you can do to help support your body while healing from an injury or surgery. When you initially get injured, there is an inflammatory process that happens in your body. Most people think of inflammation as a negative thing, but in this case, it is actually useful. The process of inflammation is actually your body sending special cells to the injury site in order to start the healing process. Nutrition can aid in this process by supplying the fuel to rebuild and repair damaged tissues.

Eat the Right Amount of Calories

This is going to look different for every person. If your injury is so severe that you cannot be as active as usual for a long period of time, you may need fewer calories than usual. This is because you are less active. Keep in mind, it is still really important to get enough calories to support recovery. If you are trying to heal soft tissue (like skin, muscle, ligaments, or tendons) or trying to heal bone, you need enough overall calories to support this process. Your body needs the building blocks to make new tissues. As always, a visit with a sports dietitian is a good idea to get specifics on what your calorie needs are during this time of bodily repair. Don't be tempted to cut your calories in order to prevent weight gain. Rock climbers are notoriously thin (because if you weigh less it's easier to climb, right? More on that in chapter 10), but undereating may prolong your healing time. You do not want to eat so little your body needs to divert energy away from repairing and rebuilding, muscle, bone, tendon, or ligament.

Eat Enough Carbohydrates

Carbohydrates are still important, even if you are not using them to actively climb while you're healing. Carbohydrates still fuel your brain (which is still working even when you're injured). And they allow the body to use carbs for fuel rather than tapping into dietary protein or (gasp!) protein stored in your body as muscle mass for fuel. Carbohydrates have another bonus attached to them: If you're eating the right kinds of foods, like whole grains, fruits, and vegetables, they have the fiber, vitamins, and minerals that all help with healing. Simple carbohydrates are best for pre- and during-workout fueling, but when you are healing from an injury it's a good time to incorporate complex carbohydrates into your diet. These contain more fiber, and usually more micronutrients as well.

> As a side note, if you are taking opioid-based pain medication, this usually causes constipation. Eating fiber with adequate water can help, but isn't always effective against the wrath of pain medication on your colon. Talk with your doctor about the correct pain-medication dosing, and also discuss using a stool softener and/or laxative in conjunction with the pain meds.

Nutrition for Injury **Recovery** (continued)

Eat Enough Protein
For a skeletal injury (like a broken bone), your muscle mass can start to atrophy within two to three weeks. So, you actually need additional protein beyond someone who doesn't have an injury. Usually about 1.6–2.5g/kg of protein is recommended. Spreading your protein intake throughout the day is a good way to maximize your protein intake. About 20–40 g at each meal (every four to six hours) is a good goal. Remember leucine, that amino acid involved with muscle building and repair? It is really important for muscle injury as well. Good sources are dairy, eggs, and meat, as well as whey protein powder. If you are vegan or vegetarian, flip to chapter 6 for more detailed information about protein sources.

Micronutrients
These three micronutrients may help heal soft tissue: vitamin A, vitamin C, and zinc. Vitamin C helps form collagen, which is connective tissue. Vitamin A synthesizes protein and promotes cell health. Zinc is master of protein and collagen synthesis and cell proliferation. Even if you don't have a major injury, but just have some shredded-up skin, these nutrients can help promote soft-tissue healing.

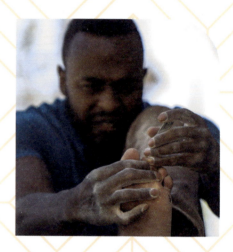

There is no evidence that you need to supplement these micronutrients—adding more won't necessarily speed up healing (unless you have a true nutrient deficiency, then supplementation is appropriate). But not eating enough foods that contain vitamins and minerals can hinder healing. Eating plenty of fruits and vegetables, whole grains, nuts/seeds, eggs, meat, and dairy can help support your healing process. Eating a variety of nutrients may also help support your immune system, which can support healthy wound healing and possibly reduce infection exposure time because it provides micronutrients and antioxidants. If you are deficient in micronutrients, it will slow down healing time. If you already have adequate micronutrients in your diet and your body stores, adding an additional supplement will not speed up healing time.

Nutrition for Injury **Recovery** (continued)

Supplements to consider

If you decide to take a supplement for any length of time, first check with your doctor to make sure it is appropriate for you. And if you are a competitive or professional climber, check with your sport's governing body to make sure you are taking a supplement that is safe for competition. Also make sure you only take supplements that are third-party tested (look for an Informed Choice or NSF Certified for Sport label). Even if you think you won't be competing for a while, make sure you understand all the rules and regulations about substances and supplements before taking something. Do not take anything that is banned. Also, be careful about the source and quality of your supplement. In the United States, the supplement industry is not well-regulated, and many contaminants, inactive substances, fillers, and banned substances have been found in supplements when they are tested in labs not associated with the manufacturer.

For soft-tissue injury, such as tendons and ligaments, you can take gelatin and vitamin C. Use 10–15 g of gelatin and 50 mg of vitamin C. Some people shake gelatin powder into their Gatorade and drink that with a vitamin C gummy. Another option is to make "Jell-O shots" by mixing a small packet of gelatin into fruit juice or Crystal Light. It is recommended to take this about 30–60 minutes before any physical therapy or training for best results.

For a skeletal injury such as a broken bone, calcium and vitamin D are important for healing. Similar to other micronutrients, you don't necessarily need to supplement (unless you are deficient). See page 109 for signs of micronutrient deficiency.

> If you don't eat a lot of fish (like three servings per week or more), supplementing with fish oil might be a good idea. It is anti-inflammatory—so after the first couple days of an injury, you want to stay away from this, because the inflammatory process is actually a good, helpful thing. After the initial injury, you can supplement at around 3-4 g/day.

Tart cherry juice is anti-inflammatory as well, and a great antioxidant. You can take this after a training or physical therapy session to help alleviate soreness. The dose is 12–24 ounces per day. Be aware that this is simply a fruit juice, so if you are not used to taking fruit juices, it will be an extra source of calories that could lead to unwanted weight gain. Be sure to take it into account when planning out your calorie needs. Some athletes also report a laxative effect when taking tart cherry juice: Consider yourself warned. In addition, tart cherry juice is a natural source of melatonin, which may make some people feel sleepy. Often people drink it at night when they are ready for bed.

Creatine is another supplement that may help. The scientific evidence isn't conclusive or overwhelming, but it won't be harmful unless you have a contraindication such as kidney disease. Creatine may prevent muscle wasting to some extent, which is desirable during a prolonged period of injury. Take 10g/day for two weeks, then 5 g/day. Check with your doctor before supplementing to make sure it is right for you.

Inflammation and Antioxidants:
Not all inflammation is bad

You may have heard about inflammation and how to reduce it in your body. There are two kinds of inflammation: chronic and acute. Chronic inflammation, which is long-term, low-grade inflammation, can be harmful to your overall health, as it is linked to heart disease, diabetes, stroke, and other health concerns.

However, acute inflammation is a bit different. This occurs when your body has an injury, such as a cut in your skin or a broken bone. Inflammation processes occur to help heal the injury. Similarly, after an intense training session or workout, there is some inflammation that occurs in your body. This signals the body to start adapting to the new stressor (the exercise). Reactive oxygen species (ROS) and reactive nitrogen species are produced due to oxidative stress from the exercise. This then helps the body produce training adaptations that improve your fitness level.

If you are regularly tamping down these signals and acute inflammatory processes by taking supplements containing antioxidants (such as vitamin C, vitamin E, coenzyme Q10, and carotenoids), you may actually be dampening your body's ability to adapt to training.

A smart approach is to get your antioxidants through food. Things like fresh fruits and vegetables, legumes, and whole grains contain antioxidants that are beneficial to your body in moderate amounts. Using vitamin or mineral supplements, shakes, or powders with high doses of vitamins/minerals, or isolated supplements, is not needed. Save your money and just eat real food!

Here's how it works:

You EXERCISE

Exercise produces FREE RADICALS
(presence of free radicals is called "oxidative stress")

OXIDATIVE STRESS signals the body to adapt to training

ANTIOXIDANTS
"neutralize" the free radicals

Nutrition for Injury **Recovery** (continued)

Crap, I got a cramp

I was at a weeklong outdoor camp for youth, and one of my fellow leaders came to our breakfast table asking if anyone had a banana. "I asked the kitchen already, and they don't have one," she said. "But I have a muscle cramp and I need some potassium." Little did she know, that I, the dietitian, was about to swoop to her rescue with my super-knowledge of cramps. Potassium was abundant at our breakfast table in the form of milk, yogurt, and oranges, but she thought only bananas were a good source. And she thought potassium was her problem–unlikely, as there is only a very small amount of potassium lost in sweat.

Cramps can feel frustrating and debilitating. Especially if they stop you from doing what you want to do. There could be a dietary cause, but there are other causes as well.

> Many people automatically think muscle cramps are a result of either dehydration or depleted electrolytes. Here are some causes of muscle cramping:
>
> » **Dehydration**
> » **Low glycogen** (you run out of fuel for your muscles)
> » **Muscle excitability from nervousness** (like climbing at a comp, attempting a project, or climbing in a new environment)
> » **Fatigue**
> » **Electrolyte imbalance** (usually sodium)
> » **Heat or humidity**
> » **Supplements or medication**
> » **Movement dysfunction,** like compressed nerves or poor blood flow (like a tough crux where you need to use muscles you never knew you had)

Cramps can be alleviated in a variety of ways, depending on the source of the problem. If it's nerves, use breathing techniques or meditation, or get help from a sports psychologist. If it's dehydration, electrolyte imbalances, or underfueling, get help from a sports dietitian to form a specialized fueling plan that works for you. If it is supplements or medication, talk to a sports dietitian and sports physician to determine what is appropriate to change, reduce, or eliminate. Good training, conditioning, and coaching can help with movement dysfunction. Cramps don't have to stop you from crushing.

7 - INJURY PREVENTION & RECOVERY

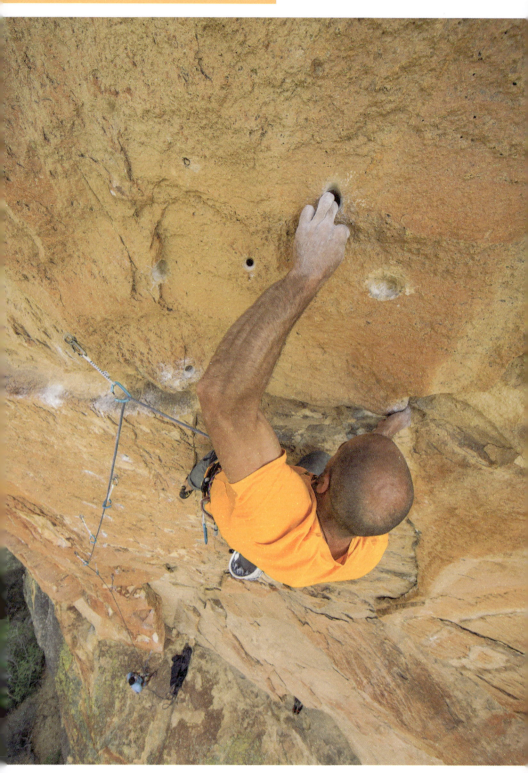

THE WRAP-UP FOR INJURIES

Injuries require different nutrition needs. You may need fewer calories than before if you can't be as active. But you need adequate calories, protein, fluids, and micronutrients in order to heal well. Supplements like collagen and vitamin C may be useful. Talk with your sports physician and sports dietitian for tailored recommendations.

CHAPTER 6 REFERENCES

Baar, Keith. 2015. "Training and Nutrition to Prevent Soft Tissue Injuries and Accelerate Return to Play." *Sport Science Exchange* 28 no. 142: 1-6.

Chan, Derwin King, Chung Chan, Nikos Ntoumanis, Daniel F. Gucciardi, Robert J. Donovan, James A Dimmock, Sarah J Hardcastle, Martin S. Hagger. 2015. "What if it Really Was an Accident? The Psychology of Unintentional Doping." *British Journal of Sports Medicine* 50 no. 15: 898-899.

Elkington, Lisa J., Maree Gleeson, David B. Pyne, Robin Callister, Lisa G Wood. 2015. "Inflammation and Immune Function." *Antioxidants in Sports Nutrition*, edited by Manfred Lamprecht, Chapter 11. Boca Raton, Florida: CRC Press/Taylor & Francis.

Flower, Alexa, Miranda Oakley. 2017. "The Deadly Valley: An analysis of Five Recent Yosemite Climbing Accidents." *Climbing* (Digital). Accessed June 4, 2018. **https://www.climbing.com/skills/the-deadly-valley-an-inside-analysis-of-five-recent-yosemite-accidents/#gid=ci021c187150002523&pid=skull-elcapfinal1.**

Grønhaug, Gudmund, 2018. "Self-Reported Chronic Injuries in Climbing: Who Gets Injured When?" *BMJ Open Sport & Exercise Medicine*, 4: e000406.

Minihane, Anne M., Sopie Vinoy, Wendy R. Russell, Athanasia Baka, Helen M. Roche, Kieran M. Tuohy, Jessica L. Teeling, Ellen E. Blaak, Michael Fenech, David Vauzour, Harry J. McArdle, Bas H.A. Kremer, Luc Sterkman, Katerina Vafeiadou, Massimo Massi Benedetti, Christine M. Williams, Philip C. Calder. 2015. "Low-Grade Inflammation, Diet Composition and Health: Current Research Evidence and its Translation." *British Journal of Nutrition* 114 no. 7: 999-1012.

Murray, Donal, Kevin C. Miller, Jeffery E. Edwards. 2016. "Does a Reduction in Serum Sodium Concentration or Serum Potassium Concentration Increase the Prevalence of Exercise-Associated Muscle Cramps?" *Journal of Sport Rehabilitation* 25: 301-304.

Nichols, Andrew W. 2014. "Heat-Related Illness in Sports and Exercise." *Current Reviews in Musculoskeletal Medicine* 7: 355-365.

Schöffl, Volker, Audry Morrison, Ulrich Schwarz, Isabelle Schöffl, Thomas Küpper. 2010. "Evaluation of Injury and Fatality Risk in Rock and Ice Climbing." *Sports Medicine* 40 no. 8: 667-679.

Schöffl, Volker, Christoph Lutter, Kaikanani Woollings, Isabelle Schöffl. 2018. "Pediatric and Adolescent Injury in Rock Climbing." *Research in Sports Medicine* 26, sup1: 91-113.

Shaw, Gregory, Ann Lee-Barthel, Megan LR Ross, Bing Wang, Keith Baar. 2017. "Vitamin C-Enriched Gelatin Supplementation Before Intermittent Activity Augments Collagen Synthesis." *American Journal of Clinical Nutrition* 105 no. 1: 136-143.

Slater, Gregory, David Pyne, Kevin Tipton. 2015. "Immunity, Infective Illness and Injury." In *Clinical Sports Nutrition*, edited by Louise Burke and Vicki Deakin, 730-750. Sydney, Australia: McGraw Hill Education.

Vitale, Kenneth, Shawn Hueglin, Elizabeth Broad, 2017. "Tart Cherry Juice in Athletes: A Literature Review and Commentary." *Current Sports Medicine Reports* 16 no. 4: 230-239.

Wall, Benjamin T., James P. Morton, Luc J.C. van Loon. 2014. "Strategies to Maintain Skeletal Muscle Mass in the Injured Athlete: Nutritional Considerations and Exercise Mimetics." *European Journal of Sport Science* 15 no. 1: 53-62.

CHAPTER 8

SUPPLEMENTS

Madisyn Cox, an elite swimmer from the United States, was abruptly banned for two years after testing positive on a routine doping test. The culprit? A contaminated multivitamin. Brant Rutemiller of Swimming World Magazine describes how Cox had been taking the vitamin for seven years and listed it on her doping control form. After taking it to a lab for testing in an attempt to clear her name, it was discovered that it was tainted with Trimetazidine, a cardiovascular drug. Once the multivitamin was revealed as the source of the banned substance, Cox's ban was reduced from two years to six months. A hard lesson to learn for an elite athlete: Be careful with your supplements.

Most athletes, whether recreational, competitive, or elite, want to know about supplements, either to improve performance, improve health, as "insurance" against a poor diet, or to get an edge over the competition.

There is a sports performance hierarchy. Picture a pyramid. At the base, sports performance is determined by genetics—they play a huge role in how well you perform. If you were lucky enough to have athletic parents, you won the rock-climbing lottery. Even better if you are naturally thin, strong, and coordinated (and have a large ape index too!) because you might pick up the sport more naturally than others. Next up on the pyramid, training and experience help your performance. If you train correctly and have a lot of experience, you will become a better climber. Next pyramid level: nutrition and hydration. Proper nutrition helps your body adapt to any training changes, build muscle, prevent injuries, etc. And finally, at the tip of the pyramid, you find supplements, which will likely play the smallest role in your climbing performance.

8 - SUPPLEMENTS

Performance Hierarchy

Some 40–100 percent of athletes report using supplements. At the time of this writing, about 71 percent of US adults (that's 170 million people!) use supplements. This is a staggering number, especially considering the state of the supplement industry. When interviewing athletes on their supplement use, one researcher found that 74 percent of an athletes' main source of information was from family and friends, followed by 44 percent from coaches, 40 percent from athletic trainers, 33 percent from doctors, and very least of all a sports dietitian.

Let's just pause a moment to think about those numbers. Athletes (at least from a few studies) value and obtain their information on supplement use from family and friends. Have you seen the meme "Do not confuse your Google search with my _____ [fill in the blank] degree?" Yeah, don't confuse your family or friend's advice, no matter how persuasive, with a professional's advice. Especially if they are selling their product via a multi-level marketing plan (recently renamed to make these sound less like pyramid schemes). Don't put your health and performance in the hands of a questionable supplement salesperson. Even your coach is likely not well-qualified to give you advice on supplement use. Seek quality information from a sports physician or sports dietitian.

Many supplements are not well researched. Their effects, side effects, safety, dosing, and efficacy is not well known. In addition, in the United States, they are not regulated. This means that what is on the label might not actually be what is in the container. They can have contaminants, fillers, banned substances, ineffective substances, or substances that may be harmful to your health. Lead, arsenic, melamine, steroids, and stimulants have been found in supplements. Some manufacturers include substances that are banned, but effective, in order to get users to achieve rapid results and continue to buy their product. This can result in severe health outcomes: People have experienced liver failure, heart problems, and even death from supplement use.

SUPPLEMENTS
NUTRITION
TRAINING
GENETICS

Many people take multiple supplements at once, even if the combined effects and risks of the supplements (and any medication you happen to be taking) are unknown.

Be careful when deciding to take supplements. Consider their safety, efficacy, side effects, and risk of contamination. Check with your physician and any and all competitive governing bodies to make sure you are in compliance with their rules and regulations. It would be a terrible thing to compete and then be suspended, banned, or fined because you took a supplement that wasn't allowed. Look for the NSF Certified for Sport logo or the Informed Choice logo. This indicates that the supplement has been third-party tested for contaminants and banned substances. Even then, if it is NSF Certified, it doesn't mean it is allowed by your sport's governing body. Use extreme caution when taking supplements of any kind.

As a general guideline, supplements are not for use in children or adolescents. Use a food-first approach with these climbers (and any climber really). Fostering a good relationship with food and fueling with a child or teen can help a young climber learn that proper fueling with real food goes a long way toward a healthy body. Relying on supplements is misguided and can lead to a belief that supplements are more important than food.

How to spot a legitimate source of nutrition information

There are probably literally millions of blog posts, books, and articles about nutrition. Many of them are very convincing, and many of them spread false information. As a dietitian, I come across articles, books, magazines, and blogs regularly that have bad information about nutrition. Some are just off by a little bit, and some are blatantly and glaringly wrong. How do you know what to believe? Here are some guidelines to help you decide if what you read is legitimate:

» **Who wrote it?** What are the credentials of the person writing it? What is their experience level? Background? Are they a professional with a degree and/or valid nutrition credentials? See page 175 for an explanation of various nutrition certifications.

» **What is the tone?** Is it absolute? Convincing? Black and white? All or nothing? Does it make extraordinary health claims? Does it state firm conclusions, such as, "If you eat fructose you will go into liver failure" or "The paleo diet cures diabetes." In nutrition, there is rarely anything that is absolute–there is a tremendous amount of nuance. Note your emotions as you read the article. Guilt, shame, confusion, or even extreme motivation to eat a certain way are all signs to be cautious before proceeding with the suggested dietary recommendations.

» **Is it well-referenced?** This may be hard to determine. Some authors cherry-pick studies and evidence to support their own claims, but ignore the larger body of research that may tell a different story. Look for articles/blogs/books that have references from peer-reviewed scientific journals.

» **Does the author agree with the general nutrition field?** Nutrition researchers and professionals generally look at the current body of evidence and make conclusions and recommendations based on what is currently known. Some authors are considered a "lone wolf," meaning they depart from the general scientific consensus and argue a contrary point of view. These authors usually misinterpret the evidence or have a heavy bias.

» **Does the author have a conflict of interest?** Is the author backed by a corporation, supplement company, or any other business that would profit from you believing their diet plan? Are there any supplements, shakes, or products for sale recommended in the publication? This doesn't automatically mean it is incorrect information, but it's wise to take a second look and see if the nutrition information is correct.

» **Does the author recognize limitations to the research?** When an author is telling the reader about nutrition information, a good author will present the known body of evidence, but also the limitations. For instance, a study design might not be robust and the researchers' conclusions may not be correct. A good author would either not even reference this study, or lay out its limitations. For example, in this book I've talked a lot about how there isn't much rock-climbing nutrition research, so I use research from other sports. I have also told you the possible benefits and limitations of using that research.

» **Does the diet or recommendation require you to give up entire food groups or drastically change your life?** If it does, it probably isn't a good diet. One that calls for giving up whole food groups limits nutrients. It is also so restrictive that it isn't sustainable. It can also lead to more anxiety around food choices, guilt, and shame. If following an extreme diet disrupts your lifestyle, family life, and social relationships, it's time to reconsider this diet.

» **Does the nutrition information rely on anecdotes and testimonials?** Good, valid nutrition information depends on science and research. If the article or book you are reading relies on testimonials or fantastical claims, it's not reliable. "I lost 50 pounds in three months," "I stopped taking my medication," or "Now all my friends and family are on this diet too," are dead giveaways that there are probably false or misleading promises.

» **Does it contain buzzwords and fads?** Things like anti-inflammatory diet, paleo, adrenal fatigue, leaky gut, low carb, high fat, keto, and intermittent fasting are all fads. Legitimate nutrition information relies on time-tested, evidence-based recommendations, not gimmicks and fads.

With that in mind, there are some supplements that are legitimate and well-researched. In addition, some supplements are appropriate to take in certain situations, particularly micronutrients. Someone with a nutrient deficiency should take a supplement to correct it, such as low vitamin D status or iron deficiency. Vegans need to take a B12 supplement or rely on fortified foods, and potentially a few others (see chapter 6 for more information on vegan climber recommendations). A climber with many food allergies or intolerances may have to eliminate key foods or food groups, which would mean missing out on nutrients. Supplements may also be needed for strategic training situations, such as taking iron before going to climb at high altitude, using creatine to increase the quality of a strength-training session, or using omega-3 oils to recover from a concussion.

8 - SUPPLEMENTS

When considering rock-climbing performance, there are a few supplements that will probably be worthwhile. Keep in mind that none of these supplements have specifically been studied in climbers. I will be drawing on studies done on athletes in other sports, as well as review papers regarding supplement use.

Please also understand that most supplements are researched in isolation. This means the subjects took just one supplement during the study. As soon as you are taking more than one supplement at a time, the effects are not known. Are they safe to take together? Do they work against or with each other? Do they interact with your medication? Do you need to take one at night and one in the morning? Or just one and no others? There is still much research to be done. Also, supplements usually aren't meant to be taken long-term. You likely need to take them for just weeks or months during a certain training phase, then discontinue use.

> Before taking a supplement, asking yourself a few questions can help you determine if it is right for you.
>
> » Where did you get your information about the supplement? Was it from a reputable, knowledgeable source?
> » What do you expect the supplement to do for you? Is there good research to back up the claims?
> » Is the supplement approved by your sport's governing body (if you compete)?
> » Are there any negative health effects or side effects?
> » Do you understand the right dose and timing protocol to make sure you take it correctly?
> » Can the health or performance benefit you are seeking be met another way, such as an adequate diet, better sleep, or strategic training methods?
> » Does the supplement fit your budget? Could you spend your money a more effective way, such as buying quality fruits, vegetables, and lean protein?

For the purpose of this chapter, I will focus specifically on supplements that are non-food supplements. Things like protein powders, sports drinks, gummies, and bars could also be considered supplements, but most people use these as a part of their training and competition food. This chapter is all about extra supplements a climber could use aside from food. I am also not including micronutrients, such as iron, calcium, and vitamin D. If you are deficient in micronutrients, it is important to identify and correct the deficiency through supplementation at proper doses as advised by your doctor. Supplements discussed in this chapter are separate ones marketed toward enhancing performance and/or recovery.

CREATINE

What It Does

Remember the phosphagen energy system? Of course you do! This is the energy system in the body responsible for explosive, powerful, strong movements. Creatine is involved with this energy system.

Creatine can help climbers by reducing fatigue, possibly reducing pump, and help you achieve greater training gains (because you're not as fatigued... you're able to go longer and harder during training). It can also increase blood flow. It's possibly an anti-inflammatory and an antioxidant. Anti-inflammatory supplements, as well as anti-inflammatory foods, can be helpful in cases of chronic inflammation (which is not desirable or healthy– if you are concerned that you are in a state of chronic inflammation, ask your doctor to test you; a common lab that indicates inflammation is called C-reactive protein). Acute inflammation, which occurs right after an injury, is a helpful body process that helps aid healing.

Potential POSITIVE Effects

More power, less pump, greater strength, longer training sessions. Increased blood flow to forearms, alleviating or reducing pump.

How to Use It

Start with a "loading dose" and then taper off into a "maintenance dose." You can do this by using creatine monohydrate as a loading dose of 20 grams per day divided into four equal daily doses (20 grams total per day, but taken at 5 grams per dose, four times per day). Do this for five to seven days. Then switch to a maintenance dose of 3–5 grams once per day.

Potential NEGATIVE Effects

There is some water-weight gain associated with creatine. Creatine is stored in your muscles with water. You might see a gain of one to five pounds, which will be lost as water weight during a training session or two. Climbers may see this as a disadvantage, because they like to feel lighter. It's hard to climb when you're feeling heavier than usual. However, any gains that you see from creatine use may offset that weight. There are no studies about climbers and creatine use to determine if the water weight is a big deal or not.

If you are vegan or vegetarian, you may see an increased advantage from creatine use, as it is not as abundant in a vegetarian diet. Omnivores get some creatine in their diet when they eat meat, but even omnivores see an advantage to supplementing with creatine.

Creatine doesn't harm the kidneys, but if you have existing kidney disease, check with your nephrologist before taking this. It is perfectly safe for those people with no kidney problems, but may be contraindicated if you have decreased kidney function.

BETA ALANINE

What It Does
Beta alanine can increase carnosine in the muscles. What is carnosine? Well, I'm glad you asked. It is made up of two amino acids (histidine and alanine). It can improve muscle function and help the muscles recover from fatigue. It can serve as a buffer during intense muscle contractions. What does this have to do with climbing? When a climber feels that burning sensation—usually in the forearms—that makes you have to pause and shake out your arms, that is possibly hydrogen ions building up in your muscles (we need more research on this, please!). Beta alanine can help buffer the hydrogen ions (acid) and decrease the burning sensation. It can potentially enhance performance and training in high-intensity exercises. It helps with movements lasting about 60–240 seconds. This would be like helping you get through a long sequence of moves (like getting through an extended crux or long boulder problem) while climbing.

There is only one small, unpublished study at the time of printing this book on beta alanine in climbers. When researchers gave climbers beta alanine, they showed an improved rate of perceived exertion, but didn't improve actual performance. This means that when they were doing a move that previously felt hard for them, it felt a bit easier when using the beta alanine. This study was limited, and much more research needs to be conducted in climbers before any conclusive recommendations can be made. That being said, beta alanine may be useful and is generally safe to use.

Potential POSITIVE Effects
You may feel less burning in your muscles and improved performance with hard, intense climbing moves.

Potential NEGATIVE Effects
Tingling sensations (the official name is paraesthesia) are often reported, especially if the person takes a higher dose and/or does not split up the dose. You can reduce the tingling by splitting the dose (see below) or by using a sustained-release formulation. As far as scientists can tell, this tingling isn't harmful. It just might be a weird or unwelcome sensation.

How to Use It
Take 4–6 grams daily for four weeks. If you feel tingling, you can split up the dose to about 1 or 1.5 grams four times per day for four weeks.

BETA-HYDROXY BETA-METHYLBUTYRATE (HMB)

What It Does

HMB is a metabolite of leucine. Leucine is an amino acid involved with muscle protein synthesis (muscle building and repair). There are a couple different forms available: HMB Calcium and HMB free acid form. Most studies have been conducted using the calcium form, and this is what is commercially available. It seems to prevent muscle breakdown, but not specifically add to muscle building.

Potential POSITIVE Effects

It may help with muscle recovery and repair. It seems to be most effective when taken two weeks prior to increasing the intensity of an exercise routine. It can help speed recovery of muscles and decreased tear-down of muscles. It can help preserve muscle mass in older people (over age 65) and those people in a calorie deficit who might otherwise lose lean mass. Overall, the data aren't convincing that it is a supplement that will have much benefit. You might be able to get the same benefit from just eating adequate, high-quality protein in your daily diet.

Potential NEGATIVE Effects

None are known. HMB seems safe to take.

How to Use It

Acute dose: Take 3 grams about 30 minutes prior to a planned intense exercise (whether a hard training session or a difficult route).

Chronic dose: Take 3 grams per day, three times per day, for two weeks before changing to a more difficult training intensity. This is not a supplement that is a must-have, but it could be useful in certain situations.

CAFFEINE

What It Does

Ah, caffeine. We all likely have had caffeine at one point or another in our lives. Many people ingest it on a regular basis in coffee and tea. It's also found in energy drinks, select sports gels, gums, and gummies, some soda beverages, chocolate, some medications (like migraine medicine), and herbal drinks like guarana and yerba maté. It's ubiquitous in many cultures worldwide. It can help with mental acuity, alertness, and fatigue.

Potential NEGATIVE Effects

Caffeine can raise your heart rate, cause jitteriness, and cause headaches and lethargy when you go through withdrawal. Use caution with caffeine and climbing—particularly outdoor climbing—because this type of climbing may raise the heart rate more than indoor climbing.

If you feel like your heart is racing, you are too jittery, you have digestive issues (like diarrhea), or you feel anxious after using caffeine, this means you either ingested too much or you do not tolerate it well. Don't use caffeine if you have these symptoms. If you take it too close to bedtime, it can also disturb sleep. This is important because sleep is when your body recovers and repairs from a day of climbing and training. Good sleep is crucial to an athlete; in fact, it is often considered the "third pillar" of training.

One other thing: If you consume caffeine on a regular basis, you might not benefit from taking some caffeine before climbing. It's less effective in some people who are already used to it.

In addition, it can cause a diuretic effect in some people, making you have to urinate more often. This doesn't mean that you will become dehydrated, however. Caffeine-containing beverages are still considered hydrating. It just might be inconvenient in some instances. In some, it also causes loose stools or diarrhea.

Potential POSITIVE Effects

Caffeine can improve endurance, delay fatigue, improve mood and alertness, improve reaction time, and decrease perceived pain. All of these can be helpful when climbing.

How to Use It

An effective dose is around 100–200 milligrams or 3 milligrams per kilogram body weight. You can take this about an hour before exercise. A cup of coffee has about 60–150 milligrams. Energy gummies have between 20–150 milligrams (check the label). Caffeinated soda pop has about 35–115 milligrams. Avoid energy drinks that have excessive amounts of caffeine or other ingredients whose effect is unknown. Always test how you respond to caffeine before taking it during an important comp or crucial climb. Test the dose that works for you, your tolerance to it, and how well you respond to it. Never try it out on a whim before climbing at a comp or in difficult climbing conditions where all variables need to be controlled as much as possible.

If you don't tolerate caffeine well, or don't want to ingest it because you want to be able to sleep later on, there is another alternative. Similar to the carbohydrate mouth rinse, you can do what is called the caffeine mouth rinse (or "swilling"). You just rinse in your mouth for 5 to 20 seconds, then spit out. Some studies have shown that simply rinsing your mouth with a beverage that has caffeine can be effective for performance enhancement. Even better, "swish and spit" with a beverage that contains both caffeine and carbohydrates. Most of the studies showing the benefits of "swish and spit" were conducted to test sprint performance (it hasn't been studied in climbers), but it could still be applicable to climbing. As with all new things, test in training! Don't try a caffeine mouth rinse the day of a comp or big climb.

NITRATE

What It Does
Nitrate is a naturally occurring substance found in beets/beet juice, green leafy vegetables (like spinach, lettuce, celery, and arugula), and some drinking water. It can be converted in the body to nitric oxide, which helps dilate blood vessels. This helps reduce blood pressure, enhance exercise tolerance, and reduce the oxygen cost of exercise. It may also help increase blood flow to muscles, as well as reduce the cost of ATP use in muscles.

Potential POSITIVE Effects
Nitrate can potentially help with pump, as well as the endurance exercise you may have to complete in the form of hiking to the crag or climbing a big wall. Nitrate may be particularly helpful at high altitudes.

Potential NEGATIVE Effects
None are known. It seems relatively safe, especially if it is consumed as food instead of a supplement. Unless you are allergic or intolerant to foods high in nitrate, you should be fine.

How to Use It
Add beetroot juice to smoothies, drink 4–6 ounces as a "shot" before workouts, or up to 16 ounces (500 milliliters) as a beverage. Add spinach, lettuce, beets, celery, and arugula (rocket) to your normal diet. BeetBoost and BeetElite are two powders marketed toward athletes. They are easy to mix into smoothies or mix with water as a "shot." Weird fun fact: Some mouthwashes seem to negate the effect of nitrate ingestion when taken close together, so avoid mouthwash right after ingesting beet juice or other foods/juices with nitrate to realize its full effects.

SODIUM BICARBONATE

What It Does
Sodium bicarbonate is plain old baking soda. It can act as a buffer in the blood and muscles to reduce that burning feeling that comes along with intense exercise.

Potential NEGATIVE Effects
You gotta really, really want to have the buffering effects that sodium bicarbonate provides to try this out. First off, it tastes terrible. Second, it can cause severe gastrointestinal side effects like diarrhea and cramping. Always, always try it first to make sure you tolerate it before using it in a big competition or on a climbing trip. Stay close to a bathroom: You may need it. That being said, it is really cheap and can be effective in enhancing your performance. If used long-term, it may reduce gastric acid, which may in turn reduce absorption of some nutrients.

Potential POSITIVE Effects
It has been shown to be effective in short bursts of intense activity lasting a few minutes or less, and also as a possible performance enhancer for activities that are intermittent (like climbing), with the effects lasting up to an hour. You may feel less burn or be able to go a bit longer or harder for short amounts of time.

How to Use It
Mix 0.3 grams per kilogram body weight of baking soda with about 8–16 ounces of water. Or 20–30 grams (5–7 teaspoons) total mixed with water. It is best to split up the doses or drink slowly over a couple of hours. Take a few hours before you're going to climb. Stay close to the bathroom.

FISH OIL

What It Does
Fish oil contains a "good" kind of fat called omega-3 fatty acids. This fat can be helpful for heart health, inflammation, and immunity, but study results are mixed.

Potential NEGATIVE Effects
They can contain contaminants. It is best to purchase a high-quality fish oil. They can also possibly increase the "bad" kind of cholesterol, called low-density lipoproteins (LDLs), as well as potential increased risk of bleeding. If you are taking any medication that can thin blood, such as warfarin (Coumadin) or aspirin, ask your doctor before supplementing with fish oil. It's always wise to ask your doctor before changing any part of your diet, supplement routine, or medications anyway.

Potential POSITIVE Effects
Fish oil can potentially help with head injuries/concussions, although climbers (hopefully!) don't get many head concussions–there is a reason you wear a helmet when climbing outdoors. Fish oil can also potentially alleviate muscle soreness and is considered anti-inflammatory. No performance benefit has been found, but that doesn't mean it isn't useful.

How to Use It
Take at least 2 grams per day. Some studies used doses up to 6 grams per day, which appears to be safe. Ask your doctor what is right for you. If you already have fatty fish such as salmon, tuna, or mackerel as part of your regular diet (at least three times per week), you don't necessarily need fish oil. If you are taking a blood-thinning medication, such as aspirin or warfarin, check with your doctor before taking fish oil, as fish oil can act as a blood thinner. Other food sources of omega-3 fats are walnuts, chia seeds, oysters, sardines, and flaxseed. If you are vegan, use algal oil, which is oil from algae.

GELATIN/COLLAGEN

What It Does
Collagen is a protein that promotes connective-tissue repair. Gelatin contains collagen. It can increase collagen production in your body, which may be helpful when healing from an injury. It also can thicken cartilage and reduce joint pain. Research is in its infancy, so these statements are made with caution, as it's not quite clear yet if gelatin/collagen is helpful and to what degree. One study looked at taking collagen right before normal training to see if this would help enhance collagen synthesis—thereby theoretically preventing injury. It seemed to work, but more research is needed, particularly in climbers—a population in which collagen has not been studied.

Potential POSITIVE Effects
It can potentially help with healing from an injury, especially one that involves ligaments, tendons, or cartilage. It can potentially decrease joint pain. Can be helpful in people with osteoarthritis.

Potential NEGATIVE Effects
It is most likely safe, as it's simply a protein.

How to Use It
For soft tissue injury (such as tendons and ligaments), or to attempt to strengthen soft tissue in order to prevent injury, you can take gelatin and vitamin C. Use 10–15 grams of gelatin and 50 milligrams of vitamin C. Alternatively, use collagen hydrolysate 10 grams per day. Some people shake gelatin powder into their Gatorade and drink that with a vitamin C gummy. Another option is to make "Jell-O shots" by mixing a small packet of gelatin into fruit juice or Crystal Light. It is recommended to take this about 30–60 minutes before any physical therapy or training for best results.

BCAAs: Help or hype?

Branched chain amino acids, or BCAAs, are certain amino acids that are helpful for muscle building, repair, and recovery. Specifically, they are leucine, isoleucine, and valine. BCAAs are common supplements, but are they worth the price? Not necessarily. Most BCAA supplements have around 1 to 3 grams of leucine, 0.5 to 1 grams of isoleucine, and 0.5 to 1 grams of valine.

Contrast this to 3 ounces of cooked chicken breast, which contains 2.23 grams of leucine, 1.3 grams of isoleucine, and 1.25 grams of valine. Two chicken eggs give you 1.1 grams of leucine, 0.7 grams of isoleucine, and 0.9 grams of valine. One 16-ounce glass of milk contains 1.5 grams of leucine, 0.8 grams of isoleucine, and 1 gram of valine. BCAAs can be easily obtained through normal food. Bonus: Food tastes better, is more filling, and contains many more micro- and macronutrients than BCAAs.

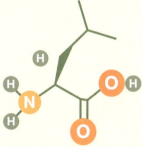

BCAAs are basically a really expensive, incomplete protein. In addition, recent research is showing that all amino acids may be useful for overall muscle building and repair. While it's true that BCAAs have been shown to be particularly necessary, all other amino acids may be important as well.

If you are vegan, you may benefit from BCAAs if you are getting a limited supply in your normal diet. But most people eat enough protein to negate the need for a specific BCAA supplement. Be sure to include around 20-30 grams of high-quality protein in your post-workout meal or snack, and you will be well on your way to recovery, minus the high-priced supplement.

Pick a **Protein Powder**

Type of powder	Definition	Qualities	Complete protein?
WHEY HYDROLYSATE	"Pre-digested," broken-down whey isolate particles for quick digestion	Easily digested, high-protein source with quality amino acids, contains lactose.	Yes
WHEY ISOLATE	Pure form of whey protein. Filtered from cow's milk. Usually about 90% protein.	High-protein source with quality amino acids, low lactose.	Yes
WHEY CONCENTRATE	Less filtered than whey isolate—some carbohydrates still present from natural sugars (lactose) in the milk. Usually about 70-80% protein	Good protein source. Contains lactose.	Yes
CASEIN	Another milk protein	Slowly digested. Best for right before bedtime. Contains lactose.	Yes
PEA	From ground peas with the fiber and starch removed	Slowly digested. Good vegan option.	No
SOY	From ground soybeans	Good vegan option.	Yes
HEMP	From the hemp plant (not marijuana)	Use caution—may contain trace amounts of THC, which would cause a positive doping test. Higher in fiber, slowly digested.	Yes
COLLAGEN PROTEIN	Made from bones, skin, and cartilage of animals.	May help with soft-tissue injuries.	No
PLANT-PROTEIN BLEND (SOY, PEA, HEMP, ETC.)	From ground plant proteins	May have better amino acid profile due to a variety of plants used. Good vegan option. Not superior to whey.	Depends on the blend, but whey is still likely higher in leucine
EGG	Made from dehydrated chicken eggs	Easily absorbed and digested.	Yes

Protein powder is useful for a few purposes: It's easy to transport and mix up for a quick recovery drink if food might be unavailable. And it can be an easy way to boost a smoothie. But usually just eating food is superior to using a protein powder. If you do want to use one, ask yourself a few questions first.

- » Is it NSF Certified for Sport or Informed Choice Certified?
- » Does it fit your budget? How much does it cost per serving?
- » Do you like the taste?
- » Could you get your protein from food instead?
- » Is it the right kind for your goals and nutrition needs?
- » Is it a complete protein (meaning it contains all essential amino acids)?

Pumped?

Here are some supplements that may help with pump. See chart on the next page for usage information.

➤ Creatine   ➤ Beta Alanine   ➤ Nitrate   ➤ Sodium bicarbonate

Supplement Usage Information

Supplement	Potential Benefits	Potential Drawbacks	How to Use
CREATINE	Reduced fatigue, increased blood flow, less pump, better strength-training sessions	Water-weight gain	Loading dose: 10-20 g/day divided into 4 doses x 5-7 days. Maintenance dose: 3-5 g/day
BETA ALANINE	Buffer for lactate in muscles (less "burn")	Tingling sensation	4-6 g/day x 4 weeks.
BETA-HYDROXY-BETA-METHYL-BUTYRATE (HMB)	Muscle recovery and repair	None known	Take 3 g 30 minutes prior to exercise. Or take 3 g/day, 3 times per day x 14 days prior to increasing training intensity.
CAFFEINE	Improve endurance, delay fatigue, improve alertness, improve reaction time, decrease pain	High heart rate, jitteriness, withdrawal symptoms, sleep disturbances, increased urination, loose stools	100-200 mg or 3 mg/kg body weight. Always test for tolerance.
NITRATE	Increased blood flow, less "pump"	None known	Eat beets, spinach, celery, lettuce, and arugula (rocket) regularly. Can use powdered beet supplement in smoothies or mixed with water.
SODIUM BICARBONATE	Less "burn"	Diarrhea, stomach cramping	Mix 0.3 g/kg body weight with 8-16 ounces of water. Drink slowly over a few hours before your climbing session.
FISH OIL	Alleviate muscle soreness; anti-inflammatory	Could contain contaminants	Take 2 g daily.
GELATIN/ COLLAGEN	Injury prevention and healing of soft tissues	None known	Collagen hydrolysate 10 g/day or 10-15 g gelatin + 50 mg vitamin C. Take 30-60 min before training.

THE WRAP-UP FOR SUPPLEMENTS

Supplements are the last line of performance enhancement. Good genetics, training, and nutrition will all be more helpful to becoming a better climber. If you choose to use a supplement, make sure you understand the risks and benefits, and always check with your doctor. Very few supplements are well-researched, and many have contaminants and unknown substances. Supplements that are third-party tested have decreased risk for contaminants. If you are a competition climber who gets blood-doping tests, be sure to check with your sport's governing body to make sure you are complying with all supplement regulations.

CHAPTER 8 REFERENCES

Beaven, Martin C, Peter Maulder, Adrian Pooley, Liam Kilduff, Christian Cook. 2013. "Effects of Caffeine and Carbohydrate Mouth Rinses on Repeated Sprint Performance." *Applied Physiology, Nutrition, and Metabolism* 38: 633-637.

Benzi, G, A. Ceci. 2001. "Creatine as a Nutrition Supplementation and Medicinal Product." *Journal of Sports Medicine and Physical Fitness* 41: 1-10.

Bescós, Raul, Antoni Sureda, Josep A Tur, Antoni Pons. 2012. "The Effect of Nitric-Oxide-Related Supplements on Human Performance." *Sports Medicine* 42 no. 2: 99-117.

Clark, Kristine L, Wayne Sebastianelli, Klaus R. Flechsenhar, Douglas F. Aukermann, Felix Meza, Roberta L. Millard, John R. Deitch, Paul S. Sherbondy, Ann Albert. 2008. "24-Week Study on the Use of Collagen Hydrolysate as a Dietary Supplement in Athletes With Activity-Related Joint Pain." *Current Medical Research and Opinion* 24 no. 5: 1485-1496.

Clarke, Neil D, Evangelos Kornilios, Darren L. Richardson. 2015. "Carbohydrate and Caffeine Mouth Rinses Do Not Affect Maximum Strength and Muscular Endurance Performance." *Journal of Strength and Conditioning Research* 29: 2926-2931.

de Moraes, Roger, Diogo Van Bavel, Beatriz Serpa de Moraes, Eduardo Tibiriçá. 2014. "Effects of Dietary Creatine Supplementation on Systemic Microvascular Density and Reactivity in Healthy Young Adults." *Nutrition Journal* 13: 115.

Engel, Florian Azad, Billy Sperlich, Urs Stöker, Peter Wolf, Volker Schöffl, Lars Donath. 2018. "Acute Responses to Forearm Compression of Blood Lactate Accumulation, Heart Rate, Perceived Exertion, and Muscle Pain in Elite Climbers." *Frontiers in Physiology* 9: 605.

Evans, Mark, Peter Tierney, Nicola Gray, Greg Hawe, Maria Macken, Brendan Egan. 2017. "Acute Ingestion of Caffeinated Chewing Gum Improves Repeated Sprint Performance of Team Sports Athletes with Low Habitual Caffeine Consumption." *International Journal of Sports Nutrition and Exercise Metabolism* 28 no. 3: 221-227.

Garthe, Ina, Ronald Maughan. 2018. "Athletes and Supplements: Prevalence and Perspectives." *International Journal of Sports Nutrition and Exercise Metabolism* 28: 126-138.

Jäger, Ralf, Martin Purpura, Andrew Shao, Toshitada Inoue, Richard B. Kreider. 2011. "Analysis of the Efficacy, Safety, and Regulatory Status of Novel Forms of Creatine." *Amino Acids* 40 no. 5: 1369-1383.

Jones, Andrew M. 2014. "Dietary Nitrate Supplementation and Exercise Performance." *Sports Medicine* 44 Suppl 1: S35-S45.

Juliana, Marcou, Savva Rafaella-Maria. 2017. "Does Caffeine Enhance Athletic Performance?" *Arab Journal of Nutrition and Exercise* 1 no. 1: 52-62.

Kizzi, Joseph, Alvin Sum, Fraser E. Houston, Lawrence D. Hayes. 2016. "Influence of a Caffeine Mouth Rinse on Sprint Cycling Following Glycogen Depletion." *European Journal of Sport Science* 16 no. 8: 1087-1094.

Kreider, Richard B, Douglas S. Kalman, Jose Antonio, Tim N. Ziegenfuss, Robert Wildman, Rick Collins, Darren G. Candow, Susan M. Kleiner, Anthony L. Almada, Hector L. Lopez. 2017. "International Society of Sports Nutrition position stand: Safety and Efficacy of Creatine Supplementation in Exercise, Sport, and Medicine." *Journal of the International Society of Sports Nutrition* 14 no 1: 18.

Masschelein, Evi, Ruud Van Thienen, Xu Wang, Ann Van Schepdael, Martine Thomis, Peter Hespel. 2012. "Dietary Nitrate Improves Muscle but Not Cerebral Oxygenation Status During Exercise in Hypoxia." *Journal of Applied Physiology* 113: 736-745.

Maughan, Ronald J, Louise M. Burke, Jiri Dvorak, D Enette Larson-Meyer, Peter Peeling, Stuart M. Phillips, Eric S. Rawson, Neil P. Walsh, Ina Garthe, Hans Geyer, Romain Meeusen, Lucas J.C. van Loon, Susan M. Shirreffs, Lawrence J. Spreit, Mark Stuart, Alan Vernec, Kevin Currell, Vidya M. Ali, Richard G.M. Budgett, Arne Ljungqvist, Margo Mountjoy, Yannis P. Pitsiladis, Torbjørn Soligard, Ugur Erdener, Lars Engebretsen. 2018. "The IOC Consensus Statement: Dietary Supplements and the High-Performance Athlete." *British Journal of Sports Medicine* 52: 439-455.

Maughan, Ronald J, Susan M. Shirreffs, Alan Vernec. 2018. "Making Decisions About Supplement Use." *International Journal of Sports Nutrition and Exercise Metabolism* 28: 212-219.

McNaughton, Lars R, Jason Siegler, Adrian Midgley. 2008. "Ergogenic Effects of Sodium Bicarbonate." *Current Sports Medicine Reports* 7 no. 4: 230-236.

Martínez-Sans, José Miguel, Isabel Sospedra, Christian Mañas Ortiz, Eduard Baladía, Angel Gil-Izquierdo, Rocio Ortiz-Moncada. 2017. "Intended or Unintended doping? A Review of the Presence of Doping Substances in Dietary Supplements Used in Sports." *Nutrients* 9 no. 10: 1093.

Peeling, Peter, Martyn J. Binnie, Paul S.R. Goods, Marc Sim, Louise M. Burke. 2018. "Evidence-Based Supplements for the Enhancement of Athletic Performance." *International Journal of Sports Nutrition and Exercise Metabolism* 28: 178-187.

Pomportes, Laura, Jeanick Brisswalter, Laurence Casini, Arnaud Hays, Karen Davranche. 2017. "Cognitive Performance Enhancement Induced by Caffeine, Carbohydrate and Guarana Mouth Rinsing During Submaximal Exercise." *Nutrient* 9: 589.

Rawson, Eric S, Mary P. Miles, D. Enette Larson-Meyer. 2018. "Dietary Supplements for Health, Adaptations, and Recovery in Athletes." *International Journal of Sports Nutrition and Exercise Metabolism* 28: 188-199.

Rutemiller, Brent. "Madisyn Cox Eligible to Compete After Source for Banned Substance Found in Multivitamin." Swimming World Magazine. Accessed September 4, 2018. https://www.swimmingworldmagazine.com/news/madisyn-cox-declared-eligible-to-compete-after-source-for-banned-substance-fou/

Shaw, Gregory, Anne Lee-Barthel, Megan L.R. Ross, Bing Wang, Keith Baar. 2017. "Vitamin C-Enriched Gelatin Supplementation Before Intermittent Activity Augments Collagen Synthesis." *American Journal of Clinical Nutrition* 105: 136-43.

Spriet, Lawrence. 2014. "Exercise and Sport Performance with Low Doses of Caffeine." *Sports Medicine* 44 Suppl 2: S175-S184.

Townsend, Jeremy R, Jay R. Hoffman, Adam M. Gonzalez, Adam R. Jajtner, Carleigh H. Boone, Edward H. Robinson, Gerald T. Mangine, Adam J. Wells, Maren S. Fragala, David GH. Fukunda, Jeffry R. Stout. 2015. "Effects of-hydroxy-methylbutyrate Free Acid Ingestion and Resistance Exercise on the Acute Endocrine Response." *International Journal of Endocrinology* article ID 856708.

Trexler, Eric T, Abbie E. Smith-Ryan, Jeffrey R. Stout, Jay R. Hoffman, Colin D. Wilborn, Craig Sale, Richard B. Kreider, Ralf Jäger, Conrad P. Earnest, Laurent Bannock, Bill Campbell, Douglas Kalman, Tim N. Ziegenfuss, Jose Antonio. 2015. "International Society of Sports Nutrition Position Stand: Beta-Alanine." *Journal of the International Society of Sports Nutrition* 12: 30.

Van Cutsem, Jeroen, Kevin De Pauw, Samuele Marcora, Romain Meeusen, Bart Roelands. 2017. "A Caffeine-Maltodextrin Mouth Rinse Counters Mental Fatigue." *Psychopharmacology* 235: 947-958.

Wilson, Jacob M, Peter J. Fitschen, Bill Campbell, Gabriel J. Wilson, Nelo Zanchi, Lem Taylor, Colin Wilborn, Douglas S. Kalman, Jeffrey R. Stout, Jay R. Hoffman, Tim N. Zegenfuss, Hector L. Lopez, Richard B. Kreider, Abbie E. Smith-Ryan, Jose Antonio. 2013. "International Society of Sports Nutrition Position Stand: Beta-Hydroxy-Beta-Methylbutyrate (HMB)." *Journal of the International Society of Sports Nutrition* 10: 6.

Woessner, Mary, James M. Smoliga, Brendan Tarzia, Thomas Stabler, Mitch Van Bruggen, Jason D. Allen. 2016. "A Stepwise Reduction in Plasma and Salivary Nitrite with Increasing Strengths of Mouthwash Following a Dietary Nitrate Load." *Nitric Oxide* 54: 1-7.

Wood, Dan. 2018. "The Effects of Beta-Alanine on Indoor Bouldering Performance." Poster presented at the 4th Research Congress of the International Rock Climbing Research Association July 13, 2018. Chamonix: France.

United States Anti-Doping Agency. 2013-2014. "Marijuana FAQ: Your Questions Answered." Accessed August 7, 2018. **https://www.usada.org/thc-and-hemp-sos-winter-2013-2014/**

CHAPTER 9

NUTRITION PERIODIZATION, WEIGHT MANAGEMENT, & CHANGING YOUR BODY COMPOSITION

A truthbomb of an article appeared on Climbing Magazine's website. Wearing nothing more than underwear, and standing on a scale with a boulder behind him, was climber-writer **James Lucas**. In one hand, outturned like a waiter holding a platter, was a plate piled high with a stack of donuts. In the other hand, a plate with a single broccoli floret. A picture worth 1000 words. Does a climber need to sacrifice enjoyable food to remain thin and send a higher grade? Can donuts and climbing co-exist peacefully? Lucas describes climbers who fasted, rejoiced in food poisoning and the weight they dropped as a result, or skipped sugar for a month. The reward for their self-deprivation was feeling lighter and sending a grade level above their previous record. He writes, *"So how skinny do I—or any of us—really need to be to crush? Where do you draw the line between strategic dieting and an unhealthy eating disorder?"* That, my friends, is the million-dollar question. But, there is more to consider than just the "skinny" factor–let's explore.

Most athletes, at one time or another, have tried to lose weight.

Often there is a perception that if you are lighter you will be faster, stronger, or just plain better. With climbing, there is a definite strength-to-weight ratio factor. You don't see a lot of heavy climbers at the elite level climbing in comps. A study of elite climbers by Phillip Watts showed them to be on average lighter and shorter than other athletes.

If you are seeking better performance, you might be tempted to try to lose some weight. This may be prudent if you are actually carrying excess fat. But be cautious when deciding to lose weight. What you think of as excess weight or fat might actually be the perfect amount your body needs to be healthy. Climbers are often lighter than the general population. If a climber who's light already decides to lose weight, it can lead to health problems—both mental and physical.

One study by Krystal Merrells and her colleagues followed two university students over a five-week climbing trip. The researchers simply wanted to follow two climbers over their trip to observe what they ate, and what changes occurred in their bodies. These two students had a $1 (Canadian) per day budget for food, and "received donations from visitors" on the weekends. OK first, let's pause to chuckle about this: poor college students receiving food donations. OK, moving on...they brought bannock (I had to Google this–it is a wide flatbread or scone), soup, tuna, peanuts, and white rice to eat.

Over the course of this five-week climbing trip, they were only eating about 40 percent of their estimated needs. They did not eat enough protein or carbs, and missed out on several vitamins and minerals.

One climber lost 4 percent of his body mass, and the other lost 7 percent of his body mass. This amount of body mass lost in a short amount of time is a huge health and performance concern. To lose that much weight from not eating enough over the course of several weeks likely means lost fat (which many view as good, although getting too lean is actually unhealthy), lost muscle mass, decreased organ function, and compromised climbing performance because if you're not eating enough, you can't climb as well.

All people need some fat on their bodies to be healthy. Fat serves to cushion organs, secrete hormones, provide insulation to regulate body temperature, absorb vitamins, and as an extra energy reserve (like an insurance policy for your body) if you get sick or injured. Fat is an essential organ. A general healthy range of body fat for males is about 5–20 percent and for females is about 12–26 percent. These numbers vary based on which data you consult, but this is a general range.

If you are a competition climber, you probably are already aware that many organizations (including the International Federation of Sport Climbing) check competitors' Body Mass Index (BMI) to make sure a climber is above 17. Climbers are not allowed to compete if they are less than this.

BODY-COMPOSITION TESTS

Fat-free mass is anything that isn't fat, and includes muscle, organs, and bone. You can find out an approximation of your body fat and fat-free mass by getting a reliable body-composition test done.

Common body-composition-test options include:

- **Dual Energy X-ray Absorptiometry (DEXA):** A machine that measures body composition as well as bone density. Considered the gold standard of body-composition tests. This looks like a table that you lay on with a scanner arm on top. It is an expensive machine and usually only available at medical facilities or universities.

- **Air displacement plethysmography (BodPod):** This is a machine that looks like a big white egg. You get inside it with minimal clothing on, like just a bathing suit, and sit quietly for about three minutes. The accuracy of the test depends on not eating before the test, not having a full bladder or bowels, and a few other things. It is considered very accurate. Again, this is an expensive machine and usually is only found at universities or high-end fitness facilities specializing in sports performance.

- **Ultrasound:** This is also an accurate measurement and gets a good result without relying on the person's hydration status, bowel/bladder status, clothing, and other factors. It sends a signal through tissues to detect thicknesses in fat and muscle.

- **Skinfold calipers:** This can be accurate if the person measuring you knows what they are doing. Look for someone trained and certified by the International Society for the Advancement of Kinanthropometry. If you get your body composition measured by your average Joe Trainer at the local gym, it's likely not going to be accurate.

- **Bioelectric Impedance (BIA):** This machine measures your body composition by shooting an electric current through your body (yikes!). It sounds scary, but it is completely safe, painless, and harmless. This has a larger margin of error (about ±4 percent), and accuracy depends on the quality of the machine, your hydration status, if you are fasting, and if you have emptied your bowels/bladder. An InBody or Seca brand machine is much more accurate than a handheld device (gym trainers are guilty of using these a lot) or a BIA bathroom scale.

Things To Consider
Before Losing Weight

Before you decide to lose weight, first consider if you even need to. You may be tempted to lose weight thinking it will help you send that project, climb a higher level of difficulty, or be a better overall climber. And maybe it will...if you are truly packing around excess fat. But if you are an appropriate weight and body composition, losing more weight may actually lead to performance losses. If you are thinner than you should be, or in a state of low energy availability, you may experience:

» **Loss of muscle mass**
» **Less overall power**
» **Fatigue**
» **Increased injuries**
» **Moodiness and irritability**
» **Loss of your period or irregular periods (women)**
» **Decreased ability and performance**
» **Nutrient deficiencies such as anemia**
» **Decreased training adaptations**
» **Disordered eating patterns**
» **Increased anxiety around food**
» **Increased dissatisfaction with body image**

If you do have some excess fat to lose, dieting may be right for you...for a certain period of time. Long-term dieting isn't wise and usually leads to decreased performance and the other negative effects mentioned above. Here are some potential positive outcomes of losing excess fat:

» **Decreased risk of heart disease, diabetes, and stroke**

» **Increased performance due to improved strength-to-weight ratio**

» **Improved eating habits (i.e., eating more fruits/vegetables, whole grains, lean proteins, and healthful fats rather than heavily processed foods, reduced sugar intake, etc.)**

Periodization

Here's the thing with dieting: It only works until it doesn't. Dieting can be effective in the short-term. But if you have to alter your diet, exercise, or lifestyle substantially in order to achieve a lower weight, this type of dieting is not sustainable. Fighting against your natural body weight is a losing, time-consuming, and depressing battle. What's the solution if you want to lose weight for better climbing, but don't want to diet forever? Enter the concept of periodization.

Nutrition periodization refers to strategic timing of food intake to support certain nutrition, training, and performance goals. It is also sometimes called "nutritional training." It simply means eating differently depending on your goals and training. For example, if you are a climber who is also a runner, you may eat more carbohydrates on your running days since you will be using more carbs as fuel that day. A climber going for a long backcountry trip that includes climbing and hiking would eat more food each day than a climber who works a desk job and then climbs for a couple hours in the evening. Periodization means you could be lighter for part of the year (like, say, your comp season), and go back to your usual weight in the off-season.

Asker Jeukendrup, a well-respected top international sports nutrition researcher, defines nutrition periodization as "a long-term progressive approach designed to improve athletic performance by systematically varying training throughout the year." And "a planned, purposeful, and strategic use of specific nutritional interventions to enhance the adaptations targeted by individual exercise sessions or periodic training plans, or to obtain other effects that will enhance performance longer term." Nutrition periodization simply means changing your nutrition intake during certain periods of training.

You can periodize your food intake based on day-to-day activity levels. Eating adequate protein after a strength-training workout, or eating quick-to-digest carbohydrates during a speed-climbing session, are examples of micro-periodization. You can also periodize your food intake based on overall training and body-composition goals for an entire season or year. This is macro-periodization.

Types of Periodization

Training "low": Training "low" means to train with low or limited carbohydrate availability. This would occur if you didn't eat enough carbs, trained in the morning before breakfast in a fasted state (when your liver has used up all its glycogen, or storage sugar, overnight to keep blood sugar stable while you sleep), or trained with low muscle glycogen stores (like if you work out in the morning, don't do a good recovery meal with carbs, then work out in the afternoon). You can also sleep "low" by training in the evening, then going to bed without eating carbs as a recovery meal. And finally, you could train "low" long-term by going on a low-carb or ketogenic diet.

Why would someone want to do this?
After all, we know that exercise, including climbing, uses carbohydrates. Intense moves, quick bursts of strength, or climbing at high altitude all need carbs. A climber might train "low" on select occasions in order to stimulate training adaptations in the body. A person who trains "low" teaches the body to use fat for fuel more efficiently. Although this may sound good on the surface, it actually could decrease performance. If you feel more fatigued, feel that you have higher perceived exertion or effort, or have mood disturbances, training low may not be a good idea.

In addition, if you train "low," you can train your body to oxidize ("burn") fat more effectively, but this may downregulate your body's ability to "burn" carbohydrates. Which means in movements and training where you are doing things that demand carbs (such as a dyno), you may not be able to perform as well because your body is now trained to use fat instead of carbs. So, training "low" makes sense if you are combining some endurance exercise with climbing—like, maybe you are a runner and want to be able to use fat stores more effectively on your runs. But training "low" when you are specifically training to climb likely may not be appropriate.

Before we move on from the train "low" section, just a word about high-fat or ketogenic (keto) diets. While there may be a few people who feel better on a keto diet, these are outliers. For a climber, keto probably doesn't make sense (although there have been no studies on keto diets for climbers). Out of all the studies exploring athletic performance with ketogenic diet, not one of them has shown improved performance. Most show the same performance as a diet with adequate carbohydrates. The only difference is the keto athletes felt more fatigue, and sprint and power performance decreased. What would that mean for a climber? That getting through a crux, a dyno, or any other powerful move may feel harder.

You may read all sorts of blogs or articles about how the keto diet is amazing and everyone should do it. You may read about how people have lost weight on it. Here's the thing: Any diet that has a restriction will lead to weight loss. There is a commonality with all these diets: They have reduced calories.

Think about it—the keto diet eliminates almost all carbohydrates. There goes your fruit, grains, dairy products, beans, and starchy vegetables. Buh-bye, calories and nutrients. Even when you are left eating high-fat and high-calorie foods such as bacon and beef, if weight loss occurred, there was a calorie deficit. In fact, the keto diet is very limited in what you can eat and demands about 80-90 percent of your intake come from fat. Ketosis is a convoluted metabolic state your body is trying to achieve because you aren't feeding it properly.

All other diets—intermittent fasting, paleo, vegan, Whole30, and others—all have one thing in common: restriction. They restrict what you eat, how much you eat, or when you eat-or even entire food groups. This leads to a calorie deficit. This is what makes you lose weight-the calorie deficit itself, not some magical property of the promoted diet. Many popular diets claim to have the special sauce that sets them apart from other diets. Claims about diets changing insulin or other hormones, claims about fat-melting, claims about anti-inflammation—all of this is mostly pseudoscience to get you to buy into a particular diet. If you take a look at the research, and all we know about nutrition and the body, these diets aren't special or magical. They just restrict in one way or another, which leads to eating fewer calories than you used to. And then you lose weight.

Whole30 FAIL:

Whole30 is a popular diet plan claiming to help with gut health, hormone balance, inflammation, energy levels, and more. You can read all sorts of glowing testimonials about how this diet changed people's lives. Does it warrant your attention? Let's take a closer look to see if it is a legitimate source of information.

» **Who wrote it?** Melissa Hartwig, a Certified Sports Nutritionist through the International Society of Sports Nutrition. This certification can be obtained online and doesn't require a four-year degree in anything related to nutrition, biology, or other health sciences. This isn't a robust qualification. Hartwig's degree comes from an online, unaccredited program; she lacks understanding and education in basic physiology, biochemistry, nutrition, and biology. Dallas Hartwig, the co-author, actually has some good credentials, with an undergrad in anatomy and physiology (but not nutrition). It all falls apart when you realize Dallas has a sketchy certification in "functional medicine" (often described as an approach to treating a patient by looking at the whole body, and environmental and lifestyle factors around a person–still not nutrition).

» **What is the tone?** The Whole30 website claims it can improve or cure a myriad of diseases and ailments, including Crohn's disease, type 1 and type 2 diabetes, arthritis, infertility, and more. It is extreme in its language and lacks nuance. It evokes strong emotions like extreme hope ("If I follow this, I can cure my diabetes") or guilt ("I ate a forbidden food"). Words like "good," "bad," "toxic," "clean," "miracle," and "life-changing" are big red flags. It claims, "One bite of pizza, one spoonful of ice cream, one lick of the spoon mixing the batter within the 30-day period and you've broken the 'reset' button, requiring you to start over again on Day 1." OK, let's just think about this on a physiological basis. Your body doesn't have a reset button. If you eat a spoonful of ice cream, your body just digests and metabolizes it as carbohydrate, protein, and fat (a very small amount, I might add). Your body doesn't know the difference between ice cream and any other food with a similar nutrient profile. It just sees the molecules and digests accordingly. To posit that if you eat one bite of pizza, your body will react in an extreme way is nonsense. Unless you are truly allergic to a food, one bite of anything is no big deal.

» **Is it well-referenced?** Nope. Not at all. There is a lack of peer-reviewed articles. The claims made about nutrition and health are not backed up by science.

- » **Does the author agree with the general nutrition field?** Um, no. Hartwig goes off the deep end, with fantastical and wild claims about how Whole30 can help with all sorts of ailments. The book states things with black-and-white certainty, while the remainder of the nutrition science field expresses caution, nuance, and "more research is needed" on a variety of issues.

- » **Does the author have a conflict of interest?** Yes. She has incentive to continue with her inaccurate claims, because sensation is what sells. The Whole30 website also has numerous links to various foods available for purchase, including bars, meal kits, nut butters, bone broth, and more.

- » **Does the author recognize limitations to the research?** No, because there isn't any mention of research to begin with. A hallmark of quality nutrition information is presenting the limitations to the research and recognizing the nuance in the recommendations, as well as analyzing if the research study was well-designed and can be considered valid.

- » **Does the diet or recommendation require you to give up entire food groups or drastically change your life?** Yes, yes, yes, yes! Whole30 eliminates healthful foods like beans, grains, and dairy. It calls for drastic changes in lifestyle. It lacks compassion and is judgmental. It carries the tone of, "If you can't follow this diet, you are weak." The fact that this diet is only in place for 30 days means it is not intended to be a permanent, sustainable lifestyle change. The diet calls for re-introduction of other foods after 30 days, which could prove troublesome if your body has down-regulated its ability to digest those foods you just eliminated for 30 days.

- » **Does the nutrition information rely on anecdotes and testimonials?** Oh, my, yes. This is basically all it is. There is no way to know if these are true. There is no way to know if these people were paid to write the testimonials. There is no way to determine if these people merely felt better (whatever that means) from the placebo effect. Robust science is lacking on all fronts. Even the testimonials from health professionals on the website are lacking in critical thinking.

- » **Does it contain buzzwords and fads?** This is basically all it contains. Here are some buzzwords I picked up from their website:

    - Miracle
    - Gut-damaging
    - Inflammation
    - Cravings
    - Whole
    - Clean
    - Sugar
    - Approved
    - Toxic
    - Cheat
    - Incredible
    - Forever

THE BOTTOM LINE: Whole30 is not backed by science, basic biology, or anything else valid. It is a diet based on testimonials and conjecture. It recommends potentially dangerous nutrition interventions and sells false hope.

> **?** Start to become a critical thinker. Analyze any diet program with a cynical view. Tread carefully when making any diet changes. Be careful that you do not fall into disordered eating patterns. Don't sell yourself short—make sure you fully understand diet changes, the reasoning and science behind them, and how they fit with your lifestyle, health history, needs, and goals.

When thinking about dieting or trying to lose weight in order to be a better climber, you don't need to pick a diet that never lets you eat beans or potatoes, or fruit or anything else. Just eat food. In general, a diet based on vegetables, fruits, beans, nuts, seeds, lean proteins, and whole grains is about as healthy as you can get. The key to losing weight happens in a calorie deficit. While again, specific diets have not been studied for climbing performance, I would guess based on research and clinical judgment that climbers on keto diets have decreased climbing performance. If they feel stronger with a keto diet, it may be because they lost a bit of weight, but not because they are in ketosis.

Dieting can also lead to hyper-awareness of food intake. Portion sizes, types of food, hunger levels, and more can become all-consuming if the diet isn't carefully managed. This can lead to eating disorders or disordered eating patterns. Two research studies looking at people who used MyFitnessPal (a calorie-tracking smartphone app) came to some disturbing conclusions. One showed that 38 percent of males using MyFitnessPal felt that their use of the app led to disordered eating. Another showed that college students who had a higher level of dietary restraint and fitness tracking were associated with eating disorder symptoms. If tracking your calories and exercise makes you anxious or more restrained or feel guilt or shame, or a general feeling of being out of control, it's time to stop using the app. See chapter 10 for more details on disordered eating patterns.

Training "high"

This means training with high carbohydrate availability. It means starting exercise with adequate glycogen stores in your muscles and liver. It can also mean eating carbs during exercise as a source of fuel.

You as a climber would want to use this approach to fuel climbing sessions. As you learned in earlier chapters, carbohydrates are useful for climbing. They fuel steady endurance climbing lasting several minutes up to several hours, as well as shorter, more intense sequences and sessions. Eating enough carbs, as well as starting out with adequate glycogen stores, will help you fuel your climbing or training session. It also helps reduce fatigue, aids training adaptations, and helps you keep your blood sugar normal to prevent it from becoming too low.

For those climbers who experience gastrointestinal distress when climbing, training with carbohydrates can help "train" your gut to tolerate them better. Gastrointestinal problems mainly occur in endurance athletes, but climbers can also experience problems from time to time. Getting used to eating foods during long climbing sessions can help your gut adapt and accept the fuel that you are giving your body.

Training with supplements

If you choose to use supplements, not all useful and effective supplements (see chapter 8) are needed all the time. Some supplements can be used strategically with the periodization concept in mind. For example, you may want to utilize creatine's performance-enhancing effects when you are in a strength-building or competition phase of your training cycle. Then, when you switch over to the off-season, you could stop using creatine for a time. You may use collagen during a period where you are healing and recovering from injury, but not otherwise. And caffeine may be ingested only when you really need it, such as a competition or a tough new route you're trying to send–though you wouldn't want to use it as a regular thing, since habitual use can lessen its effects.

Once you understand the concept of periodization, you can translate that concept over into weight loss. If you choose to try to drop some weight, you can periodize your diet to be in a calorie deficit temporarily when you need to, then go back to normal during the off-season. For instance, you may want to train at your body's natural set-point weight, then lose a few pounds/kilos for a hard grade or competition.

Weight Loss: All the Details

It may make sense to lose weight for a competition phase of your training, or if you are trying to send a huge project. Anecdotally, some climbers have "trained heavy" and "competed light," meaning you train with a few extra pounds/kilos on purpose, then cut some weight for the competition so you feel lighter when you climb. This hasn't ever been studied in climbers, so it's unknown if this is a smart tactic or is detrimental to your performance.

However, there are a few problems that could arise. If you lose weight right before you need to have enhanced power and performance, your power and performance could be compromised either from lean-muscle-mass loss or lack of adequate energy, or both. If you lose mostly water weight, you are likely climbing while either dehydrated or with depleted glycogen stores, or both. This would mean decreased power and performance, despite the fact that you weigh less. We know from research on weight-category athletes like boxers and wrestlers that when they lose weight in order to make their weight category, they can have decreased performance, dehydration, decreased nutrient intake, and abnormal hormone levels.

Keep all this in mind before you decide to lose weight. If you do end up actively trying to lose weight, read on to learn how to do it.

Hire a Dietitian

Seriously, you've heard me say it before, but you need a dietitian. Too many people try to lose weight on their own. They often become bogged down by misinformation, conflicting information, trends, and fads. If you want to lose weight safely and effectively without compromising climbing performance, seek the help of a sports dietitian or other qualified nutrition professional (emphasis on *qualified*). Dietitians depend on science and evidence rather than trends or quackery, so you will be getting useful advice for your training goals.

There are many people who call themselves "nutritionists" who aren't actually qualified. In the United States, "nutritionist" is not a regulated term. This means anyone can call themself one, even with zero training or experience. In addition, many "nutritionists" don't have the depth of knowledge in biology, biochemistry, nutrition, and science to give accurate information to their clients. Even doctors, physical therapists, chiropractors, and naturopaths are not qualified to give you nutrition advice. I have seen far too many clients who've gotten well-meaning but incorrect information from their healthcare providers. Just see a dietitian. Since nutrition is ALL dietitians do, we are very good at it!

A good dietitian will consider your lifestyle, food preferences, health history, current labs, activity level, training and health goals, cooking ability, and more. He or she will then craft a plan that is tailored to your individual needs.

United States Nutritionist Experience
WHICH PERSON WOULD YOU CHOOSE?

Registered dietitian: Minimum 4 years of college at an accredited university, 1200 hours of an internship, pass an exam, and continuing education (master's degree requirement as of 2024)

Certified Specialist in Sports dietitian: All the requirements of a registered dietitian, plus 2000 hours of sports nutrition experience, pass an exam, and continuing education

Health coach: 0–6 months

Holistic nutritionist: 6 months

Functional nutrition practitioner: 80 hours

Intuitive health coach: 200 hours

Nutrition & wellness certification: 6 months

Typical medical doctor: 25 hours of nutrition education

Weight Loss: (continued)

Get in a Calorie Deficit

In order to lose weight, you need to be in a calorie deficit. This means either eating less or exercising more, or a combination of both. Losing weight is a tricky business. Your body wants to be a certain weight, and you are basically trying to fight against your biology. To borrow an analogy from *Intuitive Eating*, by Evelyn Tribole, it is like trying to change your shoe size. If you currently are a size 8 (or maybe 39 if you're in Europe), it's like trying to shrink your foot into a size 6 (size 37).

You may have heard the old losing weight "math" that a pound of fat is equal to 3500 calories. So to lose one pound per week, you have to be in a calorie deficit of 500 calories per day (500 calories per day x 7 days = 3500 calories = 1 pound of fat). Here's the thing: Your body isn't a math equation.

Things like metabolism, your gut microbiome, stress hormones, hunger/satiety hormones, and genetics all determine how many calories you actually absorb and use. Calories (energy) you eat can have a few different pathways in your body: They can be absorbed, they can be used as energy, and they can be stored.

If two people both eat 2000 calories a day, they can use those calories differently depending on their body's metabolism and overall energy balance. The body doesn't magically or automatically store or burn calories just because you ate more or less.

The usual equation you'd see when thinking about weight loss goes something like this: Estimated calories your body needs to live + calories you need for exercise and activities = total calories needed each day.

Total calories needed each day - *total calories you actually ate* = calorie surplus or deficit.

Your body isn't a math equation, but food labels, tracking apps, and logging your food are pretty straightforward, right? Um, actually no.

Let's start with your estimated calorie needs. How did you determine that? There are many predictive equations that dietitians use to estimate calorie needs. These equations take into account your height, weight, age, gender, and activity level. If you know your body composition, a dietitian can also calculate your calorie needs based on your lean and fat mass (see Chapter 6 sidebar under "Female Athletes" for more information on body-composition testing, page 113). If you're lucky enough to have ever gotten calorie needs measured by an indirect calorimeter, you've got a pretty accurate calorie-needs goal. Otherwise, all the equations have a margin of error.

Let's say you do know your estimated calorie needs. Great. We know it's just an estimate, but it's a starting place. Next step is to know how many calories you are using every day. Take your baseline calorie needs (basic energy needed to support your body's normal processes like heart rate and respiration for 24 hours while lying still at a comfortable temperature). Multiply that by an activity factor. Then add in any calories burned while exercising.

Oh, you know how many calories you burned while exercising because your device told you? Great. Except that these have a margin of error, too. A wide and alarming one, apparently. Researchers who measured seven wrist-worn devices, including the FitBit and the Apple Watch, found that actual energy expenditure (calories burned) was so different than what the devices showed that the readings weren't even remotely reliable. Heart rate was, but not calories burned. The most accurate device they looked at (Apple Watch) was still 20 percent off from an indirect calorimetry measurement.

OK, so let's recap. First you need to know your estimated calorie needs. We know that there is a margin of error there. Next you need to know your calories burned. Definitely a margin of error there if you're relying on a device. Still a (narrower) margin of error if you are using a dietitian to help you calculate this otherwise.

Next you need to know how many calories you have eaten. How do you know that? You could look at food labels and nutrient database information. You could track your calories in an app, like MyFitnessPal (which, by the way, is notorious for underestimating actual calories you need to live and be nourished). But...you guessed it...there is a margin of error there, too. Calories reported on a food label can be up to 20 percent different than what is actually in the package. Estimated portion sizes on food without a label, like an apple, are even harder. A "medium" apple could be 83–116 calories. A third of a cup of peanuts could be 213–276 calories.

Weight Loss: Get in a Calorie Deficit (continued)

Then think about how you prepare the food. Cooking methods further change how many absorbable calories are available for your body. Cooking meat or an egg increases the amount of calories your body can absorb. Fibrous foods like vegetables, beans, and nuts are absorbed differently based on your gut bacteria. And food itself takes some energy (calories) just to digest.

Now you need to know how many calories your body is actually using and absorbing. This can vary based on gut microbiome, stress levels, hormones, the type of food it is, how the food is prepared, and other factors. There is absolutely no way to know how many calories your body is absorbing and using once you put it in your mouth.

Your body also will downregulate other body processes if you're in a calorie deficit for too long. Think of it as a calorie budget, just like your household budget. You have money for rent/mortgage, car/transportation, healthcare, food, clothing, and other things. If you have extra money, you can afford to buy something extra, or maybe save it. If you don't have enough money, you really cut back on expenses. Maybe you get a smaller, cheaper place to live. Or you don't spend money on entertainment. You don't buy extra clothes.

Your body is the same. If you have enough energy (calories), it can use it for all the things it needs, like maintaining bone health, immune function, heartbeat, respiration (breathing), reproduction (menstrual cycle for women), and so on. If you have extra calories, it stores energy for later use. But if you have a calorie deficit, it loses something. Your body could lose fat mass or lean muscle mass. But if you are not careful and go into too much of a deficit, your body starts to prioritize. Just like someone on a tight household budget, the body makes sure the necessities are "paid" for first. Maintaining heart rate and breathing is pretty important. But bone health, immunity, and reproduction could all be downregulated until you feed yourself enough overall calories to support these things.

You can see that if you are tracking your calories to get in a deficit, you may be wildly inaccurate. And also, a deficit may be harmful to overall health and performance. Here's a summary of how aiming for an energy deficit to lose weight by having your calories out > calories in can break down and eventually become meaningless.

Weight-loss steps

⬇

1: ESTIMATE BASAL CALORIE NEEDS

⬇

2: ESTIMATE CALORIE NEEDS FOR ACTIVITY LEVEL

⬇

3: ESTIMATE CALORIES EATEN

⬇

4: TRACK CALORIES BURNED

Where it can go wrong

⬇

MARGIN OF ERROR IN PREDICTIVE EQUATIONS

⬇

MARGIN OF ERROR IN ESTIMATING CALORIES BURNED USING ACTIVITY FACTORS AND TABLES

⬇

FOOD LABELS AND DATABASES CAN BE OFF BY 20 PERCENT

⬇

INACCURATE DEVICE READINGS

Net result
ARE YOU IN A CALORIE DEFICIT? NO WAY TO KNOW FOR SURE!

9 - NUTRITION PERIODIZATION

THE FAT-LOSS PYRAMID

BY ALAN ARAGON - @thealanaragon - alanaragon.com

This pyramid, created by Alan Aragon (used with permission), shows the essentials of weight loss. How many grams of carbs or fat you eat is much less important than maintaining an overall calorie deficit when trying to lose weight.

DIMINISHING IMPORTANCE →

- Supplementation
- Linear Versus Nonlinear Weekly Intake Tailored to Individual Preference
- Carbohydrates & Fat Intake Tailored to Individual Preference
- Sufficient Daily Protein within a Meal Pattern that Fosters Adherance
- Net Caloric Deficit, Realistic Progress Targets

REFERENCES: 1) Manore MM. *Int J Sport Nutr Exerc Metab*. 2012 Apr; (2): 139-54. 2) Aragon AA, et al. *J Int Soc Sports Nutr*. 2017 Jun 14; 14: 16. 3) Morton RW, et al. *Br J Sports Med*. 2018 Mar; 52(6): 376-384.

Sleep (minimum of 7 hours on average), patience (lots of it, kiddo), stress management, sound training, maximally satiating food choices, proper hydration, & essential micronutrition covered.

There is no strong or consistent research evidence that a specific supplement will produce significant fat loss (> 2 kg), especially over the long-term.[1] It's best to save your money, avoid undue adverse potential, and let diet and training do the magic.

Nonlinear caloric intake through the week has the potential benefit of increasing adherence. Claims of hormonal advantages through cyclical macro-nutrient intake (i.e., via increased carbs) are merely speculative. When there is one or more higher-calorie days per week, it gives the dieter a temporary break from the psychological (and in some cases physical) fatigue of dieting. This in turn can bolster adherence.

For the goal of fat loss, the proportion of carb and fat in the diet has a wide range of possibilities for individualization. What matters is honoring personal preference, since impact on body composition is primarily determined by protein and total calories.[2] Prefer low-carb? Perfectly fine. Keto? Great. High-carb, low-fat? Wonderful. Do you, as along as you can adhere to what you're doing in the long-term.

Total daily protein for maximizing muscle gain in non-dieting conditions is 1.6m–2.2 g/kg.[3] In lean, resistance-trained individuals, 2.3–3.1 g/kg of lean mass (roughly 1.8–2.6 g/kg of total bodyweight) optimizes muscle retention in hypocaloric condition.[4] Unlike the case of maximizing muscle gain,[5] muscle retention while dieting is possible at a very wide range of meal frequencies–as low as 2–3 meals, and as high as 6 or more.[2] Go with what you prefer, and can stick to.

The more fat to lose, the greater the deficit can be and still preserve lean muscle mass. Larger deficits (20–30 percent below maintenance) can be effective at the start of programs for obese and overweight individuals, while smaller deficits (10–20 percent below maintenance) are appropriate for those closer to their goal body-fat level. A loss of 0.5–1.0 kg (0.5–1.0 percent) per week is best for lean mass retention.[6]

4) Helms ER. et al. *Int J Sport Nutr Exerc Metab.* 2014 Apr; 24(2): 127-38. 5) Schoenfeld BJ, Aragon AA. *Journal of Orthopediac & Sports Physical Therapy*, 2018; 48(12): 911-914. 6) Helms ER, Aragon AA, Fitschen PJ. *J Int Soc Sports Nutr.* 2014 May 12; 11: 20.

Is Counting Calories a Lost Cause?

If there is no way to truly know precisely how many calories you need and burn, and how many calories you are eating, is counting calories a lost cause? Not necessarily. It can be eye-opening for people to do it, especially if you never have before. You might discover that you can do easy swaps throughout the day that will save calories, even if you don't know exactly how many you are eating. Journaling or tracking food intake can increase awareness, which can in turn help you lose weight.

For example, tracking calories might help you discover that you are drinking an extra 300 calories just in soda, juice, or beer. Cut that out and you're well on your way to being in a calorie deficit. You might learn that your favorite yogurt is 100 calories more than a different yogurt that you also enjoy. Swap it out. Or maybe you find you are overeating at night, mindlessly munching on snacks while watching TV. Just fuel yourself throughout the day so you're not hungry at night. Switch potato chips for air-popped popcorn. Easy changes can add up.

Alphabet Soup:
Ever wonder what all the acronyms mean? Here's a handy guide

BEE: Basal energy expenditure. Energy needed to carry out basic metabolic functions, such as breathing, normal cell turnover, enzymatic reactions, heart rate, etc.

BMR: Basal metabolic rate. Calories needed to support respiration, heart rate, etc. while at rest.

BPM: Beats per minute. Heart rate measured in number of beats per minute.

EPOC: Excess post-exercise oxygen consumption. Amount of oxygen required to restore the body to resting metabolism after a workout. Results in increased calorie burning after working out.

HIIT: High-intensity interval training. Specific training that uses high-intensity, anaerobic intervals with periods of recovery.

NEAT: Non-exercise activity thermogenesis. Movements other than purposeful exercise, such as fidgeting, etc.

RMR: Resting metabolic rate. Calories needed for BMR plus eating.

RPE: Rate of perceived exertion. A measure on a scale of 6–20 (or 1–10, based on which scale you use) of how hard you are working. The highest number indicates maximal exertion.

TEE: Total energy expenditure. Calories used from all activities and body processes.

VO2 Max: Volume of oxygen maximum. The amount of oxygen uptake used during exercise at maximum intensity.

Is Counting Calories a Lost Cause? (continued)

Be cautious not to go too low in calories. Consuming under about 1500 calories means you probably won't be able to eat all the required vitamins and minerals you need to be healthy. Cutting out too many calories also means your performance will suffer, and you are more prone to injuries. A general rule of thumb is to reduce your current calorie intake by about 10 percent to have a slow, gradual weight loss.

Another thing to keep in mind:

If you cut out carbohydrates, you will initially lose water weight. This is because glycogen, storage sugar in your liver and skeletal muscle, is stored with water. Since your body has to tap into those glycogen stores (since you aren't eating carbs), it will also shed some water weight. At first, you might see rapid weight loss, but it's not fat loss–it's just water and glycogen.

A better approach is to preserve carbs in your diet in order to fuel your climbing, but slowly reduce your calorie intake a bit at a time to encourage fat loss.

Many studies have also shown that eating enough protein can help with weight loss. This is because protein is very satisfying, so it helps keep you feeling full longer, curbing hunger. It is also because higher protein intake will preserve lean muscle mass as you are losing weight (as long as you are still working out). Current protein recommendations to preserve lean muscle mass while losing weight range from 1.6 to 3 grams per kilogram per day.

Keep in mind that, if you are aiming to lose weight, you won't simultaneously build muscle at the same time. Losing weight is a catabolic process, meaning it breaks down body tissues. This requires a calorie deficit. Building muscle is an anabolic process, meaning it builds new body tissue, which means your body needs calories to do so. Some studies show that people can indeed build muscle while losing fat, but this is a difficult balance. However, muscle mass can usually be maintained by continuing strength exercises while eating adequate protein during the fat-loss phase.

Need for Sleep

When thinking about trying to lose weight and enhance climbing performance, don't discount the importance of a good night's sleep. Sleep is often undervalued and overlooked as a part of becoming a better athlete. Your body repairs and restores itself while sleeping. If you don't get enough sleep, your performance will suffer...but so may your weight. Some studies show that people who get less sleep have higher body weights than those who get adequate sleep. Not enough sleep can increase your risk for type 2 diabetes, hypertension (high blood pressure), and cardiovascular disease. This is likely due to the fact that sleep disrupts hunger and satiety hormones, glucose regulation, and the production of other hormones like cortisol and insulin.

Just remember that consistently getting adequate sleep can help you in your weight and performance goals. You can't be a great climber without enough sleep. Lack of sleep also leads to mood disturbances (irritability) and lack of focus–not ideal conditions when trying to send a problem or crush a route.

Alcohol and Weight Loss

Consider this: 43 percent of Climbing Magazine's readers say that a cold beer is their post-climb drink of choice. While many people probably couldn't imagine climbing without the beer, it's time to re-think that post-climb beverage. Here's the thing: If you aren't worried about the next day—like you aren't going to climb again, do any training, or have to compete—beer after your climb is probably fine. But if you are serious about making training gains or losing weight, alcohol is just extra calories your body doesn't need.

Dropping alcohol is a simple way to cut out excess calories without changing other parts of your diet. Some people drop weight quickly just from abstaining from alcohol. This may happen if you are a semi-regular to regular drinker.

Alcohol also interferes with training adaptations in a number of ways (read on). So, if you want to get next-level climbing ability, consider cutting out alcohol, at least temporarily. Think of it as periodizing your alcohol intake. No alcohol during climbing season; add it back in during the off-season or if you don't have any big climbs coming up.

Here's what alcohol does to thwart your training:

» It interferes with other foods you could be eating instead. This means reduced opportunity for quality protein to repair muscles and quality carbs to restock glycogen.

» It interferes with cognition, which could lead to increased injury.

» It interferes with the availability of vitamins and minerals to the rest of the body—they are used to metabolize alcohol (a true toxin).

» It interferes with protein synthesis, which is the process that helps build and repair muscle.

» It leads to poor sleep quality. Sleep is crucial to health and athletic performance.

If you must drink alcohol, do so wisely. Don't drink it during a climbing session. This can lead to mistakes resulting in injury or death. Don't drink it if you are trying to make training gains, have a big climb or training session the next day, or you need to drive home from the crag or gym. Be smart.

Practical Weight-Loss Strategies

Considering everything you just read, I hope you critically analyze if you even want or need to lose weight. If you decide to proceed, be sure to work with a qualified sports dietitian to make sure you are eating for improved performance and supporting health as you lose weight. Also remember, you probably don't need to lose weight permanently—periodizing according to your training cycle and climbing goals is a better approach. It will allow your body to be at its natural weight for most of the time, opening up a better relationship with food and less restriction. And it allows for a lighter weight just for a short period of time when it may matter for sending a higher grade.

Eating plenty of vegetables, whole grains, legumes, fruit, nuts/seeds, and lean protein is the best approach. Avoid fad diets, extreme dieting techniques, and eliminating whole food groups.

Paying attention to hunger and fullness cues is extremely valuable for anyone, regardless of whether or not they're trying to lose weight. Your body knows better than any calorie-counting app, popular diet, "nutrition coach," supplement sales rep, or anyone else how much you need to eat. Mindful eating and intuitive eating are extremely valuable tools to maintain weight and health.

To learn how to pay attention to hunger and fullness, try rating yourself on a scale of zero to 10 throughout the day and at the beginning, middle, and end of each meal.

HUNGER/FULLNESS SCALE

0: Weak: So hungry you will gnaw your own leg off. You may feel weak, dizzy, nauseated, irritable, or find it hard to concentrate. Hunger pangs in your stomach may or may not be present.

1: Famished: You will eat anything in sight. This is the point where good food choices usually aren't made. You don't have the patience to prepare a meal; you just need to eat NOW.

2: Hungry: You are definitely needing to eat soon, but have enough time to make good food choices and prepare a quick meal or snack before you feel worse. This is the perfect time to eat—when healthful food is appetizing and you are ready to fuel yourself.

3: Mildly Hungry (or "snack hungry"): You could eat right now and feel good, but it's not urgent. You could also wait another 30–60 minutes and be OK.

4: Almost satisfied: While you are eating, you are still enjoying your food. If you stopped eating now, you would still feel like you need more.

5: Satisfied: A good place to stop eating. You feel fuller and physically heavier in your stomach. You feel like your meal was good.

6: More than satisfied: Your meal starts to not taste as good. Your stomach may expand more. You start to feel uncomfortably full.

7: Very full: The thought of more food is not appealing. Your stomach feels heavy. If you eat more, you may feel sick.

8: Overly full: Now you feel sick. You may feel heavy, nauseated, or bloated.

9: Painfully full: The thought of one more bite is horrible.

10: Just stop now: Unbutton your pants and go lie down to digest.

Your goal is to be a 2–3 when you begin eating—don't let yourself get to 0–1. And stop eating around 5–6. Hunger and fullness cues can take time to understand. Many adults have gotten out of tune with knowing when and how much to eat.

HUNGER/FULLNESS SCALE (continued)

Don't use external cues, like a diet plan, a food-label portion size, the time of day, or what someone tells you, as reasons to start or stop eating. Instead start focusing on using internal cues to know when to start and stop eating, such as the feeling in your stomach, irritability, nausea, feeling pleasantly full, etc. Trust your body. If you listen, over time you will learn to discern the cues it is telling you. It knows when, what, and how much you need to eat.

Be sure to fuel yourself regularly throughout the day. Many people gain weight by accident when they under-eat or skip breakfast, eat a small lunch, and then feel famished by dinnertime. Instead of having a normal dinner, they overeat (or choose less healthful foods), then keep eating after dinner and into the night. Not only is this a poor strategy for weight loss, it's not a good strategy for sports performance fueling either.

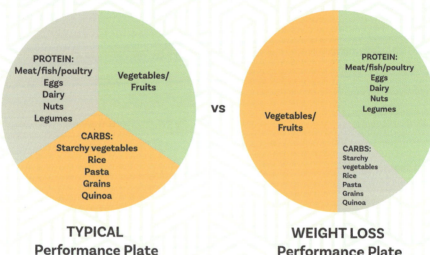

TYPICAL Performance Plate vs **WEIGHT LOSS Performance Plate**

Start each meal or snack with vegetables or fruit and protein. Then round it out with some carbohydrate. Protein and fiber help you feel full and satisfied. Here are some examples of snacks that have both protein and fiber:

- Hummus and vegetables
- Hummus and whole-grain crackers or pita
- Apple slices and peanut butter
- Cottage cheese and berries
- Smoothie made with fruit, spinach, and yogurt
- Hardboiled egg with fruit
- String cheese with a banana
- Jerky and an orange
- Greek yogurt and berries
- Mixed nuts with raisins
- Whole-grain toast with almond butter
- Edamame

With these tips in mind, remember to also add in a sports dietitian to help you lose weight safely and effectively. There's nothing better than a qualified pro on your side to help you achieve your climbing goals.

And if you decide to diet in order to lose weight, make sure you don't continue with the diet if it becomes harmful to your health and training.

How to know when to stop dieting (even if you haven't met your goal weight):

- You are thinking about food and what to eat constantly. Food occupies a significant portion of your thoughts
- You are becoming more anxious about your food choices
- You can't find anything to eat within your diet plan when going out with friends, to restaurants, or to other social occasions
- You feel guilt or shame when you eat something "unhealthy" or not in your diet plan
- You are moody or irritable
- You plateau in your training or climbing
- Your climbing ability decreases
- You have rigid or perfectionistic thinking regarding your food and exercise choices
- You are compulsive about tracking your weight, calories, training, etc.
- Friends or family tell you that you look too thin or express concern about your relationship to food or your body
- You lose your period or it becomes irregular (females only)
- You feel fatigued
- You feel like your mind is not as focused or sharp
- You find yourself overeating or bingeing
- You become sick or injured more often
- You become anemic or have other nutrient deficiencies

These are signs that you are under-nourishing your body. Stop the diet and eat normally again. Check in with your doctor and dietitian as well. I've made the following tracking chart (page 190) for you to track your health and mood as you diet. This can help you determine if you need to stop the diet and if you're getting enough to eat. Track these symptoms weekly. If you see any negative changes, such as irritability, decreased libido, increased hunger, or increased resting heart rate, this is your body telling you that it needs more calories. Stop the diet and consult a doctor and dietitian.

9 - NUTRITION PERIODIZATION

Date	Current weight	Resting heart rate	Mood (happy, sad, irritable, etc.)	Libido 0–10	Hunger level 0–10	Any illness?	Any injury?	Fatigue level 0–10

THE WRAP-UP FOR NUTRITION PERIODIZATION

Losing weight may or may not help you with climbing. Weight loss isn't a straight math equation of calories in < calories out. Your body has complex metabolic processes that determine how much you weigh, how many calories you absorb, and how much fat you may lose. Eating adequate protein can help with feeling full and also preserve lean muscle tissue as you lose weight. Dieting can lead to serious mental and physical health consequences, as well as decreased climbing performance. Talk to a sports dietitian before implementing any weight-loss measures. Make sure you understand the reasoning and science before implementing any diet changes, to make sure they are right for you.

CHAPTER 9 REFERENCES

"American College of Sports Medicine's Resource Manual for Guidelines for Exercise Testing and Prescription." 2014. 7th edition: 304.

Bayon, Virginie, Damien Leger, Danielle Merino-Gome, Marie-Vecchierini, Chennaoui. 2014. "Sleep Debt and Obesity." *Annals of Medicine* 46 no. 5: 1-9.

Burke, Louise M. 2015. "Re-Examining High-Fat Diets for Sports Performance: Did We Call the 'Nail in the Coffin' Too Soon?" *Journal of Sports Medicine* 45 Suppl 1: 33-49.

Burke, Louise M., Greg R. Collier, Elizabeth M. Broad, Peter G. Davis, David T. Martin, Andrew J. Sanigorski, Mark Hargreaves. 2003. "Effect of Alcohol Intake on Muscle Glycogen Storage After Prolonged Exercise." *Journal of Applied Physiology* 95 no. 3: 983-90.

"Climbing Magazine Media Kit." Climbing Magazine (Digital)   Date of Access: July 2, 2018. https://www.climbing.com/page/advertise/.

Hawley, John A., Cartsen Lundby, James D. Cotter, Louise M. Burke. 2018. "Maximizing Cellular Adaptation to Endurance Exercise in Skeletal Muscle." *Cell Metabolism* 27 no. 5: 962-976.

Hector, Amy J., Stuart M. Phillips. 2018. "Protein Recommendations for Weight Loss in Elite Athletes: A Focus on Body Composition and Performance." *International Journal of Sports Nutrition and Exercise Metabolism* 28 no. 2: 170-177.

Horne, Benjamin D. Joseph B. Muhlestein, Jefferey L. Anderson. 2015. "Health Effects of Intermittent Fasting: Hormesis or Harm? A Systematic Review." *American Journal of Clinical Nutrition* 102 no. 2: 464-470.

Impey, Samuel G., Mark A. Hearris, Kelly M. Hammond, Jonathan D. Bartlett, Julien Louis, Graeme L. Close, James P. Morton. 2018. "Fuel for the Work Required: A Theoretical Framework for Carbohydrate Periodization and the Glycogen Threshold Hypothesis." *Sports Medicine* 48 no. 5: 1031-1048.

Irfan, Yildirim. 2015. "Associations Among Dehydration, Testosterone and Stress Hormones in Terms of Body Weight Loss Before Competition." *American Journal of the Medical Sciences* 350 no. 2: 103-108.

Jeukendrup, Asker E. 2017. "Periodized Nutrition for Athletes." *Journal of Sports Medicine* 47 Suppl 1: S51-S63.

Kondo, Emi, Hiroyuki Sagayama, Yosuke Yamada, Keisuke Shiose, Takuya Osawa, Keiko Motonaga, Shiori, Akiko Kamei, Kohei Nakajima, Yasuki Higaki, Tanaka Hiroaki, Hideyuki Takahashi, Koji Okamura. 2018. "Energy Deficit Required for Rapid Weight Loss in Elite Collegiate Wrestlers." *Nutrients* 10 no. 5 pii: E536.

Linardon, Jake, Mariel Messer. 2019. "My Fitness Pal Usage in Men: Associations With Eating Disorder Symptoms and Psychosocial Impairment." *Eating Behaviors* 33: 13-17.

Loucks, Anne B., Bente Kiens, Hattie H. Wright. 2012. "Energy Availability in Athletes." *Journal of Sports Sciences* 29: sup1: S7-S15.

Lucas, James. July 17, 2018. "Peaches Preaches: Confessions of a Weight-Obsessed Climber." Accessed: September 4, 2018. **https://www.climbing.com/people/peaches-preaches-confessions-of-a-weight-obsessed-climber/**

Magee, Lorrie, Lauren Hale. 2013. "Longitudinal Associations Between Sleep Duration and Subsequent Weight Gain: A Systematic Review." *Sleep Medicine Review* 16 no. 3: 231-241.

Merrells, Krystal J., James K. Friel, Maria Knaus, Miyoung Suh. 2008. "Following 2 Diet-Restricted Male Outdoor Rock Climbers: Impact on Oxidative Stress and Improvements in Markers of Cardiovascular Risk." *Applied Physiolology, Nutrition, and Metabolism* 33 no. 6: 1250-1256.

Morton RW, Murphy KT, McKellar SR, Schenfeld BJ, Henselmans M, Helms E., Phillips SM. 2017. "A Systematic Review, Meta-Analysis and Meta-Regression of the Effect of Protein Supplementation on Resistance Training-Induced Gains in Muscle Mass and Strength in Healthy Adults." British *Journal of Sports Medicine*, 52: 376-384.

Mozaffarian, Dariush, Tao Hao, Eric B. Rimm, Walter C. Willett, Frank C. Hu. 2011. "Changes in Diet and Lifestyle and Long-term Weight Gain in Women and Men." *New England Journal of Medicine*, 364: 2392-2404.

O'Connor, Helen, Alexandra Honey, Ian Caterson. 2015. "Weight Loss and the Athlete." *Clinical Sports Nutrition* edited by Louise Burke and Vicki Deakin. Sydney, Australia: McGraw Hill Education.

O' Connor, Helen. Tim Olds, Ronald J. Maughan. 2007. "Physique and Performance for Track and Field Events." *Journal of Sports Sciences* 25 S1: S49-S60.

Parr, Evelyn B., Donny M. Camera, José L. Areta, Louise M. Burke, Stuart M. Phillips, John A. Hawley, Vernon G. Coffey. 2014. "Alcohol Ingestion Impairs Maximal Post-Exercise Rates of Myofibrillar Protein Synthesis Following a Single Bout of Concurrent Training." *PLoS One* 9 no. 2: e88384.

Parr, Maria-Kristina, A. Pokrywka, D. Kwiatkowska, W. Schäzer. 2014. "Ingestion of Designer Supplements Produced Positive Doping Cases Unexpected By the Athletes." *Biology of Sport*, 28 no. 3: 153-157.

Phillips, Stuart M., Amy J. Hector. 2018. "Protein Recommendations for Weight Loss in Elite Athletes: A Focus on Body Composition and Performance." *International Journal of Sports Nutrition and Exercise Metabolism* 28 no. 2: 170-177.

Relijic, Dejan, Joachim Jost, Kirsten Dickau, Ralf Kinscherf, Gabriel Bonaterra, Birgit Friedmann-Bette. 2015. "Effects of Pre-Competitional Rapid Weight Loss on Nutrition, Vitamin Status and Oxidative Stress in Elite Boxers." *Journal of Sports Sciences* 33 no. 5: 437-48.

Shcherbina, Anna. C., Mikael Mattsson, Daryl Waggott, Heidi Salisbury, Jeffery W. Christle, Trevor Hastie, Matthew T. Wheeler, Euan A. Ashley. 2017. "Accuracy in Wrist-Worn, Sensor-Based Measurements of Heart Rate and Energy Expenditure in a Diverse Cohort." *Journal of Personalized Medicine* 7 no. 2: 3.

Simpson, Courtney, Suzanne E. Mazzeo. 2017. "Calorie Counting and Fitness Tracking Technology: Associations with Eating Disorder Symptomology." *Eating Behaviors* 26: 89-92.

Stellingwerff, Trent. 2018. "Case-study: Body Composition Periodization in an Olympic-Level Female Middle-Distance Runner Over a 9-Year Career." *International Journal of Sports Nutrition and Exercise Metabolism* 28 no. 4: 428-433.

Taylor, Jerome, Jack Geldard. 2008. "Dangerously Thin'" Climbers Face Ban." Independent (digital) **https://www.independent.co.uk/news/world/europe/dangerously-thin-climbers-face-ban-867625.html**

Tinsley, Grant M., Paul M. La Bounty. 2015. "Effects of Intermittent Fasting on Body Composition and Clinical Health Markers in Humans." *Nutrition Review*, 73 no. 10: 661-674.

Tzur, Adam, Brandon Roberts, Alex Leaf. 2018. "The Ketogenic Diet's Impact on Body Fat, Muscle Mass, Strength, and Endurance." **https://sci-fit.net/ketogenic-diet-fat-muscle-performance/**

Watts, Philip B., Martin DT, Durtschi S. 1993. "Anthropometric Profiles of Elite Male and Female Competitive Sport Rock Climbers." *Journal of Sports Science* 11 no. 2: 113-117.

Wroble, Kimberly A., Morgan N. Trott, George E. Scheitzer, Rabia S. Rahman, Patrick V. Kelly, Edward P. Weiss. 2018. "Low-Carbohydrate, Ketogenic Diet Impairs Anaerobic Exercise Performance in Exercise-Trained Women and Men: A Randomized-Sequence Crossover Trial." *The Journal of Sports Medicine and Physical Fitness* 59 no. 4: 600-607.

10 - EATING DISORDERS AND DISORDERED EATING

CHAPTER 10

HAVING A HEALTHY RELATIONSHIP WITH FOOD AND YOUR BODY
EATING DISORDERS AND DISORDERED EATING

Emily Harrington, professional climber and five-time US National Champion, has summited Mt. Everest, completed a free ascent of *Golden Gate* on El Capitan (5.13b), and has struggled with food restriction, as Nora Caplan-Bricker writes in Outside Magazine.

Sasha DiGuilian, first North American woman to climb a 5.14d, three-time US National Champion, and female Overall World Champion, has struggled with eating restrictively and then feeling guilt after indulging. She wrote in 2018 in Outside Magazine about how she is trying to change the way she thinks about her body and compare herself to others less often.

> Self-acceptance is a process, even for climbers with stunning physical achievements.

From the world's top climbers to the fledgling nine-year-old at the local indoor gym, body-image issues and disordered eating patterns can arise. If these patterns continue undetected, they can result in mental and physical health issues with profound consequences.

Rock climbing, as you know, demands a high strength-to-weight ratio. Meaning, if you can be light but also strong, you'll typically perform better. Picture someone who is very heavy—either from muscles or fat, or both—climbing up a cliff. Now picture someone who is light and small. The perception is that lighter climbers are better climbers. However, this has never been studied or proven. Bigger-bodied people can and do climb all the time! The few studies that exist regarding elite climbers' anthropometrics (measurements of the body, such as height and weight) show that most top climbers are lighter, leaner, and shorter than other athletes, which may be why there is a strong perception that to be a better climber, you need to be lighter.

10 - EATING DISORDERS AND DISORDERED EATING

There is not much known about climbers and eating disorders. At the time of this writing, there are only two studies exploring climbers' food intake and disordered eating patterns. Some anecdotal evidence suggests that some climbers may diet or have disordered eating patterns. We know that climbers don't like extra weight—on your rack or on your body—so it makes sense that there may be some disordered eating within the climbing community.

Other athletes in sports that are considered "aesthetic" (meaning, those who compete usually excel partially because of perceived body shape or beauty), like gymnastics, ballet, and synchronized swimming, are prone to disordered eating patterns. Sports with weight categories, like wrestling, rowing, and boxing, also have athletes with disordered eating patterns. These athletes alter the way they eat in a manner that helps them conform to a certain weight or body image. Still other sports like running and cycling—where you have to carry your body weight over a distance—also have athletes with disordered eating patterns. If you are lighter, it's easier to run or cycle farther, right? Cyclists spend thousands of dollars for bikes that are lighter by only a matter of grams. Why not eat less to lose body weight as well? So goes the thinking.

Climbers may be no different. I would argue that hefting your body weight up a wall with a few extra pounds is probably harder than running or cycling with a few extra pounds. So how do you shed those pounds? Dieting.

Here are some sobering statistics: **Up to 94 percent of athletes in weight-class sports use extreme weight-control methods, such as dieting, diuretics, and laxatives, in order to make weight.** Jorunn Sundgot-Borgen, an internationally known sports researcher, found that 40–42 percent of females and 17–18 percent of males in aesthetic sports (such as ice skating, dancing, and gymnastics) have disordered eating patterns. Thirty to 35 percent of females and 17–18 percent of males in weight-class sports (where there are specific weight categories, such as boxing, wrestling, and rowing) have disordered eating patterns. Twenty-eight percent of elite athletes report not being fully recovered from an eating disorder even 15–20 years later. That is a huge number of athletes affected by disordered eating patterns.

There is one unpublished study in which researchers surveyed 604 climbers to assess whether they exhibited disordered eating. They found that among sport lead climbers, about 9 percent of them engaged in disordered eating patterns. About 17 percent of females and 6 percent of males surveyed reported disordered eating patterns. In addition, elite climbers demonstrated more-disordered eating patterns. This study just scratches the surface of what research needs to be done in the climbing world. The more we understand about climbers and their eating patterns, the better we can help with overall health and performance.

This chapter is probably the most important one in the whole book. That is because eating disorders, disordered eating, and body-image issues can wreak havoc in a person's life. Even with proper treatment, it can haunt them for years in the form of negative thoughts, irreversible health consequences, and disrupted relationships with food, themselves, and others. Anyone–regardless of gender, ethnicity, body type, age, weight, socioeconomic status, or athletic ability–can develop an eating disorder. The old stereotype of a thin, white, rich female with anorexia is gone.

In sports nutrition, there is a fine line between eating well to enhance performance—eating well for the sake of health or the sport-and obsessing over eating so much that it becomes a concern. At times, athletes can exhibit disordered eating, but it isn't labeled as such, and is masked behind the more acceptable "eating for sports performance."

Throughout this chapter, I will use the phrase "disordered eating". An eating disorder is a specific condition with specific diagnostic criteria. Conditions like anorexia nervosa and bulimia nervosa come with guidelines to determine if a person is suffering from these serious mental health conditions. Disordered eating is not a clinical diagnosis, but indicates that eating patterns a climber is engaging in are not normal or supportive of mental and physical health.

For example, some anorexia nervosa diagnostic criteria include:
- Restriction of energy (calorie) intake
- Intense fear of gaining weight (or getting fat)
- Body dysmorphia, which is distortion in the way a person views their body. People with anorexia often view themselves as fat when in fact they are very thin.

Some diagnostic criteria for bulimia nervosa include:
- Episodes of binge eating that are recurrent, at least once a week for three months
- Use of purging to eliminate food from the body, such as vomiting, use of laxatives, or excessive exercise
- Body-image acceptance is tied to perceived weight or body shape

These are two commonly known eating disorders, but there are others, such as Binge Eating Disorder and Avoidant/Restrictive Food Intake Disorder.

In addition to these traditional definitions and formal diagnostic criteria for eating disorders, there is a whole spectrum of disordered eating patterns and disturbances with body image. For example, one person might have body-image dysmorphia and eat restrictively, but not necessarily meet all the criteria for a formal diagnosis of anorexia. Another person might display signs of orthorexia, which is the pursuit of eating "perfect," "clean," or "healthy" to the point that it disrupts their normal lifestyle and social interactions, as well as occupies a huge portion of their thoughts and time to learn about, procure, prepare, and eat "healthy" food.

This is why I will use the term "disordered eating" throughout the chapter. Disordered eating captures the whole spectrum of eating and behavioral patterns that might occur. I am using this phrase to capture diagnosable eating disorders, orthorexia, and everything in between.

There are serious health and performance consequences that stem from disordered eating.

When a person doesn't eat enough calories to support their body processes, sport and training, and growth (in children and adolescents), they're in a state of low energy availability, aka Relative Energy Deficiency in Sport (RED-S). Low energy intake can be intentional, such as when an athlete cuts back on calories in order to lose weight or when eating disorders occur. Or it can be unintentional, such as an athlete being too busy to eat, skipping meals, or not realizing they need to eat more in order to support their training and climbing.

In my original research on adolescent rock climbers, I found that my cohort didn't have an increased risk for disordered eating patterns, but they did under-eat overall calories, fat, and carbohydrates. Especially concerning was that these were adolescents, who need to eat enough to fuel not only their sport and daily activities, but growth and puberty as well. Under-eating whether intentionally or inadvertently can lead to health and performance problems.

Did you know your body needs calories to exist? Many clients I've met with are surprised to learn that they burn calories in their sleep. "But I'm not doing anything!" they say. Except you are. You are breathing. Your heart is beating. Your cells are turning over, getting rid of old ones and making new ones. You are healing. You are dreaming (your brain uses energy!). You are building up muscle tissue that you tore down during that climbing session.

If you simply lie down for 24 hours, you will use calories. If you are lying still in a room at a comfortable temperature, you are metabolizing anywhere from about 1100–1700 calories per 24 hours. This is called your basal metabolic rate (BMR).

Now take that BMR and add in your activity level. Did you walk around the house? Do laundry? Think? Cook? Sit at a desk? Drive? Climb? Lift weights? All of these activities use additional calories. If you aren't eating to fuel all these activities, your body starts to tap into stores it already has. Maybe it downregulates your immune system. After all, that is "optional," but breathing and circulation are not. It can break down your muscle and fat tissue, using these for energy since it's not getting enough from food. It can downregulate reproductive systems. It knows that if there isn't enough food, it's not smart to produce offspring. Your body knows to wait until there's enough food to support a growing baby. Your body can also reduce bone turnover, meaning you don't have enough bone density to last you through your adult years, increasing the risk of fracture.

Whether intentional or not, being in a state of low energy availability is harmful for your health. Depending on how long this lasts (some people live like this for months or years), permanent damage to your health can result. Here are some consequences of low energy availability.

Health consequence	Performance consequences	Possible negative outcomes
Reduced lean body mass	Plateaued training gains, or decreased climbing ability	Decreased strength
Dehydration	Decreased ability to regulate body temperature. Possibly fatal.	Death, acute renal failure
Glycogen depletion	Reduced climbing ability and endurance	Drop in blood sugar, possible medical emergency
Increased perceived exertion and fatigue	Reduced climbing ability and training adaptations	Overtraining and injury
Loss of lean muscle mass	Reduced climbing ability	Heart and other organs are sometimes compromised
Decreased training adaptations	Reduced climbing ability	Possible increased injury
Loss of bone density	Increased risk of fractures	Increased risk of osteoporosis and fractures
Increased stress	Fatigue, injuries	Long-term inflammation
Decreased immune function	Increased illnesses	Declining health, decreased climbing performance
Decreased metabolic rate	Decreased climbing performance	Difficulty losing weight, even if prudent and done in a safe manner
Irregular or missed periods (females)	Decreased climbing performance	Low bone density, osteoporosis, fractures, decreased fertility
Decreased height (adolescents)	Possible improved performance—but at what cost?	You may not grow as tall as you could have with adequate calorie intake throughout puberty
Delayed puberty (adolescents)	Possible improved performance—but at what cost?	Possible decreased fertility and inability to conceive or be virile in the future
Reproductive hormonal changes (males)	Possible decreased ability to make and maintain lean muscle mass	Possible decreased fertility, decreased testosterone
Mood disturbances	Irritability with self or teammates. Negative thoughts lead to decreased performance.	Need for mental health services and therapy long-term with diagnosis of an eating disorder
Gastrointestinal problems	Discomfort from diarrhea, constipation, and/or bloating may interfere with training and competition	Gut microbiome disturbances and gastrointestinal problems (such as killing gastrointestinal cells from frequent fasting)
Oxygen uptake	Increased rate of perceived exertion	Decreased climbing performance

10 - EATING DISORDERS AND DISORDERED EATING

Here is more information about each disordered-eating category. This section has some deep questions to ask yourself. Take time to ponder and think about them. If you feel something is amiss in your eating habits, please reach out to a qualified health professional. There is a list of resources at the end of the chapter.

Anorexia Nervosa

Anorexia nervosa is more than just starving oneself to become thin. It is a serious mental illness that needs thorough and immediate treatment. It can have lasting health implications. It has the highest mortality rate of any mental illness, and some suffering from anorexia even commit suicide. A person can be at a normal weight (or even overweight) and still be suffering from anorexia.

Here are some signs and symptoms of anorexia:
» Rapid and/or extreme weight loss
» Behavioral changes
» Mood disturbances
» Use of methods of purging calories, such as laxatives and excessive exercise
» Hair loss or thinning
» Sensitivity to cold
» Fatigue
» Lost or irregular periods
» Dizziness, especially when going from sitting to standing
» Strange eating habits or food rituals, such as separating all foods on the plate, or cutting up food into tiny pieces
» Intense fear of becoming fat
» Obsession with eating, counting calories, or over kind of diet

Health complications from anorexia can include:
» Irregular heart rhythms and cardiac arrest
» Heart, kidney, or liver failure
» Loss of bone density, osteoporosis, and increased risk of fracture
» Gastrointestinal issues, such as bloating, constipation, malabsorption, and food intolerances
» Loss of period or irregular periods
» Infertility
» Anemia

Bulimia Nervosa

When people hear the word "bulimia," they often think of someone vomiting after eating in order to maintain or lose weight. Although this can be a part of bulimia, it is a complex mental illness that demands thorough treatment and ample compassion.

People suffering from bulimia have a pattern of "bingeing" in which they overeat a huge quantity of food in a short amount of time, then "purge" by either vomiting, laxative use, excessive exercise, diuretics, or a combination of these things. It is coupled with a negative body image and desire to become thinner or prevent weight gain.

Like anorexia, bulimia carries serious health risks and long-term health complications if not treated correctly and promptly.

Some signs and symptoms of bulimia are:
» Consuming large amounts of food, usually rapidly and in secret with a feeling of loss of control
» Guilt and shame associated with the bingeing episode
» Slow heart rate
» Dizziness and/or low blood pressure, especially when going from sitting to standing
» Vomiting, spitting food out, and laxative and diuretic use
» Swelling in the cheeks or jaw (from vomiting)
» Scars on the backs of the hands (from vomiting)
» Frequent use of the bathroom after meals
» Fear of gaining weight
» Change in social routines or withdrawal from friends and family
» Worsening performance at school, sports, work, or other activities

Health complications from bulimia can include:
» Irregular heartbeat
» Heart failure
» Electrolyte imbalances
» Dehydration
» Edema (swelling in ankles from water retention)
» Ulcers
» Pancreatitis
» Tooth decay and esophageal damage from vomiting
» Digestive problems
» Fatigue

Binge Eating Disorder (BED)

Binge eating disorder is a bit different than bulimia in that a person suffering from BED would not try to purge or compensate for the binge. There is no vomiting, laxatives, diuretics, or extreme exercising. The tendency to develop BED is often genetic. There are good treatment options that have helped many people to achieve recovery.

Here are some signs and symptoms of BED:
» Eating very rapidly
» Eating until feeling very full, uncomfortably so
» Eating large amounts of food even when not hungry
» Eating alone to hide the amount of food eaten
» Feelings of guilt, embarrassment, shame, or disgust with oneself after bingeing

Health complications from BED can include:
» High cholesterol
» High blood pressure
» Increased risk for heart disease and type 2 diabetes
» Gastrointestinal problems, such as constipation, diarrhea, and acid reflux

Orthorexia

Orthorexia is a non-medical, non-specific term that was coined by Dr. Stephen Bratman to describe the pursuit of "clean," "healthy," or "perfect" eating to the extent that it interferes with someone's day-to-day life. It is an obsession with healthy eating that can be disruptive to a person's relationships with their friends and family members, as well as lead to negative health consequences. Dr. Bratman wrote a book called *Health Food Junkies*. In it, he has a self-assessment quiz designed to detect if you are developing (or have) orthorexia.*

1) I spend so much of my life thinking about, choosing, and preparing healthy food that it interferes with other dimensions of my life, such as love, creativity, family, friendship, work, and school.

2) When I eat any food I regard to be unhealthy, I feel anxious, guilty, impure, unclean, and/or defiled; even to be near such foods disturbs me, and I feel judgmental of others who eat such foods.

3) My personal sense of peace, happiness, joy, safety, and self-esteem is excessively dependent on the purity and righteousness of what I eat.

4) Sometimes I would like to relax my self-imposed "good food" rules for a special occasion, such as a wedding or a meal with family and friends, but I find that I cannot. (Note: If you have a medical condition in which it is unsafe for you to make ANY exception to your diet, then this item does not apply.)

5) Over time, I have steadily eliminated more foods and expanded my list of food rules in an attempt to maintain or enhance health benefits; sometimes, I may take an existing food theory and add to it with beliefs of my own.

6) Following my theory of healthy eating has caused me to lose more weight than most people would say is good for me or has caused other signs of malnutrition such as hair loss, loss of menstruation, or skin problems.

A "yes" answer to any of these questions means you may have or be developing orthorexia.

Used with permission from Dr. Steven Bratman

Other Specified Feeding and Eating Disorders (Osfed)

OSFED is a long and awkward acronym that refers to other eating disorders that don't quite meet the diagnostic criteria for the principal disorders. It includes orthorexia as mentioned above. It also includes exercise that is compulsive or obsessive, as well as body dysmorphic disorder, in which a person has a distorted image or obsession over their weight and body shape to the point that it interferes with normal functioning. Large amounts of time and/or money may be spent on changing the body through diet, exercise, surgery, cosmetic procedures, etc.

Here are some signs and symptoms of OSFED:
» Dieting by restricting calories or whole food groups
» Excessive exercise
» Purging with laxatives, diuretics, vomiting, or excessive exercise
» Distorted body image
» Strange food behaviors, such as cutting food into tiny pieces or having many food rules
» Obsession with eating "clean," "pure," or "perfect"
» Shame, anxiety, and guilt associated with eating
» Hiding behaviors or feeling a loss of control over behaviors, such as eating to be overly full, hiding food, or bingeing at night when no one can witness the binge

Health complications from OSFED can include:
» Unintended extreme weight loss or gain
» High or low blood pressure
» High or low blood sugar (especially in those with diabetes)
» Missing nutrients in one's diet
» Anemia

SCOFF Questionnaire

The SCOFF questionnaire was designed to detect whether a person has an eating disorder. Here are the questions.

» Do you make yourself **S**ick (vomit) because you feel uncomfortably full?
» Do you worry you have lost **C**ontrol over how much you eat?
» Have you recently lost more than **O**ne stone (about 14 pounds) in a three-month period?
» Do you believe yourself to be **F**at when others say you are too thin?
» Would you say that **F**ood dominates your life?

One point for every "yes." A score of ≥2 indicates a likely case of anorexia nervosa or bulimia.

10 - EATING DISORDERS AND DISORDERED EATING

Below is a chart designed by sports psychologist Kate Bennett. It lists characteristics of seeking athletic excellence, and then contrasts these with what exercise dependency looks like. This is similar to seeking good health through nutrition vs. what disordered eating looks like.

	Athletic Excellence	**Exercise Dependency**
EXERCISE	Builds fitness Supports Competition	Defines Identity
GOAL	Excel athletically	Alter appearance Manage internal discomfort
MINDSET	Flexible Adaptable Rational	Rigid Compulsive Anxious
INTENSITY & VOLUME	Varies Rest: Essential Sweat: Result of effort Suffering: Gains	Constant Rest: Unnecessary Sweat: Essential Suffering: Required
NUMBERS	Feedback Guidance	Obsession Preoccupation
PERFORMANCE	Incremental progress	Plateaus/Declines
PLAN	Seasonal periodization Interruption: Concern Injuries/Illness: Recover & Modify	Daily need Interruption: Intolerable Injuries/Illness: Ignore
KNOWLEDGE	Resourceful Curious Open-minded	Untrusting Resistant Close-minded
PLEASURE	Inherent sense of joy Satisfaction	Boring Obligation

Used with permission from Dr. Kate Bennett

Similarly, these principles can be applied to your relationship with food.

Healthy relationship with food: seeking athletic excellence through nutrition	Unhealthy relationship with food/ disordered eating patterns
Use food as fuel	Anxious about how much, when, and what to eat
Food can be for enjoyment and pleasure	Use food to cope with emotions
Flexibility in food choice	Rigidity in food choices
Paying attention to hunger and fullness cues—eat when hungry, stop when full. Internal cues guide food intake.	External cues guide food intake: the time, the diet rules, the coach or parent, the perceived correct portion size, etc.
Variety of food choices	Restriction in food choices
Satisfaction with food choices and amount eaten	Guilt, shame, or regret with food choices

What To Do If You Suspect Disordered Eating

If you or someone you know possibly has disordered eating, there are a few things to understand. First, it is a mental illness that needs immediate treatment. It is not something that will go away if the person "tries harder" or is convinced to think a certain way. Disordered eating is serious and can cause permanent and damaging changes to a person's health, social life, family life, and work life. Your climbing ability is also at risk if you have an eating disorder. You may feel that it's easier to climb at first if you lose some weight. But, over time, disordered eating will compromise your climbing performance.

Think of disordered eating as a medical condition that needs proper treatment, because that is exactly what it is. Treat it with gravity and respect. Get treatment from qualified, experienced medical professionals. Don't be afraid, embarrassed, or ashamed if you need help. There are wonderful resources and treatment options to help you get back on track.

How to Return to Climbing After Disordered Eating

Your treatment team, which should include a doctor, therapist, and dietitian, will help you determine when it is safe (mentally and physically) to return to climbing. It may be helpful for you to climb during treatment, but your team will guide you as to how much, how often, and how intense.

If you have been diagnosed with Relative Energy Deficiency in Sport (RED-S), which is common with disordered eating, the International Olympic Committee has formulated a set of criteria to help guide your team to know when the time is right to return to training and competition. (For more on RED-S, see chapter 6.)

This is called RED-S CAT (Clinical Assessment Tool). This rates the athlete's risk of health complications into "red light," "yellow light," and "green light" categories. "Red light" includes anorexia or other eating disorders, cardiac abnormalities, dehydration, and unstable, life-threatening conditions. This means no climbing (or other sports) until stabilized and at least partially recovered.

"Yellow light" includes abnormally low body fat, slowed growth in children, significant weight loss (5–10 percent) in one month, abnormal menstrual cycle, decreased bone-mineral density, and lack of progress. Athletes may train and compete as long as they are medically cleared and following the treatment plan.

"Green light" includes healthy eating habits, adequate bone-mineral density, and a healthy body composition. Athletes may train and compete without restrictions.

Work closely with your whole treatment team to make sure you understand what to do to get yourself healthy again. They will help guide you to the point that you are ready to train, compete, and climb again.

How to Return to Climbing After Disordered Eating (continued)

Surround yourself with positive people who will support you on your journey. Follow social media accounts that carry body-positive messages. Don't follow accounts that are steeped in dieting culture or strict rules about food, or only feature very thin or muscular people. If a coach tells you to lose weight or says disparaging things about your body, or other people in your life are harming your mental health, time to make a switch and find people who can support you.

The take-home message is this: Disordered eating can affect anyone at any time. If you feel that you or someone you care about is suffering from disordered eating, seek help immediately. This is not a shameful thing to cover up, but rather a mental illness that needs proper professional treatment and care, and a healthy dose of self-compassion.

RESOURCES:

Eating Recovery Center
Eatingrecoverycenter.com

McCallum Place (Recovery center specifically for athletes)
Mccallumplace.com

Orthorexia.com

National Eating Disorders Association (United States)
Nationaleatingdisorders.org

Academy for Eating Disorders
Aedweb.org

The Center for Mindful Eating
Thecenterformindfuleating.org

BOOKS:

Body Kindness by Rebecca Scritchfield

Intuitive Eating by Evelyn Tribole

Health at Every Size by Linda Bacon

Running in Silence by Rachael Rose Steil

Recover Your Perspective by Janean Anderson

Overcoming Amenorrhea: Get Your Period Back, Get Your Life Back by Tina Muir

No Weigh! A Teen's Guide to Positive Body Image, Food, and Emotional Wisdom by Signe Darpinian, Wendy Sterling, and Shelley Aggarwal

Finding Your Sweet Spot: How to Avoid RED-S by Optimizing Your Energy Balance by Rebecca McConville

No Period. Now What? By Nicola Rinaldi, Stephanie Buckler, and Lisa Sanfilippo Waddell.

How to Nourish Your Child Through an Eating Disorder: A Simple, Plate-by-Plate Approach to Rebuilding a Healthy Relationship with Food by Casey Crosbie and Wendy Sterling

CHAPTER 9 REFERENCES

Bratman, Steven. 2000. *Health Food Junkies: Orthorexia Nervosa: Overcoming the Obsession With Healthful Eating.* New York: Vintage Books.

Caplan-Bricker, Nora. 2017. "The Inextricable Tie Between Eating Disorders and Endurance Athletes." Outside Magazine, June 23, 2017.

Cook, Brian, Stephen A. Wonderlich, James Mitchell, Ron Thompson, Roberta Sherman, Kimberli McCallum. 2016. "Exercise in Eating Disorders Treatment: Systematic Review and Proposal of Guidelines." *Medicine & Science in Sports & Exercise,* 48 no 7: 1408-1414.

THE WRAP-UP FOR DISORDERED EATING

Eating disorders comprise serious mental illnesses that need full and immediate medical treatment. Dieting and restriction can lead to disordered eating patterns. Disordered eating and eating disorders can also lead to permanent negative health consequences. If you or someone you know is suffering from disordered eating, get help right away.

CHAPTER 9 REFERENCES (CONTINUED)

DiGiulian, Sasha. 2018. "Sasha DiGiulian on Accepting Her Body." Outside Magazine Online, June 15, 2018. https://www.outsideonline.com/2171566/sasha-digiulian-female-athlete-body-image

Joubert, Lanae, Abigail Larson, Gina Blunt-Gonzalez. 2018. "Prevalence of Disordered Eating Among International Sport Lead Rock Climbers." Oral presentation July 13, 2018, at the 4th Research Congress of the International Rock Climbing Research Association; Chamonix, France.

Joy, Elizabeth, Andrea Kussman, Aurelia Nattiv. 2016. "2016 Update on Eating Disorders in Athletes: A Comprehensive Narrative Review With a Focus on Clinical Assessment and Management." *British Journal of Sports Medicine* 50 no. 3: 154-162.

Mehler, Philip S, Arnold E. Anderson. 2017. *Eating Disorders: A Guide to Medical Care and Complications.* Baltimore: Johns Hopkins University Press.

Michael, Marisa K., Lanae Joubert, Oliver C. Witard. 2019. "Assessment of Dietary Intake and Eating Attitudes in Recreational and Competitive Adolescent Rock Climbers: A Pilot Study." *Frontiers in Nutrition* 6: 64.

Morgan, John F., Fiona Reid, J. Hubert Lacey. 1999. "The SCOFF Questionnaire: Assessment of a New Screening Tool for Eating Disorders." *British Journal of Medicine* no. 7223, 1999: 1467-1468.

Mountjoy, Margo, Jorunn Sundgot-Borgen, Louise Burke, Susan Carter, Naama Constantini, Nanna Meyer, et al. 2014. "The IOC Consensus Statement: Beyond the Female Athlete Triad—Relative Energy Deficiency in Sport (RED-S)." *British Journal of Sports Medicine* 48 no. 7: 491-497.

Mountjoy, Margo, Jorunn Sundgot-Borgen, Louise Burke, Susan Carter, Naama Constantini, Constance Lebrun, Nanna Meyer, et al. 2015. "Authors' 2015 Additions to the IOC Consensus Statement: Relative Energy Deficiency in Sport (RED-S)." *British Journal of Sports Medicine* 49 no. 7: 417-420.

Mountjoy, Margo, Jorunn Sundgot-Borgen, Louise M. Burke, Kathryn E. Ackerman, Cheri Blauwet, Naama Constantini, Constance Lebrun, et al. 2018. "International Olympic Committee (IOC) Consensus Statement on Relative Energy Deficiency in Sport (RED-S): 2018 Update." *British Journal of Sports Medicine* 52 no. 11: 678-697.

Mountjoy, Margo, Jorunn Sundgot-Borgen, Louise Burke, Susan Carter, Naama Constantini, Constance Lebrun, Nanna Meyer, et al. 2015. "The IOC Relative Energy Deficiency in Sport Clinical Assessment Tool (RED-S CAT)." *British Journal of Sports Medicine* 49: 412-423.

Petkus, Dylan L., Laura E. Murray-Kolb, Mary Jane De Souza. 2017. "The Unexplored Crossroads of the Female Athlete Triad and Iron Deficiency: A Narrative Review." *Sports Medicine* 47, no. 9: 1721-1737.

Sundgot-Borgen, Jorunn, Ina Garthe. 2011. "Elite Athletes in Aesthetic and Olympic Weight-class Sports and the Challenge of Body Weight and Body Compositions. *Journal of Sport Sciences* 29 no. sup1: S101-S114.

Sundgot-Borgen, Jorunn, Nanna Meyer, Timothy G. Lohman, Timothy R. Ackland, Ronald J. Maughan, Arthur D. Stewart, Wolfram Müller. 2013. "How to Minimise the Health Risks to Athletes Who Compete in Weight-sensitive Sports Review and Position Statement on Behalf of the Ad Hoc Research Working Group on Body Composition, Health and Performance, Under the Auspices of the IOC Medical Commission." *British Journal of Sports Medicine* 47 no. 16: 1012-1022.

Watts, Phillip B, David T. Martin, Shirley Durtschi. 1993. "Anthropometric Profiles of Elite Male and Female Competitive Sport Rock Climbers." *Journal of Sports Science* 11 no. 2: 113-117.

11 - RECIPES AND MENUS

CHAPTER 11

RECIPES AND MENUS

Mug Recipes

Mug recipes are great for hotel-room and college-dorm cuisine. All you need is a microwave and a mug! Be sure to use good food-handling practices: Clean your hands and dishes before and after eating. If using meat or eggs, sanitize the surfaces. Do not use the same knife for produce and raw eggs/meat without washing first. Do not place fresh produce on top of a surface that had raw egg or meat without first cleaning it thoroughly. Microwave times in recipes are suggestions—you might need to do more or less time, depending on your microwave.

Quick Scrambled Eggs

INGREDIENTS:
- 2 eggs
- A few spinach leaves
- 2 cherry tomatoes, cut in half
- A pinch of shredded cheese

SPRAY mug with cooking spray. Crack 2 eggs into the mug and stir. Microwave for about 45 seconds. Stir, then microwave again another 45 seconds. Add toppings, microwave again for about 30 seconds. Make sure egg sets up. Enjoy!

Apple-Banana Oatmeal

INGREDIENTS:
- 1/2 cup (40 g) quick-cooking oats
- 1 tbsp (7 g) ground flax seed
- 1 egg
- 1/2 cup (120 mL) milk
- 1/3 of a banana, mashed
- 1/4 tsp (pinch) cinnamon
- 1/2 of an apple, chopped
- 1 tsp (4 g) honey

ADD oats, flax, egg, and milk in a mug. Stir well with a fork. Add banana, cinnamon, apple, and honey. Stir again until fully combined. Cook in microwave on high for 2-3 minutes. Fluff with a fork.

Macaroni & Cheese

INGREDIENTS:

- 1/2 cup (100 g) whole grain shells
- 1/2 cup (120 mL) milk
- 1/2 cup (170 g) finely shredded cheddar cheese

ADD noodles and milk to an oversized mug. Place the mug on a large plate. Microwave for 1 minute, then stir, making sure noodles do not stick to the bottom. Microwave for an additional 1 minute and stir again. Noodles should be almost cooked at this point. Add in cheese and stir until melted. Microwave another 20 seconds if cheese is not completely melted.

Chocolate "Cake"

INGREDIENTS:

- 1 small ripe banana
- 1 egg
- 1–3 T (14–42 g) cocoa powder

BLEND all ingredients until a batter is formed. If you don't have a blender, mash banana and then whisk ingredients very well. Spray second mug with cooking spray; pour in batter. Microwave about 60 seconds.

Home Recipes

These recipes are great if you have access to a full kitchen. Make at home and enjoy often.

Overnight Oatmeal

INGREDIENTS:

- 1 c rolled oats
- 1/2 c yogurt (or soy, almond, or coconut yogurt)
- 1 c milk (cow's, almond, soy, coconut, etc.)
- 1 Tbs honey

This is a super-easy breakfast that you can prep the night before in only a few minutes. Start your day off right with a filling breakfast option.

MIX all ingredients in a small bowl. Put in refrigerator overnight (or for at least two hours to let milk soak into oats). Serve warm or cold. Top with berries, granola, banana slices, or nuts as desired.

Coconut Curry

INGREDIENTS:

- 1 Tbs olive oil
- 1 chicken breast, diced (can use canned chicken breast or frozen, cooked chicken breast strips) (omit if vegan—can substitute with tofu, or lentils on the side)
- 1 sweet potato, peeled and diced
- 1 carrot, peeled and sliced into coins
- 1 can (16 oz) coconut milk
- 1 c chicken broth (or vegetable broth if vegan)
- 1 c broccoli florets
- 1 c sugar snap peas or snow peas
- 1 zucchini, sliced into coins
- 2 Tbs curry powder
- 2 cups cooked brown rice or cooked quinoa

ADD the olive oil to large saucepan. Add chicken breast (or tofu), sweet potato, and carrots. Sauté for about 5 minutes. Add coconut milk, chicken broth, and curry powder. Bring to a boil and simmer about 15 minutes, or until chicken is cooked through. Add the remaining vegetables (broccoli, peas, and zucchini) and cook 3–5 more minutes, or until tender. Serve over rice. Makes 4 servings. Note: This recipe is versatile and can use any vegetables you have on hand.

On-the-Go Egg Cups

A great high-protein breakfast or snack. Pair with fruit salad and some whole-grain toast for a complete meal.

INGREDIENTS:

- 12 eggs PLUS any of the following mix-in options:

- Veggies
Diced bell peppers, chopped spinach or kale, sliced mushrooms, diced tomato, diced onion.

- Savory Options
Shredded cheese, such as cheddar, mozzarella, or feta; bacon bits (fully cooked); minced garlic; sausage crumbles (fully cooked); diced ham (fully cooked).

- Herb/Seasoning Options
Chopped basil, chopped chives, oregano, garlic powder, truffle zest.

PREHEAT oven to 350°. Spray a nonstick muffin tin with cooking spray. Crack eggs into a bowl. Whisk until combined. Pour beaten egg into each muffin tin, filling about 2/3 of the way up. Sprinkle desired toppings onto each egg "muffin." You can do the whole pan the same way, or make a variety of "muffins" based on your own desire. Bake for 20 minutes or until egg is set, and a toothpick comes out clean when the "muffin" is poked with one.

Keep in the refrigerator and reheat as many as needed at a time in the microwave–about 30 seconds for each egg cup. You may need more or less time depending on how powerful your microwave is.

Energy Bites

INGREDIENTS:

- 1 c (340 g) rolled oats
- 1 c (340 g) coconut flakes
- ¼ c (85 g) sunflower seeds, chopped peanuts, or chopped walnuts
- ½ c (170 g) chocolate chips
- ½ c (170 g) creamy peanut butter
- 1/3 c (113 g) honey (use agave syrup if vegan)
- ½ tsp (5 g) vanilla

Perfect for after a workout, as a snack, or to take on an outdoor climb.

MIX together in a big bowl. Scoop with a spoon and form into 1" balls. Refrigerate until firm. Keep refrigerated to help maintain their shape until you're ready to enjoy them. Makes approximately 20 bites.

Fruit, Spinach & Yogurt Smoothie

A great after-workout drink that provides energy, protein, fiber, and antioxidants.

INGREDIENTS:

- ¾ c (255 g) frozen berries, such as strawberries, raspberries, blueberries, or a mix
- 1 handful fresh, washed baby spinach (about ¼–1/3 cup)
- 4 oz (112 g) vanilla or plain yogurt, or almond, coconut, or soy yogurt
- ½ banana
- 1 Tbs (14 g) chia seeds or ground flaxseed
- Water (add to get correct consistency—about ½ cup—just enough to get it to blend, but not so much to make it watery)
- **Optional add-ins:** Beet powder, protein powder, avocado

BLEND in a small blender cup. Enjoy immediately!

Roasted Brussels Sprouts & Apples

Don't be scared by the term "Brussels sprouts." Give it a try—this recipe is really good as a side dish with tofu, chicken, pork, or fish. The apples provides a sweetness that cuts the bitterness of the Brussels sprouts. Roasting them and adding Parmesan cheese gives a nice balance of bitter, salty, sweet, and savory all in one dish.

INGREDIENTS:

- 1 lb Brussels sprouts, chopped finely so they look shredded
- 2 apples, thinly sliced
- 2 Tbs olive oil
- Salt and pepper to taste
- Parmesan cheese to taste (omit for vegan option)

BLEND Pre-heat oven to broil. Place Brussels sprouts and apples on a sheet pan. Drizzle olive oil on top and toss to coat. Sprinkle salt and pepper to taste. Place in oven. After 2-3 minutes, check oven and stir Brussels sprouts and apples if needed to prevent uneven cooking. Remove from oven when tender, or after about 5 minutes. Sprinkle Parmesan cheese over pan. Allow to melt 1-2 minutes. Enjoy hot.

Protein Power Pancakes

INGREDIENTS:

- 2 bananas
- 2 eggs
- 2 scoops protein powder (use only NSF or Informed Choice certified to avoid contaminants)
- 2 Tbs flour
- 1 tsp baking powder
- ½ tsp vanilla extract
- ¼ tsp cinnamon

MASH the bananas in mixing bowl. Add in remaining ingredients. Heat skillet. Spray non-stick cooking spray if needed. Pour in 1/3 cup of batter. Flip when the first side is done cooking—the batter will start to get bubbles and appear drier. After flipping, cook another 1-3 minutes or until both sides are golden brown. Serve with fruit, nut butter, maple syrup, or banana slices.

Loaded Quesadillas

INGREDIENTS:

- 1 c frozen corn
- 1 c grated zucchini (juice squeezed out–see right)
- ½ bunch cilantro, chopped
- 1 can black beans, rinsed and drained
- ½ tsp cumin
- 2 c mozzarella cheese, shredded
- 1 c shredded chicken
- 12 tortillas

BLEND Combine everything in a bowl except for the tortillas. To squeeze out the zucchini, place grated zucchini on paper towels, or on a clean, cloth dish towel. Roll it up and squeeze over the sink until most of the juices are gone. Warm skillet on stove on medium heat. Place one tortilla in pan; place bean mixture on one half of the tortilla. Fold the tortilla over the top of the bean mixture. Cook on one side, then flip to cook the other side. Repeat for each tortilla. Serve warm. Makes 12 quesadillas.

Recovery Power Bowls

These bowls are simple to prep ahead of time. When you are done with a hard training or climbing session, simply assemble the ingredients and heat up in the microwave. It makes an easy recovery meal packed with protein, vitamins, and minerals. (Recovery power bowls are simply grain bowls with protein and vegetables added in.)

Step 1: Pick your base
Step 2: Add your protein
Step 3: Top with veggies
Step 4: Select a flavor

Some tips: Think of what variety of spices, flavorings, sauces, or ethnic flavors you'd like before building your bowl. This will guide your choices. For example, a Mexican bowl might have quinoa as the base, black or refried beans with cheese as the protein, salsa, tomatoes, olives, and avocado as the veggies, and sour cream and cilantro for added flavor. An Asian bowl might have rice as the base, teriyaki chicken as the protein, onion and bok choy for the veggies, and some ginger and soy sauce for added flavor.

Easy Grain Tips:
Batch-cook larger quantities ahead of time, such as quinoa, rice, or pasta. Keep in the fridge for up to seven days. Portion out only what you need and microwave individual portions each day.

Alternatively, buy pre-cooked shelf-stable or frozen grains, such as rice and quinoa, and microwave individual portions as needed.

Easy Protein Tips:
You can buy fully cooked canned lentils, black beans, refried beans, kidney beans, and other types of beans for easy prep. Purchase canned or pouch tuna and salmon. Use canned chicken or rotisserie chicken for an easy no-bake protein option. Scrambled, poached, or fried eggs only take a few minutes to prepare and are an affordable source of quality protein.

Easy Veggie Tips:
Frozen vegetables are a good option because they are easy to store and prepare, and last longer than fresh vegetables. If using fresh vegetables but you have limited time to wash and chop them, many grocery stores sell pre-chopped and pre-washed peppers, carrots, lettuce, spinach, and more.

Tasty combos:

SOUTHWEST BOWL: Quinoa, grilled chicken, black beans, avocado, salsa, sour cream, shredded cheddar, cilantro, and a squeeze of lime juice

CURRY BOWL: White rice, tofu cubes, sweet potato, carrots, diced onion, and yellow curry

OPEN-FACED SANDWICH: Whole-grain bread, slice of ham, shaved Parmesan cheese, fried egg with a side of asparagus

PASTA BOWL: Whole-grain pasta, ground beef, marinara sauce, Parmesan cheese, and zucchini

A few ideas for your recovery power bowl. Mix and match food from each column to create your own ideal meal.

BASE	PROTEIN	VEGGIES	FLAVOR
Quinoa	Chicken	Onion	Curry sauce
White rice	Fish	Carrots	Teriyaki sauce
Brown rice	Ground beef	Zucchini	Cumin
Pasta	Beef strips	Broccoli	Chili powder
Mixed greens	Tofu cubes	Asparagus	Marinara sauce
Teff	Chickpeas	Green beans	Salad dressing
Freekeh	Black beans	Cauliflower	Garlic
Barley	Lentils	Cucumber	Parsley
Oatmeal	Refried beans	Eggplant	Cilantro
Bread	Cheese	Sweet potatoes	Thyme
	Eggs	Potatoes	Salt/pepper
	Pork	Bell peppers	Dill
	Nuts/nut butters	Squash	
	Pumpkin or sunflower seeds		

Outdoor Recipes

Outdoor recipes are great when you're on multi-day climbing trips and will be cooking outside with limited equipment. Some of these may require the use of a camp stove or backpacking stove.

Chocolate Peanut Butter Milk

INGREDIENTS:

- 1/3 c whole milk powder
- 1 packet Carnation Instant Breakfast Essentials powder– chocolate flavor
- 3 Tbs dried peanut butter powder (such as PB Fit)

AT-HOME DIRECTIONS:
Put all ingredients in a bag or container to be used in the backcountry.

FIELD DIRECTIONS:
Add 8 oz cold water to bag or container. Stir or shake vigorously to mix well. Massage bag with fingertips if peanut powder clumps. Enjoy!

Recipe credit: Aaron Owens Mayhew at backcountryfoodie.com (used with permission).

Parmesan Pesto Ramen

INGREDIENTS:

- 1 package ramen noodles
- 1/8 c Parmesan cheese
- 1/8 c pine nuts
- 1/8 tsp garlic powder
- 1 Tbsp dried basil
- 1/8 tsp salt
- 3 Tbsp olive oil

SUBSTITUTIONS: Rice ramen noodles may be used as a gluten-free alternative

AT HOME "PREP" DIRECTIONS:
1) Discard ramen noodle spice packet
2) Put noodles in a bag or container to be used in the backcountry.
3) Put remaining dry ingredients in a second bag to be stored inside the noodle bag.
4) Pack 3 Tbsp olive oil in a leak-proof container to be added to meal when consumed.*

*Recommend double-bagging the oil in the event there is a leak.

FIELD DIRECTIONS:
1) Remove the pesto packet.
2) Add 6 oz hot/cold water, or enough to cover the noodles.
3) Let stand, allowing noodles to rehydrate.
4) Consume or properly discard the noodle broth to practice Leave No Trace principles.
5) Add pesto packet and 3 Tbsp olive oil to noodle bag.
6) Stir well and enjoy!

Note: Shelf life will be extended if single-serving packets of Parmesan cheese are added at time of consumption, or the meal is frozen until consumed.

Recipe credit: Aaron Owens Mayhew at backcountryfoodie.com (used with permission).

Chocolate Granola

10 servings | 15 min prep | 12 min cooking | 66.2g / serving

Each portion of ¾ cup contains 9g of protein and is low in fat. Add Greek yogurt or cottage cheese and fruits (I like frozen raspberries and cherries) to this granola to make a complete meal.

INGREDIENTS:

- 3 cups (750 ml) old-fashioned oats
- ½ cup (125 ml) oat bran
- ¼ cup (60 ml) cocoa
- ½ cup (125 ml) milk powder
- ½ cup (125 ml) sliced almonds
- ½ cup (125 ml) sweetened coconut flakes
- 1 pinch of salt
- 3 egg whites
- ¼ cup (60 ml) honey

PREPARATION

1) In a large bowl, mix all the dry ingredients together.
2) In another bowl, mix the egg whites and honey.
3) Add the liquid ingredients to the dry ones. Mix well.
4) Spread on 2 baking sheets covered with parchment paper and spray with oil.
5) Bake in the oven at 375° F (190°C) for 12 minutes.
6) When cooled down, break the large pieces into smaller ones, and put in smaller bags or containers for preservation. Keeps for one month.

Recipe: Geneviève Masson at gourmethiking.com (used with permission).

Berry Granola

The freeze-dried berries bring a nice freshness to this quick breakfast recipe. High in protein (21g/serving) and ridiculously easy to make on the trail or at the cliff, this breakfast will allow you to get an early start. Substitute the skim milk powder with full-fat milk powder to add 80 calories to your meal.

INGREDIENTS:

- ¾ cup (175 ml) homemade chocolate granola (see above)
- 4 Tbs (60 ml) skim milk powder
- 4 Tbs (60 ml) freeze-dried raspberries
- 4 Tbs (60 ml) freeze-dried blueberries

EQUIPMENT

- Spork or spoon

BEFORE TRIP

1) Mix in a plastic bag: all the ingredients.

AT CAMP

1) Pour about ¾ cup (175 ml) of cold water in the bag.
2) Mix well and enjoy!

Recipe: Geneviève Masson at gourmethiking.com (used with permission).

Morrocan Apricot Chickpeas

2 hungry backpackers | 5 min prep | 20 min cooking | 191.5g / serving

Warm, comforting, and sweet, this dish will transport your taste buds somewhere else, to add variety to your backpacking meals. And you will not believe that this vegan recipe contains 28 g of protein and 6.1 mg of iron (thanks go to the dried apricots for this nice contribution!).

INGREDIENTS:

- ½ cup (125 ml) dry couscous
- Salt and pepper, to taste
- 1 cup (250 ml) dehydrated, fast-cooking chickpeas*
- ¼ cup (60 ml) dried onion flakes*
- ½ cup (125 ml) dehydrated apricots, chopped into small cubes
- ½ tsp (2 ml) ground coriander seeds
- ½ tsp (2 ml) ground ginger
- ½ tsp (2 ml) cumin
- ¼ tsp (1 ml) cinnamon
- ¼ tsp (1 ml) paprika
- ¼ tsp (1 ml) salt
- 1 pinch of cayenne pepper
- 1/3 cup (80 ml) roasted almonds

Readily available for order from amazon our other bulk-food websites.

EQUIPMENT

- Stove + fuel
- Pot large enough for 1.5 liters (6 cups)
- Wooden spoon to mix
- At least one bowl or other container to hydrate the couscous
- Sporks or spoon

AT HOME

1) In bag #1, mix the couscous with salt and pepper to taste.
2) In bag #2, mix the chickpeas with the dried onions, the apricots, and all the spices.
3) In bag #3, pack the roasted almonds.
4) Write recipe instructions on bags.

AT CAMP

1) Bring to boil 2½ cups (625 ml) of water.
2) Pour the contents of bag #1 in a small container and pour about ½ cup (125 ml) of boiling water on top. Cover it so it stays warm.
3) Add the contents of bag #2 to the pot with the boiling water and let simmer for about 15 minutes or until the chickpeas are cooked.
4) Serve the chickpeas on top of the couscous and sprinkle with the almonds.
5) Enjoy!

Recipe: Geneviève Masson at gourmethiking.com (used with permission).

DIY Trail Mix

This trail mix has no rules! Mix-and-match any combination you'd like–and any amount you'd like! Select at least one item from each column and mix it up, then place in a sealed bag. Voilà! *(I personally prefer lots of chocolate in mine.)*

Crunchy options	Chewy options	Nutty options	Sweet options
Pretzels	Raisins	Walnuts	Mini-marshmallows
Oat-circle cereal	Diced, dried apricot	Pecans	Candy-coated chocolate candies
Rice-square cereal	Diced dates	Cashews	Chocolate chips
Cheddar fish crackers	Coconut flakes	Almonds	Butterscotch chips
Oyster crackers	Banana chips	Peanuts	White chocolate chips
Graham bear-shaped crackers	Dried diced pineapple	Brazil nuts	Cocoa nibs
Seasoned small crackers	Dried cherries	Macadamia nuts	Carob chips
Sesame sticks	Dried blueberries	Sunflower seeds	Yogurt pretzels
Popcorn	Dried cranberries	Pumpkin seeds	Chocolate pretzels
Puffed rice	Wasabi peas	Hazelnuts	Yogurt raisins
Shredded wheat squares	Dried strawberries	Pistachios	Chocolate raisins
Seaweed rice crackers	Dried kiwi		
Granola	Dried figs		

DIY Sports Drink

INGREDIENTS:

- 3 c (700 mL) water or coconut water
- 1 c (240 mL) orange juice
- ¼ c (300 mL) lemon juice
- 3 Tbs (14 g) honey or ¼ c (85 g) sugar
- ¼ tsp salt (1.25 g)

Mix all ingredients until dissolved. Enjoy chilled or with ice.

Citrus Sports Drink

INGREDIENTS:

- 7 oz (200 mL) orange juice concentrate
- 28 oz (800 mL) water and ice
- ¼ tsp (1.25 g) salt

Mix together and enjoy chilled.

Sample Menus

Ever had the feeling that you are hungry, so you wander into the kitchen, open the fridge, stare blankly into the void, then close it and wander away? Sometimes it's hard to know what to eat, how much to eat, and how to prepare a meal.

The sample menus outlined in this chapter then presented in detail in chapter 12 are designed to give you ideas about what, when, and how much to eat on any given day. There are different calorie levels—just pick a calorie level that most closely matches your estimated energy needs. How do you know? Well, see a dietitian of course! A general rule of thumb is about 30–45 calories per kilogram of body weight, but this is a very rough estimate. Some people may need more or less than this. Adolescents and youth climbers may need a different calorie level, as might older climbers. The highest calorie level listed on these menus is 3000 calories per day. You may need more than this. Again, see a dietitian for help if you aren't sure where to start.

The menus are designed to correspond with *The Rock Climber's Training Manual: A Guide to Continuous Improvement* by Michael L. Anderson and Mark L. Anderson. In this manual, there are different training phases.

Imagine my dilemma—trying to create menus for each possible person who may want to use them for each training phase. It's complicated! Obviously, nutrition needs vary from person to person. Your height, weight, age, gender, training status, training goals, body composition, health status, medications, and activity level all determine your nutrient needs. Then, take into consideration that most individuals eat differently from day to day. An individual typically eats a varied amount of calories, protein, carbs, and fat from one day to the next. If you look at the average trend over a week or a month, that's when it all starts to even out. On one given day, you aren't likely to eat the exact calorie, macronutrient, and micronutrient goal that's perfect for your body. And that's OK. We eat differently from day to day, and it evens out over time.

So, I created menus that also vary from day to day.

The menus average a baseline of about 200 grams of carbs daily and about 120 grams protein daily, regardless of the training phase. From there, you can add in a carb-rich snack before a workout, especially if you are in the Power or Power-Endurance Phase. You can eliminate a high-protein snack if you weigh less or don't have a heavy strength-training day.

The menus are just a starting point: You don't need to follow them religiously. It's a framework to understand what you might eat and when you would eat it, and offer a wide variety of nutrients to support health and training. There are meal and snack times listed as suggestions, and as a way to illustrate that your nutrition intake spread out over the course of a day will help maximize and support performance and training gains. Don't feel like you have to eat at exactly the designated time as listed on the sample menu. Usually, eating according to hunger and fullness cues is best.

I designed these menus to be simple. Some foods are repeated, because that's how most kitchens are set up. You want to buy ingredients that you can use for several meals—this saves time and money. Most people don't have completely different foods from one day to the next—they have carrots in their fridge, and end up using the carrots for a salad, a soup, and a snack.

These menus don't take a lot of cooking know-how or a lot of time to prepare. They are simple, basic ideas that will get you started on the age-old question: What should I eat? Now that you know the intent behind them, let's take a look at each training phase from *The Rock Climber's Training Manual: A Guide to Continuous Improvement,* and their nutrition implications.

Note: The following suggestions are based on my clinical and professional judgment, as well as the scientific evidence that is available regarding nutrition for sports performance. There are no studies specifically in climbers to explore which nutrition recommendations are most effective at each training phase. I give a range for my recommendations, because each person is different and intake varies from day-to-day. The key is to have overall adequate nutrition to support training adaptations in each phase.

Note: Each training phase needs to include fat in the diet. Since there isn't a lot of research on fat and athletic performance, I did not include specific guidelines. See chapter 1 for more information on fat.

Sample Menus (continued)

1) Base Fitness Phase: *Building up a base fitness level at the beginning of a season or training cycle. This usually consists of about 60-90 minutes of climbing three to four days per week, with some optional aerobic training mixed in.*

- » **Calorie needs** vary based on your height, weight, age, gender, activity level, and other factors. But in general, your calorie needs are a bit higher than when resting, though lower than when engaging in more-vigorous training.

- » **Protein needs** also vary, but are slightly higher than at rest, and lower than vigorous training cycles. Aim for about 1.1-1.6 grams per kilograms per day.

- » **Carbohydrate needs** are similar to calorie and protein needs, as they are a bit higher than rest to support your activity level, but lower than intense training. Aim for around 3-5 grams per kilogram per day.

2) Strength Phase: *This is focused on muscle hypertrophy—building up muscle mass and strength for climbing-specific skills such as crack climbing, multi-pitch, or bouldering. This involves training three to five times per week for up to three hours daily, with aerobic exercise tapering off toward the end of the phase. These workouts are longer and more intense than the base fitness phase.*

- » **Calorie needs** again vary from person to person, but are higher than the Base Fitness Phase, depending on how much optional exercise you do–likely up to 300-700 calories more on heavy training days. You need increased overall calorie intake to build any new tissues in your body—including muscle tissue-as well as repair and recover from heavy training sessions.

- » **Protein needs** are higher during this phase, as muscle building does take additional protein. Aim for about 1.8-2.5 grams per kilogram per day. A person may also benefit from creatine supplementation during this phase. (Always check with your doctor before adding any supplements, as well as your sport's governing body like the International Federation of Sport Climbing, to make sure they are allowed.) Using casein protein or eating foods with casein (milk, cottage cheese) as a nighttime snack will help your body repair and rebuild muscle while sleeping.

» **Carbohydrates** are needed to fuel muscle contraction during workouts, as well as replenish any depleted glycogen stores from the workouts. Needs are similar to the Base Fitness Phase.

3) Power Phase: *Different from strength, the power phase is designed to train muscle fibers to be recruited in such a way as to increase the force of a movement- like a dyno-contracting muscles with speed, strength, and impact. This training phase involves plyometrics, which are exercises that require the muscles to exert maximum force with intervals, such as box jumps or training on the campus board. This phase requires very intense interval climbs followed by rest within the climbing session. In this phase, you would work out three to four days per week, for 60-90 minutes each time. If you need to cut weight (check with a dietitian and doctor first!), this is the phase where you would do so.*

» **Calorie needs** of course vary, but are likely lower than the Strength Phase of training. You need enough overall energy (calories) to fuel intense interval workouts and have mental stamina to commit to this kind of training, but the physical demands are less than those of the strength-training phase.

» **Protein needs** are likely similar to the Strength Phase. Your muscles are going through a period of adaptation, in which they will be rebuilding and repairing after a training session. Adequate protein is essential. Creatine can help with power moves. You can try this during the power phase to see if it helps you train better and harder. If the water weight you may gain with creatine supplementation is bothersome or makes you feel heavy, you can easily stop supplementing. Usual usage of creatine is one to two months.

» **Carbohydrate** needs are likely higher than the Strength Phase, as many of the movements are utilizing the anaerobic energy system. These explosive types of movements use carbohydrate almost exclusively. Aim for around 3-7 grams per kilogram per day. You can experiment to see what works for you. If you are under-eating on carbohydrates, you may feel too tired to complete the workout, or you may not have enough energy to perform powerful, explosive moves. If you are not making training gains as expected, add in more carbohydrate to your daily intake, especially 30-60 minutes before a training session.

4) Power-Endurance Phase: *This phase is designed to train the body to perform at near-maximal levels without rest in a sustained climbing effort lasting two to four minutes at a time—difficult enough to get through a crux or other scenario in which you can't shake out your arms, rest on the wall, or easily chalk up. The training plan calls for 40-60-minute workouts, three days per week.*

> » **Calorie needs** vary, as always, but you need to eat enough calories overall to fuel training adaptations. If you find yourself plateauing or decreasing in fitness level, time to add more calories.
>
> » **Protein needs** are likely a bit less than the Strength Phase, as you are not actively trying to build new muscle tissue. But you are still using muscles at a high capacity, which requires protein (and calories) to rebuild and repair muscle, as well as allow training adaptations to occur. Aim for about 1.6-2.0 grams per kilogram of protein per day, spaced evenly throughout the day with meals and snacks.
>
> » **Carbohydrate needs** are still there, as the energy systems for movements in this training phase demand carbohydrate. Aim for about 3-7 grams per kilogram per day.

5) Rest Phase: *This phase is exactly what it sounds like—rest. There are no menu plans for the Rest Phase, as it's intended to be a phase during which nutrition doesn't have to be as dialed-in to achieve training gains.*

In general, it's good to just eat according to hunger and satiety levels. Don't overthink it. You are not training or competing, so it's a great time to take advantage of just enjoying eating, rather than over-analyzing how many grams of protein you are getting in each meal. If your rest is forced upon you because of injury, flip to chapter 7, which offers good tips on what you can do to promote healing and recovery. Of course, it's always wise to seek out the help of a sports dietitian.

It's OK to gain weight during this phase, especially if you purposefully lost weight during the other training phases. Let your body come back to its natural set point, and gently nourish it with foods you enjoy.

CHAPTER 12

MENUS AND RECIPES FOR CLIMBERS

Base Fitness Menus	228
Strength Phase Menus	238
Power-Endurance Phase Menus	248
Power Phase Menus	258
Workout-Oriented Suggestions	268

These menus are designed to be a framework for you. They are guidelines designed to help you understand what, how often, and how much to eat.

Each person has different food tastes, preferences, tolerances, budgets, and cooking skills, so keep in mind that these menus are an adaptable meal pattern for you to follow (or not) according to what works best for you.

Meals and snacks are laid out at regular intervals, because to be a better climber you need to feed your body throughout the day. This helps you be fueled to peform and train. It also helps you recover and make fitness adaptations and training gains.

Seeking out the help of a sports dietitian will help you determine your personalized calorie and macronutrient needs. Be sure to consult with your healthcare provider before undergoing any diet changes to make sure they're right for you and your medical history.

12 - MENUS AND RECIPES FOR CLIMBERS

BASE FITNESS MENUS
Day 1

Meal	Time Eaten	Food	1800-calorie
BREAKFAST	7:00 AM	Scrambled eggs	2 eggs
		Whole-grain toast	1 piece
		Butter	1 tsp (5 g)
SNACK	10:30 AM	Protein bar	1 bar (approx 250 calories)
LUNCH	1:00 PM	Salad with:	1 cup (94 g) shredded lettuce
		Grilled chicken strips	6 oz (16 g)
		Veggies of choice	1 cup chopped (94 g)
		Dressing of choice	1 Tbs (15 g)
SNACK	3:00 PM	Energy Bites	2 balls
		(see recipe page 212)	
DINNER	6:30 PM	Macaroni and cheese	1 recipe / 1 serving
		(see recipe page 210)	
		Green beans	1 cup (125 g)
SNACK	9:00 PM	Sliced cucumber, peppers, and carrots	1 cup veggies (100 g)
		with hummus	2 Tbs (30 g)
AVG CHO*			CHO: 144 g
AVG PRO*			PRO: 115 g

* CHO is an abbreviation for carbohydrates, and PRO is an abbreviation for protein.

DRINK WATER throughout the day according to thirst and urine color

2100-calorie	2500-calorie	3000-calorie	Vegan/Vegetarian option	
2 eggs	3 eggs	3 eggs + 1/4 c (28 g) shredded cheese	Soy yogurt	
2 pieces	2 pieces	3 pieces		
1 Tbs (15 g)	1 Tbs (15 g)	1 Tbs (15 g)	Jam	
1 bar (approx 250 calories)	1 bar (approx 250 calories)	1 bar (approx 250 calories)		
1 cup (94 g) shredded lettuce	1 cup (94 g) shredded lettuce	1 cup (94 g) shredded lettuce		
6 oz (16 g)	6 oz (16 g)	6 oz (16 g)	Chickpeas	
1 cup chopped (94 g)	1 cup chopped (94 g)	1 cup chopped (94 g)		
1 Tbs (15 g)	1 Tbs (15 g)	1 Tbs (15 g)		
		Add almonds (23 each)		
3 balls	2 balls	3 balls		
1 recipe / 1 serving	1 1/2 recipes	2 recipes	Use nut milk and soy cheese	
1 cup (125 g)	1 cup (125 g)	1 cup (125 g)		
1 cup veggies (100 g)	1 cup veggies (100 g)	1 cup veggies (100 g)	AVG CHO	AVG PRO
2 Tbs (30 g)	2 Tbs (30 g)	3 Tbs (30 g)	114	115
			170	123
			215	147
CHO: 170 g	CHO: 215 g	CHO: 224 g	224	167
PRO: 123 g	PRO: 147 g	PRO: 167 g	**180.75**	**138**

BASE FITNESS MENUS
Day 2

Meal	Time Eaten	Food	1800-calorie
BREAKFAST	7:00 AM	Greek yogurt	7 oz (200 g)
		Granola	1/2 ounce (15 g)
		Strawberries	1/2 c (78 g) sliced
SNACK	10:30 AM	Apple slices	1 apple
		Peanut butter	2 Tbs (24 g)
LUNCH	1:00 PM	Pita sandwich with:	1 small pita
		Turkey, cheese, and veggies	2 slices (30 g) deli turkey
		An orange	1 slice cheese
			Veggies of choice
			1 medium orange
SNACK	3:00 PM	Grapes	20 grapes (94 g)
DINNER	6:30 PM	Loaded baked sweet potato	1 medium potato
		Bacon bits	1 Tbs (15 g)
		Sour cream	2 Tbs (24 g)
		Shredded cheese	1 oz (28 g)
		Shredded chicken	3 oz (84 g)
		Side of broccoli	1/2 c (78 g)
SNACK	9:00 PM	Trail mix	2 handfuls (80 g)
AVG CHO			CHO: 194 g
AVG PRO			PRO: 62 g

DRINK WATER throughout the day according to thirst and urine color

2100-calorie	2500-calorie	3000-calorie	Vegan/Vegetarian option	
7 oz (200 g)	7 oz (200 g)	10.5 oz (300 g)	Soy yogurt	
1 oz (28 g)	1 oz (28 g)	2 oz (57 g)		
1/2 c (78 g)	1/2 c (78 g)	1/2 c (78 g)		
1 apple	1 apple	1 apple		
3 Tbs (48 g)	3 Tbs (48 g)	3 Tbs (48 g)		
1 large pita	1 large pita	1 small pita	Egg-or-tofu salad–stuffed pita	
3 slices (45 g) deli turkey	3 slices (45 g) deli turkey	6 slices (90 g) deli turkey		
2 slices cheese	2 slices cheese	2 slices cheese		
Veggies of choice	Veggies of choice	Veggies of choice		
1 medium orange	1 medium orange	1 medium orange		
20 grapes (94 g)	20 grapes (94 g)	40 grapes		
1 medium potato	1 large potato	1 large potato		
1 Tbs (15 g)	1 Tbs (15 g)	1 Tbs (15 g)	Meatless bacon bits	
2 Tbs (24 g)	4 Tbs (48 g)	4 Tbs (48 g)	Vegan sour cream	
1 oz (28 g)	1 oz (28 g)	1 oz (28 g)	Soy cheese	
3 oz (84 g)	4 oz (120 g)	4 oz (120 g)	Black beans	
1/2 c (78 g)	1/2 c (78 g)	1/2 c (78 g)	AVG CHO	AVG PRO
			194	62
2 handfuls (80 g)	1 cup (150 g)	1 cup (150 g)	170	116
			225	138
CHO: 170 g	CHO: 225 g	CHO: 256 g	256	160
PRO: 116 g	PRO: 138 g	PRO: 160 g	**211.25**	**119**

CHAPTER 12 - MENUS AND RECIPES FOR CLIMBERS

BASE FITNESS MENUS
Day 3

Meal	Time Eaten	Food	1800-calorie
BREAKFAST	7:00 AM	Oatmeal	1 cup (80 g)
		Banana slices	1/2 banana (48 g)
		Walnuts	1/4 c chopped (40 g)
SNACK	10:30 AM	Mozzarella cheese stick	1 oz
		Whole-grain crackers	40 small crackers (40 g)
LUNCH	1:00 PM	Rice bowl with:	1 c (200 g) brown rice
		Black beans	1/2 c cooked (120 g)
		Salsa	4 Tbs (72 g)
		Avocado	1/3 avocado (20 g)
		Cheese	1/2 oz (14 g)
SNACK	3:00 PM	Carrots	10 baby carrots
		Hummus	2 Tbs (14 g)
DINNER	6:30 PM	Grilled chicken with:	4 oz (120 g)
		Brussels sprouts and apples	1 cup
		(See recipe page 212)	
SNACK	9:00 PM	Energy Bites	1 ball
		(See recipe page 212)	
AVG CHO			CHO: 179 g
AVG PRO			PRO: 62 g

2100-calorie	2500-calorie	3000-calorie	Vegan/Vegetarian option
1 1/2 cup (120 g)	1 1/2 cup (120 g)	1 1/2 cup (120 g)	
1 banana (101 g)	1 banana (101 g)	1 banana (101 g)	
1/4 c chopped (40 g)	1/4 c chopped (40 g)	1/4 c chopped (40 g)	
1 oz	1 oz	2 each (2 oz)	Nut-butter spread
40 small crackers (40 g)	40 small crackers (40 g)	60 small crackers (60 g)	
1 c (200 g) brown rice	1 1/2 c (404 g)	1 1/2 c (404 g)	
1/2 c cooked (120 g)	1 c (240 g)	1 1/2 c (480 g)	
4 Tbs (72 g)	4 Tbs (72 g)	4 Tbs (72 g)	
1/3 avocado (20 g)	1/3 avocado (20 g)	1/3 avocado (20 g)	
1/2 oz (14 g)	1/2 oz (14 g)	1/2 oz (14 g)	Vegan cheese
10 baby carrots	10 baby carrots	10 baby carrots	
2 Tbs (14 g)	2 Tbs (14 g)	2 Tbs (14 g)	
4 oz (120 g)	4 oz (120 g)	6 oz (160 g)	Roasted tofu
1 cup	1 cup	1 cup	
1 ball	1 ball	2 balls	
CHO: 214 g	**CHO: 274 g**	**CHO: 325 g**	
PRO: 98 g	**PRO: 111 g**	**PRO: 150 g**	

DRINK WATER throughout the day according to thirst and urine color

BASE FITNESS MENUS
Day 4

Meal	Time Eaten	Food	1800-calorie
BREAKFAST	7:00 AM	Fruit, Spinach, and Yogurt Smoothie (see page 212)	1 smoothie (260 mL)
SNACK	10:30 AM	Hardboiled egg	2 eggs
LUNCH	1:00 PM	Lettuce wraps with:	4 leaves lettuce
		Teriyaki chicken	4 oz
		Mushrooms	6 chopped mushrooms (36 g)
		Green onions	1 onion, chopped
		Side of grapes	40 grapes
SNACK	3:00 PM	Rice cakes	2 cakes
		Cocoa hazelnut spread or peanut butter	4 Tbs (64 g)
DINNER	6:30 PM	Spaghetti with:	5 oz (140 g) cooked
		Marinara sauce	1/2 c (132 g)
		Meatballs (beef)	3 each (56 g)
		Garden salad	1 c
		Dressing	1 tsp (5 g)
SNACK	9:00 PM	Chocolate milk	1 c (240 mL)
AVG CHO			CHO: 127 g
AVG PRO			PRO: 106 g

DRINK WATER throughout the day according to thirst and urine color

2100-calorie	2500-calorie	3000-calorie	Vegan/Vegetarian option
1 smoothie (260 mL)	1 smoothie (260 mL)	1 smoothie (260 mL)	Use nut milk in place of yogurt
	1 medium bran muffin	1 medium bran muffin	
2 eggs	3 eggs	3 eggs	Mixed nuts
		1 protein bar (about 250 calories)	
4 leaves lettuce	4 leaves lettuce	6 leaves lettuce	
4 oz	4 oz	6 oz (120 g)	Tofu or increase mushrooms and add water chestnuts
6 chopped mushrooms (36 g)	6 chopped mushrooms (36 g)	6 chopped mushrooms (36 g)	
1 onion, chopped	1 onion, chopped	1 onion, chopped	
40 grapes	40 grapes	40 grapes	
2 cakes	2 cakes	4 cakes	
4 Tbs (64 g)	4 Tbs (64 g)	6 Tbs (96 g)	
8 oz (224 g) cooked	8 oz (224 g) cooked	8 oz (224 g) cooked	
1 c (264 g)	1 c (264 g)	1 c (264 g)	
3 each (56 g)	3 each (56 g)	6 each (112 g)	Lentils or tofu
1 c	1 c	1 c	
1 tsp (5 g)	1 tsp (5 g)	2 Tbs (32 g)	
1 1/2 c (360 mL)	2 c (480 mL)		Nut milk
CHO: 175 g	CHO: 234 g	CHO:	
PRO: 119 g	PRO: 135 g	PRO:	

BASE FITNESS MENUS
Day 5

Meal	Time Eaten	Food	1800-calorie
BREAKFAST	7:00 AM	Protein Power Pancakes (see recipe pg 213)	1/2 of recipe
		Peanut butter	1 Tbs
		Banana slices	1/2 small banana
SNACK	10:30 AM	Almonds	1 oz (23 nuts)
		Dried apricots	6 halves
LUNCH	1:00 PM	Taco wrap with flour tortilla:	8-inch tortilla
		Black beans	1/2 c (120 g)
		Mozzarella cheese	1 oz shredded (28 g)
		Salsa	2 Tbs (36 g)
		Avocado slices	1/4 avocado
SNACK	3:00 PM	Deli turkey slices	2 slices
		Cheddar cheese	2 slices
DINNER	6:30 PM	Grilled salmon with:	3 oz (85 g)
		Steamed asparagus	4 spears
		Wild rice	1 cup (164 g)
SNACK	9:00 PM	Cottage cheese with:	1/2 c (115 g)
		Strawberries	1/2 c sliced (83 g)
AVG CHO			CHO: 164 g
AVG PRO			PRO: 116 g

DRINK WATER throughout the day according to thirst and urine color

2100-calorie	2500-calorie	3000-calorie	Vegan/Vegetarian option
1/2 of recipe	1 whole recipe	1 whole recipe	Use plant protein powder
1 Tbs	2 Tbs	2 Tbs	Substitute 2 Tbs flax + 6 Tbs water for the 1 egg
1/2 small banana	1/2 small banana	2 small bananas	
1 oz (23 nuts)	1 oz (23 nuts)	2 oz (46 nuts)	
6 halves	6 halves	1 c of halves (130 g)	
8-inch tortilla	8-inch tortilla	8-inch tortilla	
1/2 c (120 g)	1/2 c (120 g)	1/2 c (120 g)	
1 oz shredded (28 g)	1 oz shredded (28 g)	1 oz shredded (28 g)	Use vegan cheese
2 Tbs (36 g)	2 Tbs (36 g)	2 Tbs (36 g)	
1/4 avocado	1/4 avocado	1/4 avocado	
2 slices	2 slices	2 slices	Mixed nuts
2 slices	2 slices	2 slices	
4 oz (113 g)	4 oz (113 g)	4 oz (113 g)	Meatless patty
4 spears	4 spears	4 spears	
1 1/2 c (246 g)	1 1/2 c (246 g)	1 1/2 c (246 g)	
1 c (230 g)	1 c (230 g)	1 c (230 g)	Vegan yogurt
1 c (166 g)	1 c (166 g)	1 c (166 g)	
CHO: 192 g	CHO: 242 g	CHO: 336 g	
PRO: 139 g	PRO: 168 g	PRO: 180 g	

STRENGTH PHASE MENUS
Day 1

Meal	Time Eaten	Food	1800-calorie
BREAKFAST	7:00 AM	Breakfast sandwich made with English muffin	1 each
		Egg	1 fried
		Pork-sausage patty	1 patty (2 oz)
		Slice of cheese	1 slice
SNACK	10:30 AM	Sunflower seeds	0
LUNCH	1:00 PM	Peanut butter and jam sandwich	
		Wheat bread	2 slices
		Peanut butter	2 Tbs (32 g)
		Jam	1 Tbs (20 g)
		Apple	1 medium
SNACK	3:00 PM	Protein bar	0
DINNER	6:30 PM	Southwest salad made with:	
		Mixed greens	2 cups chopped (110 g)
		Black beans	1/2 c (120 g)
		Avocado slices	1/4 avocado
		Cojita cheese	1/3 c crumbled (30 g)
		Corn	1/2 c (83 g)
		Tortilla chips	1 oz (28 g)
SNACK	9:00 PM	Graham crackers	1 sheet (35 g)
		Milk	1/2 c (120 mL)
AVG CHO			CHO: 171 g
AVG PRO			PRO: 70 g

DRINK WATER throughout the day according to thirst and urine color

2100-calorie	2500-calorie	3000-calorie	Vegan/Vegetarian option
1 each	1 each	1 each	
1 fried	1 fried	1 fried	
2 patties (4 oz)	2 patties (4 oz)	2 patties (4 oz)	Veggie sausage patty
1 slice	1 slice	1 slice	Vegan cheese
0	1 oz (28 g)	2 oz (57 g)	
2 slices	2 slices	2 slices	Chickpeas
2 Tbs (32 g)	2 Tbs (32 g)	2 Tbs (32 g)	
1 Tbs (20 g)	1 Tbs (20 g)	1 Tbs (20 g)	
1 medium	1 medium	1 medium	
0	approx-250 calorie bar	approx-250 calorie bar	
2 cups chopped (110 g)	2 cups chopped (110 g)	2 cups chopped (110 g)	
1/2 c (120 g)	1/2 c (120 g)	1 c (240 g)	
1/4 avocado	1/4 avocado	1/4 avocado	
1/3 c crumbled (30 g)	1/3 c crumbled (30 g)	1/3 c crumbled (30 g)	
1/2 c (83 g)	1/2 c (83 g)	1/2 c (83 g)	
1 oz (28 g)	1 oz (28 g)	1 oz (28 g)	
2 sheets	2 sheets	4 sheets	
1 c (240 mL)	1 c (240 mL)	1 c (240 mL)	Soy or nut milk
CHO: 203 g	**CHO: 250 g**	**CHO: 316 g**	
PRO: 86 g	**PRO: 101 g**	**PRO: 118 g**	

STRENGTH PHASE MENUS
Day 2

Meal	Time Eaten	Food	1800-calorie
BREAKFAST	7:00 AM	Greek yogurt with:	5 oz (150 g)
		Almonds	1 oz (23 almonds; 28 g)
		Blueberries	50 berries (68 g)
SNACK	10:30 AM	Whole grain mini-bagel with:	1 mini-bagel
		Cream cheese	1 Tbs
LUNCH	1:00 PM	Fruit and cheese board made with:	
		Apple and pear slices	1 small apple, 1 small pear
		Goat cheese (or other cheese of choice)	1 oz (28 g)
		Gruyere cheese (or other cheese of choice)	1 oz (28 g)
		Almonds (or other nut of choice)	1 oz (23 almonds)
		Walnuts (or other nut of choice)	1 oz (28 g)
SNACK	3:00 PM	Chocolate milk	1 c (240 mL)
DINNER	6:30 PM	Stir fry made with:	
		Veggies of choice	1 cup (60 g)
		Chicken strips	3 oz (120 g)
		Brown rice	1 cup (202 g)
		Soy or teriyaki sauce	1 tsp
SNACK	9:00 PM	Protein shake	0
AVG CHO			**CHO:** 157 g
AVG PRO			**PRO:** 101 g

DRINK WATER throughout the day according to thirst and urine color

2100-calorie	2500-calorie	3000-calorie	Vegan/Vegetarian option
5 oz (150 g)	5 oz (150 g)	10 oz (300 g)	Soy or almond yogurt
1 oz (23 almonds; 28 g)	1 oz (23 almonds; 28 g)	2 oz (57 g)	
50 berries (68 g)	50 berries (68 g)	1 c berries (148 g)	
1 mini-bagel	2 mini-bagels	2 mini-bagels	
1 Tbs	2 Tbs	2 Tbs	Jam or nut butter
1 small apple, 1 small pear	1 small apple, 1 small pear	1 large apple, 1 large pear	
1 oz (28 g)	1 oz (28 g)	1 oz (28 g)	Vegan cheese
1 oz (28 g)	1 oz (28 g)	1 oz (28 g)	Vegan cheese
1 oz (23 almonds)	1 oz (23 almonds)	1 oz (23 almonds)	
1 oz (28 g)	1 oz (28 g)	1 oz (28 g)	
1 c (240 mL)	1 1/2 c (360 mL)	2 cups (480 mL)	Nut milk
1 cup (60 g)	1 1/2 cups (90 g)	1 1/2 cups (90 g)	
3 oz (120 g)	4 oz (160 g)	4 oz (160 g)	Tofu or meatless patty
1 cup (202 g)	1 1/2 cups (303 g)	1 1/2 cups (303 g)	
1 tsp	1 tsp	1 tsp	
250 mL (approx 250 calories)	250 mL (approx 250 calories)	250 mL (approx 250 calories)	Plant-protein shake
CHO: 158 g	**CHO:** 214 g	**CHO:** 279 g	
PRO: 121 g	**PRO:** 145 g	**PRO:** 171 g	

STRENGTH PHASE MENUS
Day 3

Meal	Time Eaten	Food	1800-calorie
BREAKFAST	7:00 AM	Breakfast burrito made with:	
		Tortilla	8-inch tortilla
		Scrambled egg	1 egg
		Sausage crumbles	1 oz (28 g)
		Shredded cheese	1/4 c (28 g)
		Side of fruit (orange)	1 medium
SNACK	10:30 AM	Fruit Smoothie (see recipe page 212)	1 recipe/smoothie
LUNCH	1:00 PM	Chili or lentil soup with:	1 cup (248 g)
		Whole-grain roll	1 oz (28 g)
		Butter	1 tsp (5 g)
SNACK	3:00 PM	Banana with:	1 medium
		Nut butter	2 Tbs
DINNER	6:30 PM	Grilled pork chop	3 oz (80 g)
		Quinoa	1 c (185 g)
		Broccoli	1 c (156 g)
SNACK	9:00 PM	On-the-Go Egg Cup (see recipe page 211)	0
AVG CHO			CHO: 159 g
AVG PRO			PRO: 90 g

DRINK WATER throughout the day according to thirst and urine color

2100-calorie	2500-calorie	3000-calorie	Vegan/Vegetarian option
	2 burritos	2 burritos	
8-inch tortilla	2 8-inch tortillas	2 8-inch tortillas	
1 egg	2 eggs	2 eggs	Black beans
1 oz (28 g)	2 oz (56 g)	2 oz (56 g)	Meatless sausage crumbles
1/4 c (28 g)	1/2 c (56 g)	1/2 c (56 g)	Vegan cheese
1 medium	1 medium	1 medium	
1 recipe/smoothie	1 recipe/smoothie	1 recipe/smoothie	
1 cup (248 g)	1 cup (248 g)	1 cup (248 g)	
1 oz (28 g)	1 oz (28 g)	1 oz (28 g)	
1 tsp (5 g)	1 tsp (5 g)	1 tsp (5 g)	Jam
1 medium	1 medium	1 medium	
2 Tbs	2 Tbs	2 Tbs	
3 oz (80 g)	3 oz (80 g)	6 oz (160 g)	Roasted tofu or meatless veggie patty
1 c (185 g)	1 c (185 g)	2 cups (370 g)	
1 c (156 g)	1 c (156 g)	1 c (156 g)	
3 egg cups (177 g)	3 egg cups (177 g)		Plant-protein shake
CHO: 162 g	CHO: 190 g	CHO: 224 g	
PRO: 115 g	PRO: 137 g	PRO: 167 g	

STRENGTH PHASE MENUS
Day 4

Meal	Time Eaten	Food	1800-calorie
BREAKFAST	7:00 AM	Apple Banana Oatmeal	1 recipe
		(see recipe page 209)	
SNACK	10:30 AM	Carrots, sliced bell peppers, and:	As much as desired
		Sliced cucumber	
		Hummus	2 Tbs
LUNCH	1:00 PM	Bagel sandwich made with:	1 bagel (98 g)
		Turkey deli meat	2 slices (30 g)
		Lettuce	1 leaf
		Tomato	1 slice
		Cheese	1 slice
		With apple slices	1 medium apple
SNACK	3:00 PM	Grapes	1 cup (151 g)
		Almonds	0
DINNER	6:30 PM	Steak	3 oz (82 g)
		Roasted potatoes	1/2 c (78 g)
		Steamed zucchini	1/2 c (80 g)
SNACK	9:00 PM	Cottage cheese	1 cup (230 g)
		Strawberries	1 cup (166 g)
AVG CHO			CHO: 204 g
AVG PRO			PRO: 95 g

DRINK WATER throughout the day according to thirst and urine color

2100-calorie	2500-calorie	3000-calorie	Vegan/Vegetarian option
1 recipe	1 recipe	1 recipe	Use agave syrup instead of honey
		Top with walnuts 1/2 c (60 g)	Use nut milk instead of milk; omit egg
As much as desired	As much as desired	As much as desired	
2 Tbs	4 Tbs	1/2 c (123 g)	
1 bagel (98 g)	1 bagel (98 g)	1 bagel (98 g)	
2 slices (30 g)	4 slices (45 g)	4 slices (45 g)	Use veggie patty
1 leaf	1 leaf	1 leaf	
1 slice	1 slice	1 slice	
1 slice	2 slices	2 slices	Omit cheese or use vegan cheese
1 medium apple	1 medium apple	1 medium apple	
1 1/2 c (249 g)	1 1/2 c (249 g)	1 1/2 c (249 g)	
0	23 almonds (28 g)	23 almonds (28 g)	
6 oz (163 g)	6 oz (163 g)	6 oz (163 g)	Fish (if pescatarian) or tofu
1 c (156 g)	1 c (156 g)	1 c (156 g)	
1 c (160 g)	1 c (160 g)	1 c (160 g)	
1 cup (230 g)	1 1/2 c (345 g)	1 1/2 c (345 g)	Soy yogurt
1 cup (166 g)	1 cup (166 g)	1 cup (166 g)	
CHO: 237 g	**CHO: 249 g**	**CHO: 259 g**	
PRO: 119 g	**PRO: 148 g**	**PRO: 162 g**	

STRENGTH PHASE MENUS
Day 5

Meal	Time Eaten	Food	1800-calorie
BREAKFAST	7:00 AM	Granola with:	1 cup (122 g)
		Milk	1 cup (245 g)
		Raisins	1/4 c (37 g)
SNACK	10:30 AM	Whole-grain crackers with:	0
		Cheese	0
LUNCH	1:00 PM	Chilled pasta salad made with:	
		Pasta	1 c (120 g)
		Cherry tomatoes	5 tomatoes
		Spinach	1 handful
		Carrots	5 baby carrots (50 g)
		Grilled chicken strips	4 oz (120g)
		Salad dressing: vinaigrette (bottled)	1 Tbs (16 g)
SNACK	3:00 PM	Yogurt with:	0
		Blueberries	0
DINNER	6:30 PM	Coconut Curry	1/4 of the recipe (total recipe makes 4 servings)
		(see recipe page 211)	
SNACK	9:00 PM	Chocolate milk	0
AVG CHO			CHO: 261 g
AVG PRO			PRO: 92 g

DRINK WATER throughout the day according to thirst and urine color

2100-calorie	2500-calorie	3000-calorie	Vegan/Vegetarian option
1 cup (122 g)	1 cup (122 g)	1 cup (122 g)	
1 cup (245 g)	1 cup (245 g)	1 cup (245 g)	Nut milk
1/4 c (37 g)	1/4 c (37 g)	1/4 c (37 g)	
0	18 crackers (84 g)	30 crackers (140 g)	
0	1 slice (28 g)	2 slices (56 g)	Nut butter or hummus
1 c (120 g)	1 c (120 g)	1 1/2 c pasta	
5 tomatoes	5 tomatoes	5 tomatoes	
1 handful	1 handful	1 handful	
5 baby carrots (50 g)	5 baby carrots (50 g)	10 baby carrots	
4 oz (120g)	4 oz (120g)	6 oz (170 g)	Use pine nuts
1 Tbs (16 g)	1 Tbs (16 g)	1 Tbs (16 g)	
6 oz (170 g)	6 oz (170 g)	6 oz (170 g)	Soy yogurt
50 berries (68 g)	50 berries (68 g)	50 berries (68 g)	
1/4 of the recipe (total recipe makes 4 servings)	1/4 of the recipe (total recipe makes 4 servings)	1/3 of the recipe (total recipe makes 4 servings)	Substitute pre-cooked lentils for chicken
			Substitute for chicken broth–use vegetable broth
0	0	1 cup (240 mL)	
CHO: 189 g	**CHO: 239 g**	**CHO: 292 g**	
PRO: 127 g	**PRO: 143 g**	**PRO: 163 g**	

POWER-ENDURANCE PHASE MENUS
Day 1

Meal	Time Eaten	Food	1800-calorie
BREAKFAST	7:00 AM	Protein smoothie with:	
		Chocolate whey protein powder	2 scoops (57 g)
		Peanut butter	1 Tbs (16 g)
		Milk	1/2 cup
		Banana	1/2 banana
		Scrambled eggs	0
SNACK	10:30 AM	Orange	1 medium
		Greek yogurt	none
LUNCH	1:00 PM	Turkey pita with:	Two 4" pitas (96 g)
		Lettuce	4 leaves
		Cucumber	4 slices (20 g)
		Tomato	2 slices
		Side of grapes	20 grapes (94 g)
		Turkey	4 slices (60 g)
SNACK	3:00 PM	Trail mix	2 handfuls (80 g)
DINNER	6:30 PM	Soft tacos with:	
		Tortilla	1 tortilla (49 g)
		Shredded pork	2 oz (58 g)
		Salsa	2 Tbs (36 g)
		Shredded lettuce	1/2 c (22 g)
		Avocado	1/4 avocado (20 g)
		Side of grapes	20 grapes (94 g)
		Cheese	0
SNACK	9:00 PM	Protein bar	1 bar ~ 250 calories
		Chocolate milk	0
AVG CHO			CHO: 184 g
AVG PRO			PRO: 111 g

DRINK WATER throughout the day according to thirst and urine color

2100-calorie	2500-calorie	3000-calorie	Vegan/Vegetarian option
2 scoops (57 g)	2 scoops (57 g)	2 scoops (57 g)	Plant based protein powder
1 Tbs (16 g)	1 Tbs (16 g)	1 Tbs (16 g)	
1/2 cup	1/2 cup	1/2 cup	
1/2 banana	1/2 banana	1/2 banana	
0	2 eggs	2 eggs	Tofu scramble
1 medium	1 medium	1 medium	
none	1 container (170 g)	1 container (170 g)	Soy/vegan yogurt
Two 4" pitas (96 g)	Two 4" pitas (96 g)	Two 4" pitas (96 g)	
4 leaves	4 leaves	4 leaves	
4 slices (20 g)	4 slices (20 g)	4 slices (20 g)	
2 slices	2 slices	2 slices	
20 grapes (94 g)	20 grapes (94 g)	20 grapes (94 g)	
4 slices (60 g)	4 slices (60 g)	6 slices (90 g)	Chickpeas
2 handfuls (80 g)	3 handfuls (120 g)	1 cup (150 g)	
2 tortillas (98 g)	2 tortillas (98 g)	2 tortillas (98 g)	
4 oz (117 g)	4 oz (117 g)	4 oz (117 g)	Black beans
2 Tbs (36 g)	2 Tbs (36 g)	2 Tbs (36 g)	
1/2 c (22 g)	1/2 c (22 g)	1/2 c (22 g)	
1/4 avocado (20 g)	1/4 avocado (20 g)	1/4 avocado (20 g)	
20 grapes (94 g)	20 grapes (94 g)	20 grapes (94 g)	
1 oz shredded (28 g)	1 oz shredded (28 g)	1 oz shredded (28 g)	Vegan cheese
1 bar ~ 250 calories	1 bar ~ 250 calories	1 bar ~ 250 calories	
0	0	1 cup (240 mL)	Nut milk, chocolate flavor
CHO: 208 g	CHO: 234 g	CHO: 277 g	
PRO: 138 g	PRO: 173 g	PRO: 189 g	

POWER-ENDURANCE PHASE MENUS
Day 2

Meal	Time Eaten	Food	1800-calorie
BREAKFAST	7:00 AM	Omelet with:	2 eggs
		Green onion	1 Tbs (6 g)
		Spinach	1 handful
		Tomatoes	1/4 c diced
		Whole-grain toast	2 slices
		Butter	1 Tbs (14 g)
SNACK	10:30 AM	Mixed nuts	1 oz (28 g)
		Dried apricots	1/2 c (60 g)
LUNCH	1:00 PM	Peanut butter and jelly sandwich with:	
		Apple slices	1 medium apple (172 g)
		Whole-wheat bread	2 slices
		Peanut butter	2 Tbs (32 g)
		Jam	1 Tbs (20 g)
		Greek yogurt	0
SNACK	3:00 PM	Fruit, Spinach, and Yogurt Smoothie	1 smoothie (1 recipe)
		(See recipe page 212)	
DINNER	6:30 PM	Minestrone soup	10 oz (283 g)
		Whole-grain sourdough bread	1 slice (43 g)
		Garden salad	1 cup (44 g)
		Salad dressing	1 Tbs (16 g)
SNACK	9:00 PM	Protein shake	0
AVG CHO			CHO: 194 g
AVG PRO			PRO: 62 g

DRINK WATER throughout the day according to thirst and urine color

2100-calorie	2500-calorie	3000-calorie	Vegan/Vegetarian option
2 eggs	2 eggs	4 eggs	Oatmeal with nuts and berries
1 Tbs (6 g)	1 Tbs (6 g)	1 Tbs (6 g)	
1 handful	1 handful	1 handful	
1/4 c diced	1/4 c diced	1/4 c diced	
2 slices	2 slices	2 slices	
1 Tbs (14 g)	1 Tbs (14 g)	1 Tbs (14 g)	Jam
1 oz (28 g)	1 oz (28 g)	2 oz (57 g)	
1/2 c (60 g)	1/2 c (60 g)	1/2 c (60 g)	
1 medium apple (172 g)	1 medium apple (172 g)	1 medium apple (172 g)	
2 slices	2 slices	2 slices	
2 Tbs (32 g)	2 Tbs (32 g)	2 Tbs (32 g)	
1 Tbs (20 g)	1 Tbs (20 g)	1 Tbs (20 g)	
0	6 oz (125 g)	6 oz (125 g)	Vegan yogurt
1 smoothie (1 recipe)			
10 oz (283 g)	20 oz (566 g)	20 oz (566 g)	
1 slice (43 g)	2 slices (86 g)	2 slices (86 g)	
1 cup (44 g)	1 cup (44 g)	1 cup (44 g)	
1 Tbs (16 g)	1 Tbs (16 g)	1 Tbs (16 g)	
8 oz (240 mL)	8 oz (240 mL)	16 oz (480 mL)	
CHO: 206 g	CHO: 249 g	CHO: 267 g	
PRO: 94 g	PRO: 111 g	PRO: 160 g	

POWER-ENDURANCE PHASE MENUS
Day 3

Meal	Time Eaten	Food	1800-calorie
BREAKFAST	7:00 AM	Avocado toast with:	2 slices whole-wheat bread
		Fried egg on top	2 eggs
		Avocado	1/4 avocado
		Side of strawberries	1/2 cup (71 g)
SNACK	10:30 AM	Protein bar	~250 cal bar
LUNCH	1:00 PM	Chinese chicken salad with:	
		Mixed greens	2 cups (94 g)
		Chicken	2 oz (90 g)
		Mandarin oranges	1 medium orange in slices (65 g)
		Veggies of choice	As much as desired
		Dressing	1 Tbs (16 g)
SNACK	3:00 PM	Tortilla chips	1 oz (28 g)
		Salsa	1/4 cup (72 g)
DINNER	6:30 PM	Pasta served with:	1 cup cooked (107 g)
		Pesto	1/4 c (61 g)
		Salmon	3 oz (85 g)
		Steamed asparagus	8 spears (120 g)
SNACK	9:00 PM	Chocolate milk	0
AVG CHO			CHO: 137 g
AVG PRO			PRO: 95 g

DRINK WATER throughout the day according to thirst and urine color

2100-calorie	2500-calorie	3000-calorie	Vegan/Vegetarian option
2 slices whole-wheat bread	3 slices	3 slices	
2 eggs	3 eggs	3 eggs	Nut butter
1/4 avocado	1/2 avocado	1/2 avocado	
1/2 cup (71 g)	1/2 cup (71 g)	1/2 cup (71 g)	
~250 cal bar	~250 cal bar	~250 cal bar	
2 cups (94 g)	2 cups (94 g)	2 cups (94 g)	
2 oz (90 g)	2 oz (90 g)	2 oz (90 g)	Tofu or Pine nuts
1 medium orange in slices (65 g)	1 medium orange in slices (65 g)	1 medium orange in slices (65 g)	
As much as desired	As much as desired	As much as desired	
1 Tbs (16 g)	1 Tbs (16 g)	1 Tbs (16 g)	
1 oz (28 g)	1 oz (28 g)	2 oz (57 g)	
1/4 cup (72 g)	1/4 cup (72 g)	1/2 cup (144 g)	
1 cup cooked (107 g)	2 cups cooked (214 g)	2 cups cooked (214 g)	
1/4 c (61 g)	1/4 c (61 g)	1/2 c (122 g)	
6 oz (170)	6 oz (170)	6 oz (170)	Tofu or meatless patty
8 spears (120 g)	8 spears (120 g)	8 spears (120 g)	
8 oz (240 mL)	8 oz (240 mL)	16 oz (480 mL)	Nut milk, chocolate flavored
CHO: 165 g	**CHO: 208 g**	**CHO: 260 g**	
PRO: 121 g	**PRO: 138 g**	**PRO: 151 g**	

POWER-ENDURANCE PHASE MENUS Day 4

Meal	Time Eaten	Food	1800-calorie
BREAKFAST	7:00 AM	Breakfast sandwich with:	
		English muffin	1 muffin (68 g)
		Slice of cheese	1 slice (28 g)
		Slice of ham	2 slices (56 g)
		Fried egg	1 egg
		Side of orange slices	1 medium orange
SNACK	10:30 AM	Banana	1 medium (76 g)
		Peanut butter	2 Tbs
LUNCH	1:00 PM	Chilled pasta salad made with:	
		Pasta	1 cup cooked (107 g)
		Cherry tomatoes	10 each (155 g)
		Spinach	1 handful (31 g)
		Carrots	5 each (50 g)
		Bell peppers	1/2 cup sliced
		Grilled chicken strips	1 oz (45 g)
		Dressing	1 Tbs (16 g)
SNACK	3:00 PM	Cheese board with nuts and fruit	
		Cheese	1 oz (28 g)
		Walnuts	0
		Apple slices	1 medium apple (172 g)
DINNER	6:30 PM	Loaded quesadilla with:	2 quesadillas
		(See recipe page 213)	
		Garden salad	1 cup salad with vegetables of choice
		Dressing	1 Tbs (16 g)
SNACK	9:00 PM	Greek yogurt with:	0
		Blueberres	0
AVG CHO			CHO: 159 g
AVG PRO			PRO: 93 g

DRINK WATER throughout the day according to thirst and urine color

2100-calorie	2500-calorie	3000-calorie	Vegan/Vegetarian option
1 muffin (68 g)	1 muffin (68 g)	2 muffins (136 g)	
1 slice (28 g)	1 slice (28 g)	1 slices (57 g)	Vegan cheese
2 slices (56 g)	2 slices (56 g)	4 slices (112 g)	1 meat-alternative sausage patty
1 egg	1 egg	2 eggs	Egg if vegetarian; omit egg if vegan
1 medium orange	1 medium orange	1 medium orange	
1 medium (76 g)	1 medium (76 g)	1 medium (76 g)	
3 Tbsp (48 g)	3 Tbsp (48 g)	3 Tbsp (48 g)	
1 cup cooked (107 g)	1 cup cooked (107 g)	1 cup cooked (107 g)	
10 each (155 g)	10 each (155 g)	10 each (155 g)	
1 handful (31 g)	1 handful (31 g)	1 handful (31 g)	
5 each (50 g)	5 each (50 g)	5 each (50 g)	
1/2 cup sliced	1/2 cup sliced	1/2 cup sliced	
1 oz (45 g)	1 oz (45 g)	1 oz (45 g)	Vegetarian option: soft-boiled egg; vegan option: kidney beans
1 Tbs (16 g)	1 Tbs (16 g)	1 Tbs (16 g)	
1 oz (28 g)	1 oz (28 g)	1 oz (28 g)	Vegan cheese
1/2 cup (22 g)	1/2 cup (22 g)	1/2 cup (22 g)	
1 medium apple (172 g)	1 medium apple (172 g)	1 medium apple (172 g)	
2 quesadillas	3 quesadillas	3 quesadillas	
1 cup salad with vegetables of choice	1 cup salad with vegetables of choice	1 cup salad with vegetables of choice	
1 Tbs (16 g)	1 Tbs (16 g)	1 Tbs (16 g)	
0	6 oz (150 g)	6 oz (150 g)	Soy or nut yogurt
0	1/2 c (70 g)	1/2 c (70 g)	
CHO: 163 g	CHO: 197 g	CHO: 227 g	
PRO: 100 g	PRO: 127 g	PRO: 155 g	

CHAPTER 12 - MENUS AND RECIPES FOR CLIMBERS

POWER-ENDURANCE PHASE MENUS
Day 5

Meal	Time Eaten	Food	1800-calorie
BREAKFAST	7:00 AM	Yogurt parfait with:	
		Greek yogurt	4 oz (125 g)
		Granola	1/2 oz (14 g)
		Strawberries	1/2 c sliced (71 g)
SNACK	10:30 AM	Apple slices	1 medium apple (172 g)
		Almonds	1 oz (22 almonds)
LUNCH	1:00 PM	Baked potato with:	1 medium potato (173 g)
		Shredded cheese	1/4 c (28 g)
		Chili beans	1/2 c (128 g)
		Sour cream	2 Tbs (24 g)
		Side of carrot and celery sticks	As much as desired
SNACK	3:00 PM	Energy Bites	2 bites (74 g)
		(see recipe page 212)	
DINNER	6:30 PM	Spinach salad with:	2 cups fresh leaves, loosely packed (20 g)
		Grilled chicken strips	3 oz (100 g)
		Strawberries	1/2 c sliced
		Blueberries	50 berries (65 g)
		Walnuts	1/4 c chopped (30 g)
		Basalmic vinaigrette	1 Tbs (16 g)
SNACK	9:00 PM	Protein shake	0
AVG CHO			CHO: 131 g
AVG PRO			PRO: 83 g

DRINK WATER throughout the day according to thirst and urine color

2100-calorie	2500-calorie	3000-calorie	Vegan/Vegetarian option
4 oz (125 g)	4 oz (125 g)	8 oz (250 g)	Soy or nut yogurt
1/2 oz (14 g)	1/2 oz (14 g)	1 oz (28 g)	
1/2 c sliced (71 g)	1 c sliced (152 g)	1 c sliced (152 g)	
1 medium apple (172 g)	1 medium apple (172 g)	1 medium apple (172 g)	
1 oz (22 almonds)	1 oz (22 almonds)	2 oz (44 almonds)	
1 medium potato (173 g)	1 medium potato (173 g)	1 medium potato (173 g)	
1/4 c (28 g)	1/4 c (28 g)	1/4 c (28 g)	Vegan cheese
1/2 c (128 g)	1/2 c (128 g)	1/2 c (128 g)	
2 Tbs (24 g)	2 Tbs (24 g)	2 Tbs (24 g)	Vegan sour cream
As much as desired	As much as desired	As much as desired	
2 bites (74 g)	4 bites (148 g)	4 bites (148 g)	
2 cups fresh leaves, loosely packed (20 g)	2 cups fresh leaves, loosely packed (20 g)	2 cups fresh leaves, loosely packed (20 g)	
3 oz (100 g)	3 oz (100 g)	3 oz (100 g)	Soft-boiled egg or chickpeas
1/2 c sliced	1/2 c sliced	1/2 c sliced	
50 berries (65 g)	50 berries (65 g)	50 berries (65 g)	
1/4 c chopped (30 g)	1/4 c chopped (30 g)	1/4 c chopped (30 g)	
1 Tbs (16 g)	1 Tbs (16 g)	1 Tbs (16 g)	
8 oz (240 mL)	8 oz (240 mL)	16 oz (480 mL)	
CHO: 143 g	**CHO: 177 g**	**CHO: 204 g**	
PRO: 115 g	**PRO: 124 g**	**PRO: 175 g**	

POWER PHASE MENUS
Day 1

Meal	Time Eaten	Food	1800-calorie
BREAKFAST	7:00 AM	On-the-Go Egg Cups	2 egg cups
		(see recipe page 211)	
SNACK	10:30 AM	Protein shake	1 cup (240 mL)
LUNCH	1:00 PM	Grilled cheese sandwich with:	1 sandwich
		Whole-wheat bread	2 slices
		Cheddar cheese	1 oz
		Butter for grilling	1 pat
		Tomato soup	1 cup (240 mL)
		Garden salad	1 cup (44 g)
		Dressing	1 Tbs
SNACK	3:00 PM	Mixed nuts	1 oz (28 g)
DINNER	6:30 PM	Recovery power bowl	1 bowl with:
		(See recipe page 214)	1 cup grains (160 g)
			4 oz meat (85 g)
			Vegetables as desired
SNACK	9:00 PM	Cheese board with:	
		Walnuts	0
		Whole-grain crackers	0
		Grapes	0
AVG CHO			CHO: 138 g
AVG PRO			PRO: 94 g

DRINK WATER throughout the day according to thirst and urine color

2100-calorie	2500-calorie	3000-calorie	Vegan/Vegetarian option
4 egg cups	4 egg cups	5 egg cups	Soy yogurt with fruit
1 cup (240 mL)	1 cup (240 mL)	1 cup (240 mL)	Plant protein shake
1 sandwich	1 sandwich	2 sandwiches	
2 slices	2 slices	4 slices	
1 oz	1 oz	2 oz	Veggie "meat" patty
1 pat	1 pat	2 pats	Oil
1 cup (240 mL)	1 cup (240 mL)	2 cups (504 mL)	
1 cup (44 g)	1 cup (44 g)	1 cup (44 g)	
1 Tbs	1 Tbs	1 Tbs	
1 oz (28 g)	2 oz (54 g)	2 oz (54 g)	
1 bowl with:	1 bowl with:	1 bowl with:	
1 cup grains (160 g)	1 cup grains (160 g)	1 cup grains (160 g)	
4 oz meat (85 g)	4 oz meat (85 g)	4 oz meat (85 g)	Tofu, lentils, or beans
Vegetables as desired	Vegetables as desired	Vegetables as desired	
1 oz cheese (28 g)	1 oz cheese (28 g)	1 oz cheese (28 g)	Vegan cheese
1/2 c halves (23 g)	1/2 c halves (23 g)	1/2 c halves (23 g)	
20 each	20 each	20 each	
1 small bunch (100 g)	1 small bunch (100 g)	1 small bunch (100 g)	
CHO: 162 g	CHO: 169 g	CHO: 215 g	
PRO: 107 g	PRO: 129 g	PRO: 150 g	

POWER PHASE MENUS
Day 2

Meal	Time Eaten	Food	1800-calorie
BREAKFAST	7:00 AM	Granola or museli with:	3 oz (85 g)
		Milk	1 cup (240 mL)
		Berries	1/2 c (71 g)
SNACK	10:30 AM	Protein bar	1 bar ~250 calories
		Apple	0
LUNCH	1:00 PM	Greek wrap with:	1 wrap
		Flatbread	1 piece
		Lettuce	2 leaves
		Tomato	2 slices
		Feta cheese	1 oz (28 g)
		Cucumber	2 slices
		Olives	1/4 c (53 g)
		Chicken	2 oz (45 g)
SNACK	3:00 PM	Orange	1 medium
		Greek yogurt	0
DINNER	6:30 PM	Recovery power bowl	1 bowl with:
		(See recipe page 214)	1 cup grains (160 g)
			4 oz meat 85 g)
			Vegetables as desired
SNACK	9:00 PM	Salmon with:	3 oz (85 g)
		Couscous	1 cup (157 g)
		Steamed broccoli	1 cup (156 g)
AVG CHO			CHO: 188 g
AVG PRO			PRO: 92 g

DRINK WATER throughout the day according to thirst and urine color

2100-calorie	2500-calorie	3000-calorie	Vegan/Vegetarian option
3 oz (85 g)	4 oz (113 g)		
1 cup (240 mL)	1 1/2 cups (368 mL)		
1/2 c (71 g)	1 cup (143 g)		
1 bar ~250 calories	1 bar ~250 calories	1 bar ~250 calories	
0	1 medium	1 medium	
1 wrap	1 wrap	2 wraps	
1 piece	1 piece	2 pieces	
2 leaves	2 leaves	4 leaves	
2 slices	2 slices	4 slices	
1 oz (28 g)	1 oz (28 g)	2 oz (56 g)	
2 slices	2 slices	4 slices	
1/4 c (53 g)	1/4 c (53 g)	1/2 c (106 g)	
2 oz (45 g)	2 oz (45 g)	4 oz (90 g)	Chickpeas
1 medium	1 medium	1 medium	
0	0	1 container (170 g)	Soy Yogurt
1 bowl with:	1 bowl with:	1 bowl with:	
1 cup grains (160 g)	1 cup grains (160 g)	1 cup grains (160 g)	
4 oz meat 85 g)	4 oz meat 85 g)	4 oz meat 85 g)	tofu, lentils, or beans
Vegetables as desired	Vegetables as desired	Vegetables as desired	
6 oz (170 g)	6 oz (170 g)	6 oz (170 g)	Meat-alternative patty or lentils
2 cups (314 g)	2 cups (314 g)	2 cups (314 g)	
1 cup (156 g)	1 cup (156 g)	1 cup (156 g)	
CHO: 222 g	**CHO: 263 g**	**CHO: 309 g**	
PRO: 116 g	**PRO: 125 g**	**PRO: 175 g**	

POWER PHASE MENUS
Day 3

Meal	Time Eaten	Food	1800-calorie
BREAKFAST	7:00 AM	Waffles with:	2 medium (50 g)
		Maple syrup	1 Tbs (20 g)
		Butter	1 Tbs (14 g)
		Sausage patty	2 oz (57 g)
		Banana	1 medium
SNACK	10:30 AM	Greek yogurt with	7 oz (200g)
		Blueberries	50 berries (65 g)
LUNCH	1:00 PM	Egg salad sandwich	
		Whole-wheat bread	2 slices
		Eggs, hardboiled	2 eggs
		Mayonnaise	2 Tbs
		Carrot, pepper, and cucumber slices on the side	As much as desired
SNACK	3:00 PM	Kiwi	1 kiwi
		Mixed nuts	0
DINNER	6:30 PM	Pasta with:	1 cup pasta (107 g)
		Pesto	1/8 cup (31 g)
		Chicken	3 oz (120 g)
		Zucchini	1 cup (180 g)
SNACK	9:00 PM	Protein shake	0
AVG CHO			CHO: 130 g
AVG PRO			PRO: 102 g

> DRINK WATER throughout the day according to thirst and urine color

2100-calorie	2500-calorie	3000-calorie	Vegan/Vegetarian option
2 medium (50 g)	3 waffles (75 g)	3 waffles (75 g)	
1 Tbs (20 g)	2 Tbs (40 g)	2 Tbs (40 g)	
1 Tbs (14 g)	2 Tbs (28 g)	2 Tbs (28 g)	
2 oz (57 g)	4 oz (114 g)	4 oz (114 g)	Meat-alternative sausage patty or eggs
1 medium	1 medium	1 medium	
7 oz (200g)	7 oz (200g)	7 oz (200g)	Soy yogurt
50 berries (65 g)	50 berries (65 g)	50 berries (65 g)	
2 slices	2 slices	2 slices	Portabello mushroom "steak"
2 eggs	2 eggs	2 eggs	
2 Tbs	2 Tbs	2 Tbs	
As much as desired	As much as desired	As much as desired	
1 kiwi	1 kiwi	1 kiwi	
1 oz (28 g)	1 oz (28 g)	1 oz (28 g)	
1 cup pasta (107 g)	1 cup pasta (107 g)	2 cups pasta (214 g)	
1/8 cup (31 g)	1/8 cup (31 g)	1/4 c (61 g)	
3 oz (120 g)	3 oz (120 g)	6 oz (240 g)	Meatless "chicken" patty
1 cup (180 g)	1 cup (180 g)	1 cup (180 g)	
8 oz (240 mL)	8 oz (240 mL)	16 oz (480 mL)	Plant-blend protein shake (no whey or casein)
CHO: 147 g	**CHO: 171 g**	**CHO: 208 g**	
PRO: 129 g	**PRO: 142 g**	**PRO: 175 g**	

POWER PHASE MENUS
Day 4

Meal	Time Eaten	Food	1800-calorie
BREAKFAST	7:00 AM	Apple Banana Oatmeal	1 recipe/1 serving
		(see recipe pg 209)	
SNACK	10:30 AM	Carrots, celery, and bell pepper slices	As much as desired
		With hummus	1 Tbs
LUNCH	1:00 PM	Chef salad with:	
		Mixed greens	2 cups (88 g)
		Cheese cubes	8 small cubes (34 g)
		Boiled egg	1 egg
		Veggies of choice	As much as desired
		Ham cubes	2 oz (56 g)
		Dressing	1 Tbs (16 g)
SNACK	3:00 PM	Energy Bites	2 bites (74 g)
		(See recipe page 212)	
DINNER	6:30 PM	Roast beef with:	3 oz (85 g)
		Roasted potatoes	1 small potato (138 g)
		Green beans	1 cup (185 g)
		Butter	0
SNACK	9:00 PM	Cottage cheese with:	1/2 cup (115 g)
		Fresh sliced peaches	1/2 cup (77 g)
AVG CHO			CHO: 151 g
AVG PRO			PRO: 85 g

DRINK WATER throughout the day according to thirst and urine color

2100-calorie	2500-calorie	3000-calorie	Vegan/Vegetarian option
1 recipe/ 1 serving	1 recipe/ 1 serving	1 recipe/ 1 serving	Use plant protein powder
			Substitute 2 Tbs flax + 6 Tbs water for the egg
As much as desired	As much as desired	As much as desired	
1 Tbs	1 Tbs	1 Tbs	
2 cups (88 g)	2 cups (88 g)	2 cups (88 g)	
8 small cubes (34 g)	8 small cubes (34 g)	16 cubes (68 g)	Vegan cheese
1 egg	1 egg	2 eggs	Nuts or beans
As much as desired	As much as desired	as much as desired	
2 oz (56 g)	2 oz (56 g)	4 oz (112 g)	Nuts or beans
1 Tbs (16 g)	1 Tbs (16 g)	1 Tbs (16 g)	
2 bites (74 g)	4 bites	4 bites	Omit honey or use agave nectar
6 oz (168 g)	6 oz (168 g)	6 oz (168 g)	Meatless veggie patty or tofu
1 medium potato (173 g)	1 medium potato (173 g)	1 medium potato (173 g)	
1 cup (185 g)	1 cup (185 g)	1 cup (185 g)	
1 Tbs	1 Tbs	1 Tbs	Vegan butter
1/2 cup (115 g)	1/2 cup (115 g)	1 1/2 cup (345 g)	Plant-based protein shake
1/2 cup (77 g)	1/2 cup (77 g)	1 cup (154 g)	
CHO: 158 g	CHO: 188 g	CHO: 208 g	
PRO: 101 g	PRO: 108 g	PRO: 156 g	

POWER PHASE MENUS
Day 5

Meal	Time Eaten	Food	1800-calorie
BREAKFAST	7:00 AM	Bagel with:	1 bagel (98 g)
		Nut butter (almond, peanut, or hazelnut)	1 Tbs
		Banana slices	1 small banana (101 g)
SNACK	10:30 AM	Whole-grain crackers with:	1 oz (28 g)
		Cheese stick (string cheese)	1 oz (28 g)
LUNCH	1:00 PM	Ramen bowl with:	1 cup cooked noodles
		Soft-boiled egg	1 egg
		Bok choy (chinese cabbage)	2 leaves (25 g)
		Shredded carrots	1 carrot (54 g)
SNACK	3:00 PM	Apple	1 medium (157 g)
		Walnuts	0
DINNER	6:30 PM	Grilled pork loin	3 oz (59 g)
		Quinoa	1 cup (185 g)
		Corn on the cob	1 cob
SNACK	9:00 PM	Protein shake	1 cup (240 mL)
AVG CHO			CHO: 207 g
AVG PRO			PRO: 116 g

> DRINK WATER throughout the day according to thirst and urine color

2100-calorie	2500-calorie	3000-calorie	Vegan/Vegetarian option
1 bagel (98 g)	1 bagel (98 g)	1 bagel (98 g)	
1 Tbs	2 Tbs	2 Tbs	
1 small banana (101 g)	1 medium banana (118 g)	1 medium banana (118 g)	
1 oz (28 g)	2 oz (57 g)	2 oz (57 g)	
1 oz (28 g)	2 oz (57 g)	2 oz (57 g)	Vegan cheese, nut butter, or hummus
1 cup cooked noodles	1 cup cooked noodles	1 cup cooked noodles	
2 eggs	2 eggs	2 eggs	Tofu
2 leaves (25 g)	2 leaves (25 g)	2 leaves (25 g)	
1 carrot (54 g)	1 carrot (54 g)	1 carrot (54 g)	
1 medium (157 g)	1 medium (157 g)	1 medium (157 g)	
0	1/2 c pieces (23 g)	1/2 c pieces (23 g)	
6 oz (117 g)	6 oz (117 g)	6 oz (117 g)	Meatless veggie patty or lentils
1 cup (185 g)	1 cup (185 g)	2 cups (370 g)	
1 cob	1 cob	2 cobs	
1 cup (240 mL)	1 cup (240 mL)	2 cups (480 mL)	Plant-protein shake
CHO: 208 g	CHO: 223 g	CHO: 261 g	
PRO: 137 g	PRO: 153 g	PRO: 212 g	

12 - MENUS AND RECIPES FOR CLIMBERS

WHAT TO EAT BEFORE A CLIMB

IF YOU HAVE 2-4 HOURS BEFORE CLIMBING:

- » Peanut butter + jam sandwich with chocolate milk or protein shake
- » Tuna sandwich with cheese and side of fruit and yogurt
- » Oatmeal with bananas, walnuts, and milk–or almond milk
- » Fruit smoothie with yogurt (vegan–use soy yogurt) and a protein bar

IF YOU HAVE ONLY 30-60 MINUTES BEFORE CLIMBING:

- » Pretzels
- » White mini-bagel
- » Fruit
- » Dried fruit
- » Sports drink
- » Graham crackers
- » Chocolate milk
- » Animal crackers
- » Waffle or pancake (not whole grain)
- » Gels (like Gu)
- » Sports gummies and chews
- » Fruit leather

SAMPLE MENU COMP DAY: MULTIPLE ROUNDS

Portion sizes vary based on weight and hunger level of climber. Eat as much as you feel you need!

Event	Time	Time Eaten	Food
BREAKFAST	8 AM	Prior to event	Steel-cut oats with walnuts, berries, and milk. Orange juice as a beverage
ROUND 1 CLIMBING	10 AM	After event	Pretzels and sports drink
ROUND 2 CLIMBING	12:00 PM	After event	Peanut butter and jam sandwich on white bread with apple slices. Chocolate milk as a beverage
ROUND 3 CLIMBING (ISOLATION)	3:00 PM	Eat/drink as needed in isolation	Sports gummies and sports drink. Carbohydrate mouth rinse if well-hydrated.
ROUND 4 CLIMBING	5:00 PM	Prior to event as required	Raisins and sports drink
DINNER	7:00 PM	After event	Quinoa bowl with black beans, salsa, cheese, avocado, and ground beef with a fruit and yogurt smoothie

WHAT TO EAT DURING A CLIMBING SESSION

1–2 hour session:
- No food needed unless hungry

2–4 hour session:
- Pretzels
- White mini-bagel
- Fruit
- Dried fruit
- Sports drink
- Graham crackers
- Chocolate milk
- Animal crackers
- Waffle or pancake (not whole grain)
- Gels (like Gu)
- Sports gummies and chews
- Fruit leather

Longer than 4 hours
- Protein bar
- Protein shake
- Meat and cheese sandwich
- Peanut butter and jelly sandwich
- Pretzels with hummus
- Trail mix
- Banana
- Dried fruit or fruit leather
- Nut-butter squeeze pouches
- Cheese stick
- Dehydrated meals (cooked with water)
- MREs

WHAT TO EAT AFTER CLIMBING

see instructions page 38

Turkey Sandwich:
- With whole-grain bread, cheese, avocado, and tomato
  Side of carrots and hummus

Veggie Omelet:
- Side of avocado toast
- Chocolate milk

Pasta:
- With tofu, chicken, beef, pork, or fish
- Side of veggies or salad

Peanut Butter and Jelly Sandwich:
- With fruit and yogurt smoothie

Tacos:
- Made with corn or flour tortillas
- Fish, beef, pork, chicken, or beans
- Shredded cheese
- Salsa
- Guacamole
- Side of fruit

Appendix

USEFUL BOOKS:

Roar: How to Match Your Food and Fitness to Your Female Physiology for Optimum Performance, Great Health, and a Strong, Lean Body for Life, **Stacy T. Sims**

Fueling Young Athletes, **Heather R. Mangieri**

Nancy Clark's Sports Nutrition Guidebook, **Nancy Clark**

The low FODMAP Diet Step by Step, **Kate Scarlata**

Fearless Feeding: How to Raise Healthy Eaters from High Chair to High School, **Jill Castle and Maryanne Jacobson**

Intuitive Eating, **Evelyn Tribole**

Secrets of Feeding a Healthy Family: How to Eat, How to Raise Good Eaters, How to Cook, **Ellyn Satter**

Your Child's Weight: Helping Without Harming, **Ellyn Satter**

Sports Nutrition for Paralympic Athletes, **Elizabeth Broad**

USEFUL WEBSITES

Gourmet Hiking: Recipes and nutrition blog for backcountry adventures. Created by a dietitian with solid, evidence-based guidelines and advice.
gourmethiking.com

Backcountry Foodie: Recipes, nutrition blog, and information on how to create ultralight meal plans and dehydrate your own food. Created by a dietitian and thru-hiker.
backcountryfoodie.com

Examine.com: Objective and chockful of useful information and scientific references, this website breaks down quite nicely any sort of supplement you might consider taking. This also has matter-of-fact reviews on all sorts of nutrition topics and diets. It is thorough and practical in its recommendations. Most recommendations are supported by science.
examine.com

Drug Free Sport: Website dedicated to helping athletes and coaches understand drug-free sport education and policies.
drugfreesport.com

World Anti-Doping Agency: The go-to website for information on banned and permitted substances for competitive athletes in collegiate, Olympic, professional, and other competitive arenas where drug testing occurs.
wada-ama.org

NSF International Certified for Sport: A comprehensive website that lists independent testing on supplements to ensure they are free of contaminants and banned substances.
nsfsport.com

United States National Institutes of Health Office of Dietary Supplements: A science-based and objective review of supplements, their use, side effects, and more.
ods.od.nih.gov

Low-FODMAP websites for gastrointestinal issues:
myginutrition.com/
nestlehealthscience.us/lowfodmap-old/fodmap-101
blog.katescarlata.com/fodmaps-basics/
ibsfree.net/

Low-FODMAP bars and portable foods:
stellarlabsnutrition.com/ (bars and protein-shake mix)
trueselffoods.com/ (bars)
rachelpaulsfood.com/ (bars and jerky)
fodyfoods.com/ (bars and trail mix)

Make your own:
blog.katescarlata.com/2015/02/19/almond-butter-oat-bites/
blog.katescarlata.com/2014/10/22/gorilla-munch-trail-mix-treat/

Acknowledgements

Huge thank you to Dr. Lanae Joubert, who in what little spare time she had reviewed this entire book's contents for accuracy and clarity. I could not have written this book without your professional opinions, encouragement, and support. I am profoundly thankful.

Dr. Lanae Joubert
PhD, RDN, CSSD, CSCS
Associate Professor of Nutrition
Northern Michigan University
ljoubert@nmu.edu

Lori Nedescu, MS, RDN, CSSD
Hungryforresults.com
Instagram: @hungryforresults
Facebook: hungryforresults
Twitter: @Lori_sports_RD

Niki Strealy, RDN, LD
Strategic Nutrition, LLC
Diarrheadietitian.com
Instagram: @diarrheadietitian
Facebook: diarrheadietitian

Whitney Pesek
Adaptive Climbing Group,
Salt Lake City, Utah
Instagram: @whitney.pesek
Facebook: whitney.pesek

Enock Glidden
Ambassador with Paradox Sports
Bio: paradoxsports.org/staff/enock-glidden/
Blog: gobeyondthefence.com/
Instagram: @enockglidden
Facebook: gobeyondthefence
Twitter: @enock_glidden

Aika Yoshida
Ambassador with Paradox Sports:
paradoxsports.org/staff-category/ambassadors/
Instagram: @aika.yoshida
Facebook: aika.yoshida.16
Facebook Group: Indy Adaptive Climbing

Ronnie Dickson
Instagram: @rdclimber

Genevieve Masson
Gourmet Hiking
Gourmethiking.com
Instagram: @gourmethiking
Facebook: gourmethiking

Aaron Owens Mayhew
Backcountry Foodie
Backcountryfoodie.com
Instagram: @backcountryfoodie
Facebook: backcountryfoodie

Hans Florine
Hansflorine.com
Instagram: @hansflorine

Adam Ondra
Adamondra.com
Instagram: @adam.ondra

Beth Rodden
Bethrodden.com
Instagram: @bethrodden

Sasha DiGuilian
sashadigiulian.com
Instagram: @sahsadiguilian

Elizabeth Broad, PhD, RD, CSSD
United States Olympic Committee
Dietitian

Kate Bennett, PsyD
Athlete Insight, PC
livetrainthrive.com
Facebook: AthleteInsight
Twitter: @AthleteInsight

Alan Aragon
Alanaragon.com
Instagram: @thealanaragon

Biography

Marisa Michael is a registered dietitian nutritionist specializing in sports nutrition. She owns a private practice, Real Nutrition, LLC, in Portland, Oregon, USA. Marisa helps athletes and active people achieve better health and performance through nutrition.

Marisa has an undergraduate degree in Dietetics from Brigham Young University, and a master's degree in sports nutrition from the University of Stirling. She is a certified personal trainer and group exercise instructor. She holds the International Olympic Committee's Diploma in Sports Nutrition and is a Board Certified Specialist in Sports Dietetics.

She firmly believes that relationships with food and body play a huge role in mental and physical health, and applies that in her own life by thoroughly enjoying ice cream and chocolate on a regular basis.

Marisa is available for one-on-one consultations (virtual and in-person), workshops, speaking engagements, and writing for publications. You can book and appointment and find on-demand e-courses on her website at realnutritionllc.com. She is the author of Bike Shorts: Your Complete Guide to Indoor Cycling, available on Amazon.

Find her on Instagram @realnutritiondietitian
Find her on Facebook @realnutritionllc
Find her online at realnutritionllc.com

INDEX

A

Adaptive climbers 120, 121, 123, 124
Adolescent climbers 94, 96, 98, 100, 102, 133
Adrenaline 52
Aerobic glycolysis 25
Alcohol 14, 18, 24, 93, 128, 185
Alpine (Ice) climbing 73, 74
Altitude 18, 24, 41, 42, 46, 51, 52, 53, 54, 71, 72, 74, 80, 128, 147, 153, 168
Amino acids 16, 63, 86, 150, 155, 156, 157
Anaerobic glycolysis 25, 29
Anorexia nervosa 197, 200, 203
Antioxidant 11, 18, 19, 21, 38, 39, 136, 137, 138, 149, 212
Appetite 53, 82

B

Basal energy expenditure (BEE) 182
Basal metabolic rate (BMR) 112, 182, 198
Base Fitness Phase 222, 223
Beats per minute (BPM) 28, 182
Beta alanine 150, 157, 158
Binge eating disorder 197, 201
Blood sugar 15, 25, 26, 42, 43, 44, 72, 74, 108, 122, 168, 173, 199, 203
Blood work 53, 81
Body composition 42, 113, 163, 165, 166, 177, 181, 205, 220
Body-image issues 97, 114, 117, 118, 166, 196, 198, 201, 203, 206
Body mass index (BMI) 111, 164
Body-weight ratio 45, 52
Bouldering 68, 69, 70, 71, 95, 100, 222
Branch chain amino acids (BCAAs) 155
Bulimia nervosa 197, 201

C

Caffeine 36, 50, 60, 74, 93, 125, 127, 152, 158, 173
Calcium ... 18, 19, 48, 61, 82, 83, 84, 106, 109, 115, 137, 148, 151
Caldwell, Tommy 28
Calorie deficit 111, 151, 169, 172, 173, 176, 178, 179, 180, 182, 183
Calories 11, 13, 14, 15, 19, 21, 23, 24, 26, 42, 53, 54, 59, 64, 71, 73, 79, 80, 95, 98, 99, 102, 104, 107, 109, 110, 111, 112, 113, 114, 115, 116, 121, 122, 123, 134, 135, 137, 141
Carbohydrate mouth rinse 47, 152, 268
Carbohydrates 11, 14, 15, 16, 18, 21, 23, 24, 25, 26, 27, 29, 34, 36, 38, 39, 42, 43, 44, 47, 48, 52, 58, 59, 63, 67, 68, 69, 91, 95, 100, 101, 104, 105, 106, 107, 108, 121, 122, 135, 152, 156

Cardiovascular (training) 28, 143, 184
Carotenoid 138
Coenzyme Q10 138
Cold 24, 33, 45, 54, 55, 56, 63, 73, 74, 81, 122, 200
Comp (competition climbing) ... 12, 15, 17, 33, 35, 54, 60, 67, 68, 70, 71, 85, 102, 117, 120, 125, 137, 148, 153, 159, 164, 173, 174, 199, 204, 205
Core temperature 54, 73
Cortisol 52, 184
Cramp 48, 50, 56, 57, 61, 72, 91, 119, 139, 153, 158
Creatine-phosphagen 25, 29
Creatine supplement ... 67, 85, 137, 147, 149, 157, 173, 222, 223

D

Dairy products 15, 16, 17, 19, 21, 64, 82, 83, 84, 86, 106, 136, 169, 171
Dehydration 18, 42, 45, 46, 48, 49, 50, 55, 56, 57, 58, 59, 74, 93, 101, 105, 127, 139, 174, 199, 201, 205
Dietitian 5, 19, 41, 48, 50, 53, 56, 58, 60, 64, 71, 81, 87, 88, 91, 92, 93, 97, 99, 102, 104, 106, 114, 115, 121, 122, 123, 124, 129, 135, 139, 141, 144, 146, 175, 176, 177, 186, 189, 191, 205, 220, 223, 225, 227, 270, 273
DiGiulian, Sasha 117
Disordered eating 114, 118, 166, 172, 195, 196, 197, 198, 204, 205, 206, 207
Dizziness 47, 48, 74, 81, 93, 101, 200, 201
Dynos 3, 15, 23, 25, 27, 43, 85, 95, 121, 168, 223

E

Eating disorders ... 87, 114, 119, 163, 172, 195, 196, 197, 198, 199, 201, 203, 205, 206, 207
Eggs 16, 19, 21, 35, 38, 44, 53, 57, 59, 61, 64, 80, 82, 83, 84, 86, 89, 90, 91, 99, 108, 122, 127, 136, 155, 156, 178, 188
Electrolyte 18, 48, 49, 52, 55, 61, 93, 101, 105, 128, 139, 201
Endurance training 26, 28, 43, 45, 46, 47, 55, 68, 81, 93, 103, 107, 113, 152, 153, 158, 168, 173, 199, 221, 225, 227, 248
Energy expenditure ... 12, 23, 53, 99, 112, 121, 123, 177, 182
Excess post-exercise oxygen consumption (EPOC) 182

F

Fat..........11, 14, 15, 17, 18, 19, 21, 24, 25, 26, 27, 29, 35, 37, 39, 53, 62, 68, 70, 84, 93, 95, 100, 101, 105, 106, 107, 112, 117, 121, 122, 127, 147, 154, 163, 164, 165, 166, 168, 169, 170, 176, 177, 178, 180, 181, 183, 191, 195, 197, 198, 199, 200, 203, 205, 217, 220, 221
Fatigue...........13, 18, 25, 36, 42, 43, 45, 47, 48, 54, 57, 81, 82, 84, 91, 101, 106, 113, 115, 116, 128, 134, 139, 147, 149, 150, 152, 158, 166, 168, 173, 181, 189, 190, 199, 200, 201
Female athletes....107, 108, 109, 110, 111, 112, 113, 114, 116, 177
Female athlete triad 114
Fiber......12, 15, 35, 36, 37, 80, 91, 92, 93, 122, 127, 135, 156, 188
Fish oil 39, 84, 137, 154
Florine, Hans..28, 60, 272
Fluid......11, 18, 19, 21, 41, 42, 46, 47, 49, 50, 52, 54, 55, 56, 57, 59, 74, 85, 93, 101, 105, 116, 117, 122, 123, 127, 128, 141
Flying..41, 125, 128
FODMAP..91, 92, 93, 270, 271
Foggy mind 48
Fruit......14, 15, 18, 19, 21, 35, 37, 38, 39, 43, 44, 52, 59, 62, 72, 80, 90, 92, 99, 104, 106, 117, 119, 126, 127, 129, 135, 136, 137, 138, 148, 154, 166, 169, 172, 186, 188, 211, 212, 213, 217, 234

G

Gastrointestinal distress (Diarrhea)....57, 72, 91, 92, 93, 122, 127, 152, 153, 158, 173, 199, 201
Gelatin 137, 154, 158
Glycogen..........15, 26, 27, 38, 54, 67, 69, 103, 106, 113, 115, 139, 168, 173, 174, 183, 185, 199, 223

H

Heart rate...23, 24, 25, 27, 28, 29, 36, 51, 54, 112, 121, 152, 158, 177, 178, 182, 189, 190, 201
Heat......24, 41, 48, 51, 54, 55, 73, 88, 101, 122, 139, 214
Heat regulation...51
High-intensity interval training (HIIT)...................182
HMB..151, 158
Hormones....16, 17, 52, 84, 107, 108, 111, 164, 169, 176, 178, 184
Hydration......18, 21, 41, 45, 46, 49, 50, 51, 52, 54, 55, 56, 59, 62, 63, 68, 70, 71, 73, 74, 75, 93, 94, 105, 107, 119, 122, 124, 126, 134, 143, 165, 181
Hydrogen..150
Hyponatremia (Overhydration)...........46, 47, 55, 101

I

Immunity 84
Individualized nutrition 63, 124
Inflammation 83, 106, 135, 138, 149, 154, 169, 170, 171, 199
Informed choice....................................137, 145, 157, 213
Injury prevention......................................83, 133, 134, 158
Injury recovery 18, 135, 136
International Federation of
    Sport Climbing (IFSC).........................68, 70, 111
Intolerance 91, 147, 200
Iodine... 84
Iron.........18, 19, 53, 72, 80, 81, 82, 84, 106, 109, 110, 115, 147, 148, 218
Irritability 43, 74, 113, 166, 184, 188, 189, 199
Isometric contraction.....................................24, 43, 100

L

Legumes 14, 15, 16, 80, 81, 86, 92, 104, 138, 186
Leucine 16, 86, 104, 136, 151, 155, 156
Low blood sugar.....................................42, 74, 122, 203
Low energy availability.........111, 112, 113, 114, 166, 198, 199

M

Macronutrients........................11, 14, 18, 21, 52, 86, 155
Menstrual cycle....................................108, 109, 178, 205
Menus....209, 220, 221, 227, 228, 230, 232, 234, 236, 238, 240, 242, 244, 246, 248, 250, 252, 254, 256, 258, 260, 262, 264, 266
Metabolic processes (Metabolism).....18, 23, 25, 45, 80, 84, 106, 111, 113, 176, 182, 191
Micronutrients....11, 18, 19, 21, 102, 106, 109, 115, 123, 135, 136, 137, 141, 147, 148
Mug recipes 209
Muscle contraction..........15, 18, 26, 27, 38, 43, 69, 82, 85, 106, 150, 223

N

Nitrate..153, 157, 158
Non-exercise activity thermogenisis (NEAT) 182
NSF Certified 137, 145, 157, 271
Nutrition periodization 163, 167

O

Older athletes 103, 104, 105, 106
Omega 3 fats.. 84
Ondra, Adam..62
Orthorexia 198, 202, 203, 206
Other specific feeding
    and eating disorders (OSFED)..................203
Overall energy needs...42
Oxygen......14, 18, 24, 25, 27, 51, 80, 99, 103, 138, 153, 182, 199

P

Perceived exertion...................................168, 199
Physiology 5, 12, 23, 94, 170, 270
Phytate...81, 84
Power Endurance Phase 221, 225, 298-257
Power Phase 223, 227, 258, 260, 262, 264, 266
Pregnant climbers 115
Protein.....11, 12, 14, 15, 16, 17, 18, 19, 21, 23, 24, 26, 34,
35, 38, 39, 44, 53, 58, 59, 60, 61, 62, 63, 70,
71, 84, 86; 89, 99, 100, 104, 106, 107, 115, 117,
119, 121, 122, 123, 127, 135, 136, 141, 148, 149,
151, 154, 155, 156, 157, 164, 166, 167, 170, 172,
181, 183, 185, 186, 188, 191, 211, 212, 213, 214,
215, 217, 218, 220, 221, 222, 223, 225, 228,
234, 236, 238, 240, 242, 248, 252
Puberty.........23, 94, 95, 96, 97, 98, 101, 133, 198, 199

R

Rate of perceived exertion (RPE).............................182
Rebuilding..................16, 18, 38, 44, 112, 135, 206, 223
Recovery..........12, 18, 33, 38, 44, 59, 62, 70, 71, 83, 95,
99, 114, 129, 133, 134, 135, 148, 151, 155, 157,
158, 168, 182, 201, 214, 215, 225, 258, 260
Relative Energy Deficiency
in Sport (RED-S) 114, 198, 205, 206
Repair.....................................12, 16, 18, 23, 38, 44, 71, 99,
104, 106, 112, 135, 136, 151, 152, 154, 155, 158,
184, 185, 222, 223, 225
Respiration......13, 18, 24, 45, 52, 74, 98, 112, 128, 177,
178, 182
Resting metabolic rate (RMR) 182
Rodden, Beth..119

S

Salt................48, 55, 64, 84, 93, 119, 212, 215, 216, 217
Screaming barfies 74
Sleep.....39, 51, 52, 63, 113, 125, 128, 152, 158, 168,
181, 184, 185
Sodium 18, 19, 46, 47, 48, 55, 139
Sodium bicarbonate...................................153, 157, 158
Speed climbing...25, 28, 67
Sport climbing 68, 133, 164, 222
Sports dietitian 5, 41, 48, 50,
53, 56, 64, 71, 88, 104, 106, 114, 121, 123, 129,
135, 139, 141, 144, 175, 186, 189, 191, 225, 227
Sports drink 35, 43, 48, 52, 55, 101, 105, 128
Strength Phase....222, 223, 225, 227, 238, 240, 242,
244, 246
Sugar..12, 14, 15, 25, 26, 38, 42,
43, 44, 47, 48, 54, 60, 64, 72, 74, 92, 93, 101,
103, 108, 117, 119, 122, 127, 156, 163, 166, 168,
171, 173, 183, 199, 203, 211, 220
Supplements...5, 18, 36, 39,
49, 61, 63, 72, 82, 83, 85, 102, 106, 115, 125,
137, 138, 139, 141, 143, 144, 145, 146, 147, 148,
149, 155, 157, 159, 173, 222, 271

Sweat............45, 50, 52, 54, 55, 56, 85, 101, 105, 106,
122, 124, 139, 204
Sweat rate 50, 56, 105, 124

T

Tart cherry juice...39, 137
Total energy expenditure (TEE)..................................182
Traditional (Trad) climbing...71
Training...11, 12, 13,
14, 15, 16, 19, 21, 23, 26, 27, 28, 38, 39, 50, 61,
62, 63, 64, 67, 68, 86, 94, 95, 101, 102, 104,
108, 111, 113, 116, 117, 121, 123, 125, 127, 133,
134, 137, 138, 139, 143, 147, 148, 149, 150, 151,
152, 154, 158, 159, 166, 167, 168, 173, 174, 175,
181, 182, 185, 186, 189, 198, 199, 205, 214,
220, 221, 222, 223, 225, 227

U

Ultralight meal planning..57, 58
Urinalysis-urine test 49, 50
Urine specific gravity (USG) 49, 50

V

Van life..88, 89, 90
Vegan............62, 79, 85, 86, 87, 106, 109, 136, 147, 149,
156, 212, 218, 230, 232, 236, 238, 240, 242,
244, 248, 250, 254, 256, 258, 264, 266
Vegetable...14, 15, 18,
19, 21, 38, 39, 62, 63, 68, 80, 82, 86, 92, 104,
117, 126, 127, 129, 135, 136, 138, 148, 153, 166,
169, 172, 178, 186, 188, 211, 214, 246, 254,
258, 260
Vegetarian 79, 82, 85, 87, 109, 149, 254
Vitamin B12..................................18, 19, 72, 82, 103, 106
Vitamin C 18, 19, 81, 136, 137, 138, 141, 154, 158
Vitamin D.......18, 19, 61, 72, 82, 83, 106, 109, 137, 147,
148
Vitamins.........11, 18, 19, 21, 38, 104, 107, 109, 115, 135,
136, 138, 164, 183, 185, 214
VO2 max 24, 182

W

Weight management 163
Wharton, Josh..74
Whey...86, 104, 156, 248, 262
Whole30..169, 170, 171

Y

Youth climbers..94, 100, 220

Z

Zinc...18, 19, 84, 106, 109, 136